VOLUME III

MEDITATIONS
FOR ALL THE DAYS OF THE YEAR

VOLUME III

From the Second Sunday after Easter to the Sixth Sunday after Pentecost

"Take ye, and eat: This is My body. Drink ye all of this: For this is My blood."
- St. Matthew 26:26-28

FOR THE USE OF PRIESTS, RELIGIOUS AND THE FAITHFUL.

BY

REV. M. HAMON, S.S.,

Pastor of St. Sulpice, Paris, Author of "Life of St. Francis de Sales" and "Life of Cardinal Cheverus."

From the Twenty-third Revised and Enlarged Edition

BY

MRS. ANNE R. BENNETT,

(née GLADSTONE.)

WITH A METHOD OF USING THESE MEDITATIONS, BY VERY REV. A. MAGNIEN, S.S., D.D.

VOLUME III

From the Second Sunday after Easter to the Sixth Sunday after Pentecost

Originally published by:

NEW YORK, CINCINNATI, CHICAGO:
Benzinger Brothers
Printers to the Holy Apostolic See

Reprinted by Valora Media
Cover and layout by: Kenneth R. Henderson

Nihil Obstat

D. J. McMAHON, D.D.,

Censor Librorum
Imprimatur

MICHAEL AUGUSTINE,

Archbishop of New York

NEW YORK, July 14, 1894.

Printed in the United States of America

Printed in the United States of America.

Preface

To aid Christian souls better to know God with His infinite perfections and His adorable mysteries; better to love and serve Him, better to know themselves, their faults and their duties; better to reform themselves and to make progress in virtue: such is the end we have proposed to ourselves in writing this work. In this futile and frivolous age, in which hardly any one occupies himself with aught except external events, there are very few souls who seriously reflect upon these great and holy things; very few who carefully meditate every morning how much God deserves to be loved and served, how they can serve Him during the present day, and what they will do for His glory, for their own salvation, and their personal sanctification. As a remedy for this evil, we have believed it will be useful to make the very important exercise of meditation easy for souls of goodwill, by putting into their hands not a literary work which addresses itself to their minds, but a course of meditations which addresses itself to their hearts, and which should be read calmly, attentively, with reflection, with the object of entering into themselves and being awakened to a better life. May the reader thoroughly understand our design, meditate deeply and get to the bottom of each phrase, if we may so speak, penetrate himself with it and apply it to himself, by comparing what he is with what he ought to be, and deducing practical consequences for the reformation of his life, not in the distant future, but on the very same day. In the composition of his work, we have followed, step by step, if we can so say, the Roman liturgy, which has so admirably collected together the whole of religion within the course of the ecclesiastical year, and under the direction of such a sure guide we have meditated: first, upon the mysteries which are the basis of Christian virtues; second, the Christian virtues themselves, which are the edifice to be built upon this basis; third, the feasts of the most celebrated among the saints, whose life is virtue itself in action; and we have endeavored to present here these great subjects in a manner which will be equally suitable to the clergy and the faithful, so that our work may be useful to a greater number. The reader must not be astonished sometimes to meet with the same truth or the same virtue presented for meditation under different aspects. The soul needs to have the same truth often repeated to it, otherwise the impression would be effaced, until it became for us as though it had never been; it needs to reproach itself often with certain faults, otherwise it would lose sight of them, and would no longer take any care to correct them; lastly, it needs to be often raised up, because it often falls; hence our repetitions are anything but idle repetitions.

He must not be astonished, either, on the preceding evening, to find there the summary of the morrow s meditation. It is very important, in order to succeed properly in meditation, to fix precisely the subject on the preceding evening, and to arrive at the meditation of it already penetrated with what is about to occupy him. Hence, at the head of every meditation we have placed: First, an indication of the points of the meditation; Second, the enunciation of the resolutions which should be the practical consequence of it. We have added afterwards what St. Francis de Sales calls a spiritual nosegay; that is to say, a good thought which will be the sum total as it were of the meditation, and of which the perfume, embalming our heart during the whole day, recalls to us our morning meditation.

We have also placed at the beginning of each volume the usual morning and evening prayers, so that there may be no need to have recourse to another book to fulfill the daily duties of every Christian. Lastly, we have added to this third edition: First, several new meditations; second, a more careful and complete index; third, a plan of meditations for an eight day retreat; fourth, self examinations inserted in the greater part of the meditations; fifth, various developments op several subjects of meditation. May God, in His love for souls, deign to bless this new work and make it serve to His glory and to the sanctification of the elect!

℘ Contents ℘

SAINTS DAYS

Morning Prayers

In the name of the Father, + and of the Son, and of the Holy Ghost. Amen.

Place Yourself in the Presence of God, and adore His holy Name.

Most holy and adorable Trinity, one God in three Persons, I believe that Thou art here present: I adore Thee with the deepest humility, and render to Thee, with my whole heart, the homage which is due to Thy sovereign majesty.

ACT OF FAITH

O my God, I firmly believe that Thou art one God in three divine Persons. Father, Son, and Holy Ghost; I believe that Thy divine Son became man, and died for our sins, and that He will come to judge the living and the dead. I believe these and all the truths which the holy Catholic Church teaches, because Thou hast revealed them, who canst neither deceive nor be deceived.

ACT OF HOPE

O my God, relying on Thy infinite goodness and promises, I hope to obtain pardon of my sins, the help of Thy grace, and life everlasting, through the merits of Jesus Christ, my Lord and Redeemer.

ACT OF LOVE

O my God, I love Thee above all things, with my whole heart and soul, because Thou art all-good and worthy of all love. I love my neighbor as myself for the love of Thee. I forgive all who have injured me, and ask pardon of all whom I have injured.

THANK GOD FOR ALL FAVORS AND OFFER YOURSELF TO HIM

O my God, I most humbly thank Thee for all the favors Thou hast bestowed upon me up to the present moment. I give Thee thanks from the bottom of my heart that Thou hast created me after Thine own image and likeness, that Thou hast redeemed me by the precious blood of Thy dear Son, and that Thou hast preserved me and brought me safe to the beginning of another day. I offer to Thee, O Lord, my whole being, and in particular all my thoughts, words, actions, and sufferings of this day. I consecrate them all to the glory of Thy name, beseeching Thee that through the infinite merits of Jesus Christ my Savior they may all find acceptance in Thy sight. May Thy divine love animate them, and may they all tend to Thy greater glory.

RESOLVE TO AVOID SIN AND TO PRACTICE VIRTUE

Adorable Jesus, my Savior and Master, model of all perfection, I resolve and will endeavor this day to imitate Thy example, to be, like Thee, mild, humble, chaste, zealous, charitable, and resigned. I will redouble my efforts that I may not fall this day into any of those sins which I have heretofore committed (here name any besetting sin), and which I sincerely desire to forsake.

ASK GOD FOR THE NECESSARY GRACES

O my God, Thou knowest my poverty and weakness, and that I am unable to do anything good without Thee; deny me not, O God, the help of Thy grace: proportion it to my necessities; give me strength to avoid anything evil which Thou forbiddest and to practice the good which Thou hast commanded; and enable me to bear patiently all the trials which it may please Thee to send me.

THE LORD'S PRAYER

Latin

Pater noster, qui es in caelis, sanctificetur nomen tuum. Adveniat regnum tuum. Fiat voluntas tua, sicut in caelo et in terra. Panem nostrum quotidianum da nobis hodie, et dimitte nobis debita nostra sicut et nos dimittimus debitoribus nostris. Et ne nos inducas in tentationem, sed libera nos a malo. Amen.

English

Our Father, who art in heaven, hallowed be Thy name. Thy kingdom come. Thy will be done on earth as it is in heaven. Give us this day our daily bread and forgive us our trespasses as we forgive those who trespass against us. And lead us not into temptation, but deliver us from evil. Amen.

THE HAIL MARY

Latin

Ave Maria, gratia plena, Dominus tecum. Benedicta tu in mulieribus, et benedictus fructus ventris tui, Jesus. Sancta Maria, Mater Dei, ora pro nobis peccatoribus, nunc, et in hora mortis nostrae. Amen.

English

Hail Mary, full of grace, the Lord is with thee. Blessed art thou amongst women and blessed is the fruit of thy womb, Jesus. Holy Mary, Mother of God, pray for us sinners, now, and in the hour of our death. Amen.

THE APOSTLE'S CREED

Latin

Credo in Deum Patrem omnipotentem, Creatorem caeli et terrae. Et in Iesum Christum, Filium eius unicum, Dominum nostrum, qui conceptus est de Spiritu Sancto, natus ex Maria Virgine, passus sub Pontio Pilato, crucifixus, mortuus, et sepultus, descendit ad infernos, tertia die resurrexit a mortuis, ascendit ad caelos, sedet ad dexteram Dei Patris omnipotentis, inde venturus est iudicare vivos et mortuos. Credo in Spiritum Sanctum, sanctam Ecclesiam catholicam, sanctorum communionem, remissionem peccatorum, carnis resurrectionem et vitam aeternam. Amen.

English

I believe in God, the Father almighty, Creator of heaven and earth. I believe in Jesus Christ, His only Son, our Lord. He was conceived by the power of the Holy Spirit and born of the Virgin Mary. He suffered under Pontius Pilate, was crucified, died, and was buried. He descended to the dead. On the third day He rose again. He ascended into heaven and sits at the right hand of God, the Father Almighty. From thence He shall come to judge the living and the dead. I believe in the Holy Spirit, the holy catholic Church, the communion of saints, the forgiveness of sins, the resurrection of the body, and the life everlasting. Amen.

ASK THE PRAYERS OF THE BLESSED VIRGIN, YOUR GUARDIAN ANGEL, AND YOUR PATRON SAINT.

Holy Virgin Mother of God, my Mother and Patroness, I place myself under thy protection, I throw myself with confidence into the arms of thy compassion. Be to me, O Mother of mercy, my refuge in distress, my consolation under suffering, my advocate with thy adorable Son, now and at the hour of my death.

Angel of God, my guardian dear,
To whom His love commits me here,
Ever this day be at my side,
To light and guard, to rule and guide. Amen.

O great Saint whose name I bear, protect me, pray for me that like thee I may serve God faithfully on earth, and glorify Him eternally with thee in heaven. Amen.

LITANY OF THE MOST HOLY NAME OF JESUS

O Lord Jesus Christ, who hast said: Ask, and ye shall receive; seek, and ye shall find; knock, and it shall be opened unto you; grant, we beseech Thee, unto us who ask, the gift of Thy most divine love, that we may ever love Thee with all our hearts, and in all our words and actions, and never cease from showing forth Thy praise.

Latin	*English*
Kyrie eleison.	Lord, have mercy on us.
Christe eleison.	Christ, have mercy on us.
Kyrie eleison.	Lord, have mercy on us.
Jesu aucli nos.	Jesus, hear us.
Jesu exaudi nos.	Jesus, graciously hear us.
Pater de coelis Deus,	God the Father of heaven,
...Miserere nobis	...Have mercy on us.
Fill, Redemptor mundi, Deus,	God the Son, Redeemer of the world,
Spiritus Sancte Deus,	God the Holy Ghost,
Sancta Trinitas, unus Deus,	Holy Trinity, one God,
Jesu, Fili Dei vivi,	Jesus, Son of the living God,
Jesu, splendor Patris,	Jesus, splendor of the Father,
Jesu, candor lucis aeternx,	Jesus, brightness of eternal light,
Jesu, rex gloriae,	Jesus, king of glory,
Jesu, sol justitiae,	Jesus, sun of justice,
Jesu, fili Mariae Virginis,	Jesus, son of the Virgin Mary,
Jesu amabilis,	Jesus, most amiable,
Jesu admirabilis,	Jesus, most admirable,

Jesu, Deus fords,	Jesus, mighty God,
Jesu, pater f uturi saeculi,	Jesus, father of the world to come,
Jesu, magni consilii angele,	Jesus, angel of the great council,
Jesu potentissime,	Jesus, most powerful,
Jesu patientissime,	Jesus, most patient,
Jesu obedientissime,	Jesus, most obedient,
Jesu, mitis et humilis corde,	Jesus, meek and humble of heart,
Jesu, amator castitatis,	Jesus, lover of chastity,
Jesu, amator noster,	Jesus, lover of us,
Jesu, Deus pacis,	Jesus, God of peace,
Jesu, auctor vitae,	Jesus, author of life,
Jesu, exemplar virtutum,	Jesus, model of virtues,
Jesu, zelator animarum,	Jesus, zealous for souls,
Jesu, Deus noster,	Jesus, our God,
Jesu, refugium nostrum,	Jesus, our refuge,
Jesu, pater pauperum,	Jesus, father of the poor,
Jesu, thesaurus fidelium,	Jesus, treasure of the faithful,
Jesu, bone pastor,	Jesus, good shepherd,
Jesu, lux vera,	Jesus, true light,
Jesu, sapientia aeterna,	Jesus, eternal wisdom,
Jesu, bonitas infinita,	Jesus, infinite goodness,
Jesu, via et vita nostra,	Jesus, our way and our life,
Jesu, gaudium angelorum,	Jesus, joy of angels,
Jesu, rex patriarcharum,	Jesus, king of patriarchs,
Jesu, magister apostolorum,	Jesus, master of apostles,
Jesu, doctor evangelistarurn,	Jesus, teacher lists,
Jesu, fortitude martyrum,	Jesus, strength of martyrs,
Jesu, lumen confessorum,	Jesus, light of confessors,
Jesu, puritas virginum,	Jesus, purity of virgins,
Jesu, corona sanctorum omnium,	Jesus, crown of all saints,
Propitius esto,	Be merciful,
Parce nobis,Jesu.	Spare us, O Jesus,
Propitius esto,	Be merciful,
Exaudi nos, Jesu.	Graciously hear us, O Jesus.
Ab omni malo,	From all evil,
Ab omni peccato,	From all sin,
Ab ira tua,	From Thy wrath,
Ab insidiis diaboli,	From the snares of the devil,
A spiritu fornicationis,	From the spirit of fornication,

A morte perpetua,
A neglectu inspirationumtuarum,
Per mysterium sanctse incamationis tuae,
Pet nativitatem tuam,
Per infantiam tuam,
Per divinissimam vitam tuam,
Per labores tuos,
Per agoniam et passionem tuam,
Per crucem et derelictionem tuam,
Per languores tuos,
Per mortem et sepulturam tuam,
Per resurrectionem tuam,
Per ascensionem tuam,
Per gaudia tua,
Per gloriam tuam,
Agnus Dei, qui tollis peccata mundi,
Parce nobis, Jesu.
Agnus Dei, qui tollis peccata mundi,
Exaudi nos, Jesu.
Agnus Dei, qui tollis peccata mundi,
Miserere nobis, Jesu.
Jesu audi nos.
Jesu, exaudi nos.

Oremus.
Domine Jesu Christe, qui dixisti: Petite, et accipietis; qiiaerite, et invenietis ; pul sate, et aperietur vobis, quaesumus ; da nobis peteu tibus divinissimi tui amoris affectum, ut te toto corde, ore et opere diligamus, et a tua nunquam laude cessemus. Sancti Nominis tui, Domine, timorem pariter et amorem fac nos habere per petuum, quia nunquam tua gubernatione destituis quos in soliditate tuae dilectionis instituis. Qui vivis et reg. uas, etc. Amen.

From everlasting death,
From the neglect of Thy inspirations,
Through the mystery of Thy holy incarnation,
Through Thy nativity,
Through Thine infancy,
Through Thy most divine life,
Through Thy labors,
Through Thine agony and passion,
Through Thy cross and dereliction,
Through Thy faintness and weariness,
Through Thy death and burial,
Through Thy resurrection,
Through Thine ascension,
Through Thy joys,
Through Thy glory,
Lamb of God, who takes away the sins of the world
Spare us, O Jesus.
Lamb of God, who takest away the sins of the world.
Graciously hear us, O Jesus.
Lamb of God, who takest away the sins of the world,
Have mercy on us, O Jesus*
Jesus, hear us.
Jesus, graciously hear us

Let us pray.
Make us, O Lord, to have a perpetual fear and love of Thy holy Name; for Thou never failest to govern those whom Thou dost solidly establish in Thy love. Who livest and reignest, etc. Amen.

THE ANGELUS DOMINI

Latin

V. Angelus Domini nuntiavit Mariae.
R. Et concepit de Spiritu Sancto.

Ave Maria, gratia plena; Dominus tecum: benedicta tu in mulieribus, et benedictus fructus ventris tui Iesus. * Sancta Maria, Mater Dei ora pro nobis peccatoribus, nunc et in hora mortis nostrae. Amen.

V. Ecce ancilla Domini,
R. Fiat mihi secundum verbum tuum.

Ave Maria, gratia plena; Dominus tecum: benedicta tu in mulieribus, et benedictus fructus ventris tui Iesus. * Sancta Maria, Mater Dei ora pro nobis peccatoribus, nunc et in hora mortis nostrae. Amen.

V. Et Verbum caro factum est,
R. Et habitavit in nobis.

Ave Maria, gratia plena; Dominus tecum: benedicta tu in mulieribus, et benedictus fructus ventris tui Iesus.* Sancta Maria, Mater Dei ora pro nobis peccatoribus, nunc et in hora mortis nostrae. Amen.

V. Ora pro nobis, sancta Dei Genetrix,
R. Ut digni efficiamur promissionibus Christi.

Oremus. Gratiam tuam, quaesumus, Domine, mentibus nostris infunde; ut qui, Angelo nuntiante, Christi Filii tui incarnationem cognovimus, per passionem eius et crucem ad resurrectionis gloriam perducamur. Per eumdem Christum Dominum nostrum.

R. Amen.

English

V. The angel of the Lord declared unto Mary.
R. And she conceived of the Holy Spirit.

Hail Mary, full of grace; the Lord is with Thee: blessed art thou among women, and blessed is the fruit of thy womb, Jesus.* Holy Mary, Mother of God, prayer for us sinners, now and at the hour of our death.

V. Behold the handmaid of the Lord,
R. Be it done to me according to Thy word.

Hail Mary, full of grace; the Lord is with Thee: blessed art thou among women, and blessed is the fruit of thy womb, Jesus.* Holy Mary, Mother of God, prayer for us sinners, now and at the hour of our death.

V. And the Word was made flesh,
R. And dwelt among us.

Hail Mary, full of grace; the Lord is with Thee: blessed art thou among women, and blessed is the fruit of thy womb, Jesus.* Holy Mary, Mother of God, prayer for us sinners, now and at the hour of our death.

V. Pray for us, O holy Mother of God,
R. That we may be made worthy of the promises of Christ.

Let us pray.

Pour forth, we beseech Thee, Lord, Thy grace into our hearts; that, as we have known the Incarnation of Christ, Thy Son, by the message of an angel, so by His Passion and Cross we may be brought to the glory of the Resurrection. Through the same Christ our Lord.

R. Amen.

Evening Prayers

In the name of the Father, + and of the Son, and of the Holy Ghost. Amen.

Come, O Holy Ghost, fill the hearts of Thy faithful, and kindle in them the fire of Thy love.

Place Yourself in the Presence of God and Humbly Adore Him.

O my God, I present myself before Thee at the end of another day, to offer Thee anew the homage of my heart. I humbly adore Thee, my Creator, my Redeemer, and my Judge! I believe in Thee, because Thou art Truth itself; I hope in Thee, because Thou art faithful to Thy promises; I love Thee with my whole heart, because Thou art infinitely worthy of being loved; and for Thy sake I love my neighbor as myself.

RETURN THANKS TO GOD FOR ALL HIS MERCIES.

Enable me, O my God, to return Thee thanks as I ought for all Thine inestimable blessings and favors. Thou hast thought of me and loved me from all eternity; Thou hast formed me out of nothing; Thou hast delivered up Thy beloved Son to the ignominious death of the cross for my redemption; Thou hast made me a member of Thy holy Church; Thou hast preserved me from falling into the abyss of eternal misery, when my sins had provoked Thee to punish me; Thou hast graciously continued to spare me, even though I have not ceased to offend Thee. What return, O my God, can I make for Thy innumerable blessings, and particularly for the favors of this day? O all ye saints and angels, unite with me in praising the God of mercies, who is so bountiful to so unworthy a creature.

Our Father. Hail Mary. I believe.

ASK OF GOD LIGHT TO DISCOVER THE SINS COMMITTED THIS DAY.

O my God, sovereign judge of men, who desirest not the death of a sinner, but that he should be converted and saved, enlighten my mind, that I may know the sins which I have this day committed in thought, word, or deed, and give me the grace of true contrition.

Here Examine your Conscience; then say

O my God, I heartily repent and am grieved that I have offended Thee, because Thou art infinitely good and sin is infinitely displeasing to Thee. I humbly ask of Thee mercy and pardon, through the infinite merits of Jesus Christ. I resolve, by the assistance of Thy grace, to do penance for my sins, and I will endeavor never more to offend Thee.

THE CONFITEOR

Latin

Confiteor Deo omnipotenti, et vobis fratres, quia peccavi nimis cogitatione, verbo opere et omissione: mea culpa, mea culpa, mea maxima culpa. Ideo precor beatam Mariam semper Virginem, omnes angelos et Sanctos, et vobis fratres, orare pro me ad Dominum Deum nostrum. Amen.

Misereatur nostril Omnipotens Deus, et dimissis peccatis nobis, perducat nos ad vitam aeternam. Amen.

Indulgentiam, + absolutionem, et remissionem peccatorum nostrorum, tribuat nobis omnipotens et misericors Dominus. Amen.

English

I confess to almighty God, and to you my brothers and sisters, that I have sinned through my own fault, in my thoughts and in my words, in what I have done and what I have failed to do. I ask blessed Mary ever Virgin, all the angels and saints, and you my brothers and sisters, to pray for me to the Lord our God. Amen.

May Almighty God have mercy upon us, and forgive us our sins, and bring us unto life everlasting. Amen.

May the Almighty and merciful Lord grant us pardon, + absolution, and remission of our sins. Amen.

PRAY FOR THE CHURCH OF CHRIST

O God, hear my prayers on behalf of our Holy Father Pope N., our Bishops, our clergy, and for all that are in authority over us. Bless, I beseech Thee, the whole Catholic Church, and convert all heretics and unbelievers.

PRAY FOR THE LIVING AND FOR THE FAITHFUL DEPARTED

Pour down Thy blessings, O Lord, upon all my friends, relations, and acquaintances, and upon my enemies, if I have any. Help the poor and sick, and those who are in their last agony. O God of mercy and goodness, have compassion on the souls of the faithful in purgatory; put an end to their sufferings, and grant to them eternal light, rest, and happiness. Amen.

COMMEND YOURSELF TO GOD, TO THE BLESSED VIRGIN, AND THE SAINTS

Bless, O Lord, the repose I am about to take, that, my bodily strength being renewed, I may be the better enabled to serve Thee.

O blessed Virgin Mary, Mother of mercy, pray for me that I may be preserved this night from all evil, whether of body or soul. Blessed St. Joseph, and all ye saints and angels of Paradise, especially my guardian angel and my chosen patron, watch over me. I commend myself to your protection now and always. Amen.

LITANY OF LORETTO

Latin	*English*
Kyrie, eleison.	Lord, have mercy.
Christe, eleison.	Christ, have mercy.
Kyrie, eleison.	Lord, have mercy.
Christe, audi nos.	Christ, hear us.
Christe, exaudi nos.	Christ, graciously hear us.
Pater de caelis, Deus,	God the Father of heaven,
...miserere nobis.	...have mercy upon us.
Fili, Redemptor mundi, Deus,	God the Son, Redeemer of the world,
Spiritus Sancte, Deus,	God the Holy Spirit,
Sancta Trinitas, unus Deus,	Holy Trinity, one God,
Sancta Maria,	Holy Mary,
...ora pro nobis.	...pray for us.
Sancta Dei Genetrix,	Holy Mother of God,
Sancta Virgo virginum,	Holy Virgin of virgins,
Mater Christi,	Mother of Christ,
Mater divinae gratiae,	Mother of divine grace,

Mater purissima,	Mother most pure,
Mater castissima,	Mother most chaste,
Mater inviolata,	Mother inviolate,
Mater intemerata,	Mother undefiled,
Mater amabilis,	Mother most amiable,
Mater admirabilis,	Mother most admirable,
Mater boni consilii,	Mother of good counsel,
Mater Creatoris,	Mother of our Creator,
Mater Salvatoris,	Mother of our Savior,
Virgo prudentissima,	Virgin most prudent,
Virgo veneranda,	Virgin most venerable,
Virgo praedicanda,	Virgin most renowned,
Virgo potens,	Virgin most powerful,
Virgo clemens,	Virgin most merciful,
Virgo fidelis,	Virgin most faithful,
Speculum iustitiae,	Mirror of justice,
Sedes sapientiae,	Seat of wisdom,
Causa nostrae laetitiae,	Cause of our joy,
Vas spirituale,	Spiritual vessel,
Vas honorabile,	Vessel of honor,
Vas insigne devotionis,	Singular vessel of devotion,
Rosa mystica,	Mystical rose,
Turris Davidica,	Tower of David,
Turris eburnea,	Tower of ivory,
Domus aurea,	House of gold,
Foederis arca,	Ark of the covenant,
Ianua caeli,	Gate of heaven,
Stella matutina,	Morning star,
Salus infirmorum,	Health of the sick,
Refugium peccatorum,	Refuge of sinners,
Consolatrix afflictorum,	Comfort of the afflicted,
Auxilium Christianorum,	Help of Christians,
Regina Angelorum,	Queen of angels,
Regina Patriarcharum,	Queen of patriarchs,
Regina Prophetarum,	Queen of prophets,
Regina Apostolorum,.	Queen of apostles,
Regina Martyrum,	Queen of martyrs,
Regina Confessorum,	Queen of confessors,
Regina Virginum,	Queen of virgins,

Regina Sanctorum omnium,
Regina sine labe originali concepta,
Regina in caelum assumpta,
Regina sacratissimi Rosarii,
Regina pacis,
Agnus Dei, qui tollis peccata mundi, parce nobis, Domine.
Agnus Dei, qui tollis peccata mundi, exaudi nos, Domine.
Agnus Dei, qui tollis peccata mundi, miserere nobis.

V. Ora pro nobis, sancta Dei Genetrix.
R. Ut digni efficiamur promissionibus Christi.

Oremus.

> Concede nos famulos tuos, quaesumus, Domine Deus, perpetua mentis et corporis sanitate gaudere, et gloriosae beatae Mariae simper Virginis intercessione, a praesenti liberari tristitia, et aeterna perfrui laetitia. Per Christum Dominum nostrum.

R. Amen.

Queen of all saints,
Queen conceived without original sin,
Queen assumed into heaven,
Queen of the most holy Rosary,
Queen of peace,
Lamb of God, who take away the sins of the world,
spare us, O Lord.
Lamb of God, who take away the sins of the world,
spare us, O Lord.
Lamb of God, who take away the sins of the world,
have mercy upon us.

R. Pray for us, O holy Mother of God.
V. That we may be made worthy of the promises of Christ.

Let us pray.

> Grant, we beseech Thee, O Lord God, unto us Thy servants, that we may rejoice in continual health of mind and body; and, by the glorious intercession of blessed Mary ever Virgin, may be delivered from present sadness, and enter into the joy of Thine eternal gladness. Through Christ our Lord.

R. Amen

Meditations For All the Days of the Year

VOLUME III

From the Second Sunday after Easter
to the Sixth Sunday after Pentecost

THE GOSPEL ACCORDING TO ST. JOHN, 10:11-16.

"Jesus said: I am the good shepherd. The good shepherd giveth his life for his sheep. But the hireling, and he that is not the shepherd, whose own the sheep are not, seeth the wolf coming, and leaveth the sheep, and flieth; and the wolf catcheth and scattereth the sheep. And the hireling flieth, because he is a hireling, and he hath no care for the sheep. I am the good shepherd, and I know Mine, and Mine know Me. As the Father knoweth Me, and I know the Father: and I lay down My life for My sheep. And other sheep I have, that are not of this fold: them also I must bring, and they shall hear My voice, and there shall be one fold and one shepherd."

SUMMARY OF TOMORROW'S MEDITATION

e will meditate tomorrow upon the gospel of the good shepherd, and we shall see: First, all that Jesus Christ has done, as a Good Shepherd, to make us enter into His fold; Second, all that He still does every day to keep us there. We will then make the resolution. First, to keep ourselves in a state of union with Jesus Christ, as with our Good Shepherd, by means of the deepest sentiments of gratitude and love; second, to allow ourselves to be led like docile sheep by His holy inspirations. We will retain as our spiritual nosegay the words which Jesus Christ has said of Himself: "I am the good shepherd." (John 10:11)

MEDITATION FOR THE MORNING

Let us adore Jesus Christ offering Himself to us under the title of the Good Shepherd. Oh, how amiable He is under this title, which includes all His goodness towards us! Let us render Him our homage of adoration, of love, of praise, and of thanksgiving.

FIRST POINT

✝ *What Jesus has done, as the Good Shepherd, to make us Enter into His Fold*

The whole human race had wandered far away from the road leading to heaven, and was walking with closed eyes and a corrupted heart along the road which leads to perdition, when Jesus, the Good Shepherd, beheld us from the height of heaven hastening to our ruin; His heart was touched: My sheep, He said by the prophet, are scattered; I behold them a prey to wild beasts. I will go and seek them and will visit them (Ezech. 34:11). On the day decreed in the eternal councils, He lowers the heavens, and comes to gather together the lost sheep of the house of Israel (Matt. 15: 24). O gratuitous predilection which was not granted even to the angels after their fall! My God, how good Thou art to man, who nevertheless merits it so little! The Good Shepherd begins His labors. After thirty years of preparation in retreat, He spends three more in journeys, labors, fatigue, and sweat, which terminate in only bringing the twelve apostles and the seventy-two disciples into the fold, the infidel Canaanite, Mary Magdalene the sinner, and the schismatic Samaritan; and moreover, at the very moment in which He was immolating Himself for His flock, He was on the point of losing Peter, the first of His sheep, if the glance which He gave him had not brought him back to duty. In addition to that, what has He not also done? To speak only of ourselves, what have we not cost Him? From our first entrance into the fold by holy baptism, how many times have we not wandered away from Him? (Is. 53:6) We have lost ourselves in the paths of self-love and of vanity; of love of the world and its pleasures, its riches and its glory; in the crooked paths of dissipation, of frivolity, of love of our own comfort (Ps. 118:176). Touched by our wanderings, the Good Shepherd set forth to seek us, across deserts, through thorns and over rocks, that is to say, across our passions which ravage us, tear us, and render us insensible to the things of God. After having found His lost sheep, He invited it to return: it resisted Him; He was not discouraged: He remained and remains always at the door of our heart, knocking at it by all His exterior and interior graces (Apoc. 3:20; Jer. 3:12), and when the faithless sheep at last consents to return, He does not make it walk painfully in front of Him, striking it with His crook, He does not drag it along the ground; but, O touching image of the sweetness with which grace at tracts us! He takes it on His shoulders, bears it back to the fold, and holds a feast with all His friends, the angels and the saints, to celebrate His happiness in having brought us back (Luke 15:6). O Good Shepherd of my soul, how shall I ever bless Thee enough and love Thee sufficiently?

SECOND POINT

✝ *What Jesus does every Day, as the Good Shepherd, to keep us in the Fold*

So great is our misery that, after having brought as back to the fold with so much love, we are still inclined to escape through that part of ourselves which runs after the creature, after the world and its pleasures. We seem to say to Jesus Christ that He does not suffice us, that His possession without anything more is sad, that our heart has need of something else, and that something is still wanting to us. Then our imagination, our mind, our heart, and our will, set off on their way and diffuse themselves in the world; and if the Divine Shepherd did not stretch out His hand continually we should abandon the holy fold; whence it follows that Jesus Christ must constantly be at work to keep us there. He employs for that purpose three means: first, His graces, His sacraments, the exhortations of His ministers, a thousand sweet attractions, a thousand amiable controversies by which He captivates the will, whilst at the same time leaving it its free choice, disgusts it with what is evil and attaches it to what is good; second, the good examples afforded us by the just, which He places continually before our eyes; third, all the events of life which He directs towards this end. O Good Shepherd, blessed be Thou for Thy zeal for my salvation! May I henceforth better appreciate Thy goodness and profit better by it! Alas! he who should exceedingly profit by Thy grace would soon become a saint; whilst I who have received so many already, and who receive so many every day. I am still nothing more than a sinner! Pardon, O Good Shepherd! I am about to begin to lead a better life, and to give myself up to Thy guidance. *Resolutions and spiritual nosegay as above.*

Monday in the Second Week after Easter

SUMMARY OF TOMORROW'S MEDITATION

e will meditate tomorrow on the touching care of Jesus Christ, our Good Shepherd: first, in protecting and defending us against the enemies of our salvation; second, in curing all our infirmities. We will then make the resolution: First, often to recommend to Jesus Christ the needs of His Church and of the parish in which we are; second, to invoke Him under the title of the Good Shepherd in our temptations and our trials, and to present ourselves before Him as one who is sick and who asks to be cured, saying to Him, in the words of the Psalmist, which may serve as our spiritual nosegay: "Heal my soul, for I have sinned against Thee. Say to my soul, I am thy salvation." (Ps. 40:5; 34:3)

MEDITATION FOR THE MORNING

Let us adore Jesus Christ as the Good Shepherd watching day and night over His beloved sheep, in order to save them from the jaws of the wolves who want to devour them, or to cure them of their infirmities. Oh, how all these solicitudes and this zeal for our salvation merits all our gratitude and all our love!

FIRST POINT

✝ ***The Touching Care Exercised by Jesus Christ in Order to Protect us from the Enemies of our Salvation***

Our first enemy is the devil. Sin had sold us to him, and we could not be redeemed excepting at the price of blood (Heb. 9:22). Jesus Christ did not hesitate in presence of such a redemption. Before He appeared, many shepherds had been seen to defend their flocks by means of their hands and their voices; but to give their blood and their lives for their sheep was a spectacle which had never been beheld. It was the exclusive glory of our Good Shepherd to love His sheep even to this excess (Eph. 2:4) He had said, "The Good Shepherd giveth His life for His sheep," (John 10:11) and He has indeed done so. He shed His blood to redeem us; and His blood, like that of the Paschal lamb, has preserved us from the sword of the exterminating angel; and the apostle has been able to say to the faithful of all ages: "You were not redeemed with corruptible things such as gold or silver; but with the precious blood of Christ as of a lamb unspotted and undefiled." (1 Pet 1:18,19) Our second enemy is men raging with passion and hatred against the Church and her children. Here the Good Pastor does not fail us any more than in the preceding case. Let us observe with admiration and love all that He has done. During eighteen hundred years He has not ceased to protect the Church, His dear flock, which He bought at the price of all the blood in His veins. He defends it against the sword of tyrants and the hatred of the impious, against the scandals of schism and of heresy, against the reasoning spirit of a science which is proud and vain, and which calls all truth in question; and He preserves it always pure and holy, always catholic and apostolic, always the same in the midst of the eternal variations of human things, of opinions which change, of empires which crumble away. And how wonderful it is! He protects not only the body, but each member in particular. His Providence watches over each one of us with more tenderness than the tenderest mother over her child; so that we may well say with the Psalmist: "The Lord ruleth me, and I shall want nothing. He hath set me in a place of pasture. He hath brought me up on the water of refreshment. For though I should walk in the midst of the shadow of death, I will fear no evils, for Thou art with me. Thy rod and Thy staff, they have comforted me." (Ps.

22:1,2,4) What motives of gratitude for the past, of confidence in the future, of love in the present! Let our hearts overflow with these sentiments towards Jesus, the Good Shepherd.

SECOND POINT

✝ ***The Touching Solicitude of Jesus, the Good Shepherd, in Curing the Infirmities of His Sheep***

Alas! We are all of us ill. Sick in our mind, which is full of ignorance, prejudices, and errors, subject to a thousand digressions, deceived by the follies of the imagination; sick in our heart, which has in it the germ of all the vices and the principle of all the passions; sick in our body, which rebels against the law and weighs down the soul. O Good Shepherd, heal us or we are lost! Thou hast said in times past by the mouth of Ezeckiel: "I will bind up that which was broken, and I will strengthen that which was weak." (Ezech. 34:16) Thou hast accomplished the prophecy from the time of Thy arrival upon earth; Thou hast marked all Thy steps by cures and blessings (Acts 10:38); the blind have seen, the lame have been straightened, the lepers purified, the dead restored to life. Every day still how many wounds and ills are cured by Thy grace, and the vivifying virtue of Thy sacraments! How many weak and languishing sheep strengthened; how many lepers purified; how many dead restored to life! O heavenly Physician! Thou hast made of Thy blood a precious bath wherein our soul finds healing if it is sick, an increase of strength and of health if it is already in a healthy state. To the merits of Thy divine blood Thou dost add the example of Thy life, the counsels of Thy gospels, the teachings of Thy cross and of Thy sacred wounds, all the means of salvation which Thy Church and her priests put every day at our disposition. Ah, if with so many resources we still remain sick, it is, indeed, our own fault. Thanks, O Good Shepherd, who hast contrived so many remedies for our infirmities. *Resolutions and spiritual nosegay as above.*

Tuesday in the Second Week after Easter

SUMMARY OF TOMORROW'S MEDITATION

Jesus, the Good Shepherd, does not satisfy Himself with only defending and curing His sheep. He feeds them also in the most excellent manner: first, with the bread of His word; second, with the bread of His grace; third, with the bread of the Eucharist. After these considerations, we will make the resolution: first, to profit better by the word of God and His grace, living a life of faith, and never resisting a

good thought; second, to prepare ourselves better for our communions and to preserve the fruits of them better. Our spiritual nosegay shall be the words of St. Paul: "Thanks be to God for His unspeakable gift." (2 Cor. 9:15)

MEDITATION FOR THE MORNING

Let us adore Jesus Christ, the Good Shepherd, for the care which He takes to feed His sheep. He had said by Ezeckiel: "I will feed them in the most fruitful pastures, and in fat pastures upon the mountains of Israel." (Ezech. 34:14) Let us admire the manner in which He has kept His word. Without speaking of the material bread, which He never allows to fail, He gives them the bread of His word, the bread of His grace, the Eucharistic bread. What goodness! and how, for all these things, does He merit our praises and our love!

FIRST POINT

✝ ***The Excellence of the Bread of the Word with which Jesus, The Good Shepherd, feeds His Sheep***

Man does not live solely by material bread; his noble intelligence requires a better kind of bread the bread of truth. If he does not have this bread, his intelligence dies, and man becomes equal to the brute. Therefore Jesus Christ has provided it for us in an admirable manner. Whilst the greatest geniuses of antiquity, after long study, did not know what to think of God and of His providence, of the future destinies of man and the rule of his duties, the word of Jesus Christ nourishes us from our infancy with the doctrines of the most sublime theology. The divine attributes are revealed to us; the secrets of our future life shown in the light of day; the highest virtues taught; the ways of perfection opened out; the sun of justice shines for us in all its splendor. Let us appreciate this great blessing by comparing ourselves with the people who are deprived of it, and let us take heed of abusing it by not conforming our life to our faith.

SECOND POINT

✝ ***The Excellence of the Bread of Grace with which Jesus, the Good Shepherd, feeds His Sheep.***

We are so miserable that it does not suffice us to know the truth in order to believe it, nor what is right in order to practice it. For the one as well as for the other the grace of God is necessary to us, and of this grace Jesus, the Good Shepherd, is prodigal. He gives it to us by the good thought which enlightens, by the interior attraction which touches us. He offers it to whoever asks it of Him. "Ask, and it shall be given you. Seek, and you shall find. Knock, and it shall be opened to you." (Luke 11:9) He offers it to all who appreciate and desire it; He is as a rich man who stands at the door of his palace, with his hands full, calling to all the poor to come and receive his bounties, and excluding none but those who will not ask, or who ask coldly and carelessly, as if something very low in price were in question. Let us here examine ourselves. Do we esteem grace as highly as we ought to do? Do we desire it ardently? Do we ask for it earnestly? When we receive it, do we profit by it? Do we not lose it voluntarily, sometimes by levity of thought, which makes us forget it, sometimes by the cowardice which has no courage to do what it inspires?

THIRD POINT

✝ *The Excellence of the Eucharistic Bread with which Jesus, The Good Shepherd, feeds His Sheep*

It is here that the excess of the love and tenderness of the Divine Pastor is revealed. A Shepherd feeds His flock with His own flesh, and gives them to drink of His own blood! O mystery of love, which only a God could conceive, even as He alone could execute it (Is. 66:8). The parable which Nathan addressed to David is doubtless very touching: A poor man bought a sheep, giving all the money he possessed for it; he brought it up in his house, he made it eat of his bread, drink out of his cup, rest on his bosom, and he loved it as though it had been his daughter. But what a difference between the parable and the reality upon which we are meditating. Jesus Christ is indeed the poor man, since, being by His nature supremely rich, He reduced Himself, from love for us, to indigence. (2 Cor. 8:9) Our soul is indeed the sheep which He bought with all that He possessed (Acts 20: 28). But instead of making it eat of His bread and drink of His cup, He made of Himself food to nourish it and drink where with to slake its thirst. (John 6:56) O Divine Shepherd! How good Thou art, how excellent is the repast Thy love has prepared! (Ps. 22:5) Oh, I do indeed desire to love and serve Thee better, to have more zeal for communion, to prepare myself better for it, and better to profit by it. *Resolutions and spiritual nosegay as above.*

Wednesday in the Second Week after Easter

SUMMARY OF TOMORROW'S MEDITATION

fter having seen, in our preceding meditations, all that Jesus does for us as the Good Shepherd, we will now meditate upon what we ought to do for Him as sheep of His divine fold. We ought before all things to know Him; My sheep know Me, He says. This knowledge is: First, absolutely necessary to us; second, infinitely useful. These are the two points which will form the subject of our meditation. We will then make the resolution: First, to study the life of Jesus Christ, often reading the gospels, and especially that of St. John, the historian of His most intimate thoughts, and the epistles of St. Paul, who has told us so many marvelous secrets about Him; Second, we will often recall to mind, in our meditations, the life of our divine Savior, and beg of Him to make Himself intimately known to us. Our spiritual nosegay shall be the words which the Good Shepherd applied to His sheep: "My sheep know Me." (John 10:14)

MEDITATION FOR THE MORNING

Let us adore Jesus Christ as the Sovereign Pastor, whom it is exceedingly necessary that we should know intimately; let us prostrate ourselves at His feet, begging Him, like St. Augustine, to make Himself known to us, so that we may love Him and serve Him as we ought.

FIRST POINT

✝ ***The Necessity of Knowing Jesus Christ Intimately***

To know Jesus Christ is not only to know His name, His origin, and His history, as we know the name, the origin, and the history of the great men of antiquity; but it is to know His spirit, His heart, His doctrine, His virtues, His mysteries, His whole life, exterior and interior; a knowledge which, in the opinion of St. Paul, is the first of all sciences, the one which is supremely important and supremely necessary. All seemed but as vile clay in the esteem of this great apostle compared with the supereminent science of Jesus Christ (Philipp. 3:8), and He falls prostrate on His knees before God the Father to conjure Him to give this inestimable knowledge to all His dear children of Ephesus. All other sciences are, in fact, of no importance whatever in regard to health of this present life, nor to happiness in the future life; whilst to know Jesus Christ is the key of heaven (John 17:3), the road to eternal life (Ibid. 14:6), and the soul of all the virtues. We shall never know what it is to be meek and humble of heart until we have thoroughly studied the meekness and humility of Jesus; never shall we possess perfect abnegation and true detachment, if we do not mould ourselves in accordance with the well-known and well-considered model of Jesus poor and divested of all things; never shall we subject the resistance made by the heart to contempt and suffering, if Jesus, known and meditated upon, does not present Himself to us in order to make all our murmurings cease; never, above all, shall we love Jesus as we ought if we do not thoroughly know Him, for we only love that which we know to be amiable and in proportion as we know it to be more or less amiable. Jesus Christ only superficially known will be to us but as one of those personages belonging to ancient history or to fable, whose real or imaginary existence may indeed amuse our curiosity, but not excite our love. Let us judge from hence how necessary it is for us to study, in order to know it thoroughly, the exterior and interior life of Jesus Christ.

SECOND POINT

✝ *The Utility of the Knowledge of Jesus Christ*

All kinds of virtue enter into the soul, as though in company, with the knowledge of Jesus Christ. It is impossible in the calmness of reflection to contemplate such tender and compassionate charity, gentleness so attractive, such patience shown exteriorly by an unalterable equanimity of the soul and an unruffled face, such profound humility united with such elevated sentiments, the whole person, in a word, of the Savior, without being enamored of the beauty of virtue, without loving it, without desiring it, without being impelled to tend towards it with our whole strength. It is, above all, impossible to consider in the silence of meditation all the perfections of the Man-God, the mystery of His greatness, the infinite need which we have of His mediation, the immense riches of redemption, the wisdom of His maxims, the holiness of His example and of His actions, of which each one is a lesson, the excess of love revealed by His incarnation, His passion, His death, His sacraments, above all that of the Eucharist, without the heart being in flamed with love; and if in the practice of virtue some difficulties are met with they disappear in presence of this simple reflection: "A God suffered so many humiliations, so many sorrows, and should not I bc without excuse if I were to refuse to suffer infinitely less? A God practiced this or that virtue to so high a degree, and is it not incumbent on me to wish to do likewise?" Happy then is he, O Jesus, who knows Thee, even though he be ignorant of everything else, and unhappy he who knows everything, if he does not know Thee. O Jesus, may I always know Thee ever more and more, so that I may always serve Thee better, always love Thee more. *Resolutions and spiritual nosegay as above.*

Thursday of the Second Week after Easter

SUMMARY OF TOMORROW'S MEDITATION

We will meditate tomorrow on the second duty of the sheep of the Good Shepherd: My sheep, He says, follow Me, and they do not follow a stranger (John 10:4,5). By these words Jesus Christ: First, forbids souls who desire to belong to Him to follow the world; Second, He commands them to follow Him alone. After these considerations we will make the resolution: First, to correct everything in us which is touched with the spirit of the world, its immoderate luxury, its effeminacy, its sensuality, and its idle joys; Second, to propose to ourselves, as the rule of our conduct, the example and the maxims of Jesus Christ. Our spiritual nosegay shall be the words of Our Lord: "The sheep follow the Shepherd, but a stranger they follow not."

MEDITATION FOR THE MORNING

Let us adore the Good Shepherd calling upon us to follow Him and summoning us all to His fold, that He may lead us from there to heaven. Happy he who listens to the voice of Jesus and walks in His footsteps! Woe to him who listens to another voice, and follows another master! Let us bless the Good Shepherd for His gracious invitation.

FIRST POINT

✝ *He who Desires to Follow Jesus Christ ought not to Follow the World*

"No man can serve two masters" (Matt. 6:24), God and the world. There is between the two a complete opposition. The love of the world is incompatible with the love of God, and he who is a friend of the world renders himself the enemy of God (James 4:4). "Love not the world nor the things which are in the world" (1 John 2:15), the Holy Spirit says. The world is wholly given up to evil; its ways, its laws, its examples, its maxims breathe nothing but what is evil (Ibid. 5:19). It esteems nothing but gold and silver, magnificence and greatness, pomp and profane amusements, pleasure and enjoyment, applause and praise. The way in which it walks is wide, spacious, and sown with roses; they feel at their ease there; they are rendered comfort able, they laugh, they amuse themselves, and they lead a life of pleasure. But also they forget there, their salvation and their eternity. Seduced by a false appearance of happiness, they think only of pleasing the world and of being loved by it; they occupy themselves with nothing but its feasts and its events, its spectacles and its society, with all that favors the passions, develops self-love and vanity in the heart, ambition to acquire honors and riches. In a word, they live only for the present, and they have no more care for the world to come than as though it did not exist. Now, it is evident that in following such a path as this we cannot any longer belong to Jesus Christ; we cease to be sheep of His fold, and we cannot hope to be introduced by Him into the eternal pastures. Let us here enter into ourselves and examine whether our heart does not still hide within it many remains of the spirit of the world, the love of a sensual life, the continual seeking our own comfort, uneasiness with regard to human respect, the susceptibilities of self-love.

SECOND POINT

✚ *He who Desires to belong to Jesus Christ ought to Follow in His Footsteps*

The Divine Pastor has Himself said so. My sheep follow Me, He tells us. "I have given you an example, that as I have done so do you also." (John 13:15) Jesus Christ, willing to reform the world, willed that this reform should be accomp-lished still more by way of example than by the language of precepts. Every Christian, says St. John, ought to walk in the footsteps of Jesus Christ (1 John 2:6). It is our vocation (1 Pet. 2:21). In conformity with this rule, God the Father declares to us by St. Paul that He will receive into His kingdom those only who bear a resemblance to His Son (Rom. 8:29). This is why the Apostle said to the faithful: "Be ye followers of me, as I also am of Christ." (1 Cor. 11:1) A Christian, in the language of the Fathers, is another Jesus Christ, and Christianity is an imitation of Jesus Christ. This path, very different from that of the world, is narrow, stony, sown with thorns; that is to say, we must endure discomfort and suffering in it; but it is the path of Jesus Christ, and it is a sure path to heaven. What more is necessary in order to make us resolved to embrace it, and often to ask ourselves during our progress through life: Is it thus that Jesus Christ would think and speak and act? Is this His humility, His charity, His meekness, His patience? How much should we gain if we were frequently to put this question to ourselves! *Resolutions and spiritual nosegay as above.*

SUMMARY OF TOMORROW'S MEDITATION

We will meditate tomorrow on our third duty towards Jesus Christ, considered as the Good Shepherd, a duty which consists in listening to His voice; and we shall see: First, that this Good Shepherd speaks to us; second, that we ought to listen to Him; third, that we ought to obey Him and do all that He tells us. We will then make the resolution: first, to maintain ourselves in an habitual state of recollection, in order to listen to the words which Jesus speaks to us interiorly, avoiding everything which may make the soul give itself up to outward things. Second, never to resist good inspirations and to obey promptly, generously, lovingly, all that grace asks of us. We will retain as our spiritual nosegay the words of David: "I will hear what the Lord God will speak in me." (Ps. 84:9)

MEDITATION FOR THE MORNING

Let us recollect ourselves at the feet of Jesus, the Good Shepherd; let us offer Him our homage of adoration, praise, and love.

FIRST POINT

✝ ***Jesus, the Good Shepherd, Speaks to us.***

The Divine Shepherd loves us too much not to enlighten us by His counsels respecting all we have to do; to console us in our trials, to encourage us in our weaknesses, to recall us to order in our wanderings. He does this sometimes by oral instructions or spiritual reading, sometimes by the good examples He sets before us; at other times by the good thoughts He suggests to us, by the secret touches of His grace, the encouragements He infuses into our hearts, and the good movements of all kinds which He excites in us. We sometimes take these holy interior words to be a product of our own hearts; we are pleased with them, and our pride congratulates itself upon them. Forgive us, Good Shepherd; we attribute to ourselves that which comes from Thee; we steal Thy own property from Thee. I see it now; all that is supernatural in us comes from Thee alone; our evil nature can produce nothing but what is evil. To Thee be honor for all that is good; to us, shame and confusion in all things, and forever and ever (Baruch 1:15).

SECOND POINT

✝ ***We ought to Listen to the Voice of the Good Shepherd.***

What is it to listen to the voice of Jesus Christ within us? It is to maintain the powers of the soul in a great interior silence, to be attentive to the slightest inspirations, recollected and prostrated, as it were, at the feet of Jesus, like Mary, the sister of Martha, that we may listen to Him with reverential respect. If all is not calm and peaceful within us; if the tumult of exterior things penetrates therein, preoccupies, agitates, and troubles us, we shall no longer hear the voice of Jesus. For why should He speak to anyone who does not listen to Him? Hence the unhappiness of wandering thoughts, which deprive the soul of all graces; hence the damnation of the world, which is eternally given up to wandering thoughts, which thinks of everything excepting its salvation and its God; hence the necessity of recollection, of that vigilance over ourselves which opens the ear of the heart to the interior voice. When Jesus finds a soul which is recollected and listening attentively, He speaks to it, He enlightens it, He touches it, and He converts it and sanctifies it. "I will hear," says the Royal Prophet, "what the Lord God will speak to me." (Ps. 84:9) "Speak, Lord," said the young Samuel, "Thy servant heareth." (1 Kings 3:10) "Happy the soul that thus listens within itself! Happy the ears which, closed to all external sounds, open and are attentive to the voice which speaks within." (3 Imit. 1:1) Is it thus that we listen to the words of the Good Shepherd? Are we attentive and careful not to lose a single word He speaks?

THIRD POINT

✝ ***We must Obey the Voice of the Good Shepherd.***

When the Good Shepherd finds nothing in the soul but a cowardly and pusillanimous will, which only obeys in matters which are pleasing to it; which recoils in presence of a sacrifice, and leaves on one side that which annoys and incommodes it, or which does not come back to Him, He is silent, and abandons it to its miserable state, and it is thereby lost. This Divine Pastor requires strong and generous souls, disposed to do all which He asks of them, whatever it may cost them; souls to which He says: Do this, and they do it; go, and they go; speak, and they speak; keep silence, and they are silent. When He finds souls of this kind, He takes possession of them, directs them, animates them, encourages them, and makes them advance rapidly along the road to heaven. It is in this way that saints are made. Is it thus that we obey grace? What a subject of remorse for the past! What matter for resolution for the future! *Resolutions and spiritual nosegay as above.*

Saturday in the Second Week after Easter

SUMMARY OF TOMORROW'S MEDITATION

e will meditate tomorrow on the three special virtues which Jesus, the Good Shepherd, demands from His flock; that is to say: first, innocence; second, meekness; third, docility. We will then make the resolution: first, to infuse a great deal of simplicity and of meekness into all our relations with our neighbor; second, to delight to take the advice of others, and thus to unite their wisdom with our own. Our spiritual nosegay shall be the words of Our Saviour: "Learn of Me, because I am meek and humble of heart." (Matt. 11:29)

MEDITATION FOR THE MORNING

Let us come back to the feet of Jesus, the Good Shepherd; let us adore Him, let us love Him, let us pray to Him to instruct us in the virtues He asks from His sheep.

FIRST POINT

✝ ***The First Virtue the Good Shepherd Asks of us is Innocence.***

Of all animals, the sheep is the least vicious. It goes on its way quietly in the pastures where it is taken, without attacking any one, without righting the other sheep; it is the type of innocence which never does harm to anyone; of that innocence which is the first condition the Good Shepherd requires from His sheep. He wills that they should never do harm to others; that they should be without envy, without hatred, without aversion for others; that they should never wish any one ill; that they should, still less, do any ill themselves; and that candor and innocence should preside over all the acts of their lives, all their designs and their projects; so that, instead of anyone having to complain of them, all should be rendered happy in the intercourse they have with them. Do we possess this primary character of the sheep of the Good Shepherd?

SECOND POINT

✝ ***Meekness, the Second Virtue which the Good Shepherd Demands from His Sheep.***

A sheep is essentially meek, and so meek that it allows itself, without complaint, to be shorn and taken to the slaughter-house. If, then, Our Lord calls us His sheep, it is that we should possess their principal characteristic, which is meekness. He Himself appeared on earth with the meekness of a sheep; (Acts 8:32) and He will recognize as His sheep only those who are marked with the seal of meekness. In order to obtain it, the passions which give birth to impatience must doubtless be mortified; the desires which are annoyed if they are not satisfied must be repressed; the character which is easily hurt must be reformed; the heart must be filled with the charity which endeavors to give pleasure to its neighbor in all things. (1 Cor. 10:33) But how well are we compensated for all our trouble by the tranquility of soul which we enjoy through peace with God, our neighbor, and with ourselves, which is, even here below, our recompense. "Blessed are the meek, for they shall possess the land." (Matt. 5:4) Let us make trial of it. Meekness gains us friends; the want of meekness brings us trouble.

THIRD POINT

✝ ***Docility, the Third Virtue which the Good Shepherd Requires from His Sheep.***

A sheep easily allows itself to be led, it attaches itself to its shepherd, it follows his voice or the indication given by his crook; and if it wanders, it comes back as soon as its shepherd calls it. There is a great lesson to be learnt in this docility of the sheep. Docility allowing itself to be led by obedience is the most distinguishing characteristic of true and solid piety (John 5:45). It is the sure path, the royal road of salvation which Jesus Christ has taught us by His example (Heb. 5:9). Possessed of this docility, we are always at peace, always contented, always sure of being in the right path; whilst, with attachment to our own ideas, to our own will, we are always taking the wrong road; no one is sufficient to himself, says St. Basil; and it is folly, adds St. Bernard, to wish to make one's self master of one's own conduct. Without docility in allowing one's self to be led, all piety is false and wrongly understood: it is nothing but pride and presumption. What are our dispositions in regard to this subject? *Resolutions and spiritual nosegay as above.*

Third Sunday after Easter

THE GOSPEL ACCORDING TO ST. JOHN 16:16-22

"At that time Jesus said to His disciples: A little while and now you shall not see Me: and again a little while and you shall see Me: because I go to the Father. Then some of His disciples said one to another: What is this that He saith to us: A little while and you shall not see Me: and again a little while and you shall see Me, and because I go to the Father, They said therefore: What is this that He saith, A little while? We know not what He speaketh. And Jesus knew that they had a mind to ask Him; and He said to them: Of this do you inquire among yourselves, because I said: A little while and you shall not see Me; and again a little while and you shall see Me? Amen, amen, I say to you, that you shall lament and weep, but the world shall rejoice; and you shall be made sorrowful, but your sorrow shall be turned into joy. A woman when she is in labor hath sorrow, because her hour is come; but when she has brought forth her child she remembers no more the anguish, for joy that a man is born into the world. So also you now indeed have sorrow, but I will see you again, and your heart shall rejoice; and your joy no man shall take from you."

SUMMARY OF TOMORROW'S MEDITATION

e will meditate tomorrow on three subjects for consolation offered by the gospel of the day to souls tried by suffering: First, sufferings here below are of short duration; second, supported in a Christian manner, they are the source of the greatest blessings; third, they are preferable to all worldly joys. After these considerations we will make the resolution: First, cheerfully to accept all the trials which may happen to us during the day; second, to look with pity at all the prosperity and all the joys of this world, as being false and vain. Our spiritual nosegay shall be the words of the gospel: "You shall lament and weep, but the world shall rejoice and you shall be made sorrowful, but your sorrow shall be turned into joy, and your joy no man shall take from you."

MEDITATION FOR THE MORNING

Let us adore Jesus Christ, the good Master and Shepherd of our souls. He sees from afar the persecutions, the sufferings, and the trials of all kinds which await His dear disciples; He is touched, and He addresses to them in the gospel of today the words which are the best suited to console them and to encourage them. Let us thank Him for these good words, and let us beg of Him to enable us to understand them and to love them in our hearts.

FIRST POINT

✝ ***The Sufferings of this Life are Short.***

A little while, says Jesus Christ, and after having lost Me, you will see Me again (John 16:16). Therefore, here below our trials are of only short duration. It is true that they seem long whilst we are suffering from them. A single day, a night, even an hour of suffering, how long sometimes it seems! But there are three ways of abridging the duration of our trials. The first means is not to add to present suffering the sufferings of an unknown future which perhaps we shall never see. Sufficient unto each moment is the evil thereof; why take thought for a morrow which is uncertain? Why suppose that this morrow, even if it exist for us, will not be accompanied by better conditions than is the present moment? Let us then accept the present moment without thinking of the following one; our sufferings will then seem only to endure for a short time. The second means is to look at time and eternity together, and not separately. Looked at thus, oh, of what short duration our sufferings will seem to be! From the depths of eternity, from the depths of a hundred millions of ages, the duration of our trials will seem hardly as a flash of lightning which disappears almost at the same moment that we see it; like yesterday, which already exists no longer (Ps. 89:4). Our Lord, in His love, offers us a third means for abridging the time of suffering: He permits us to mingle with it certain recreations which turn away our thoughts from suffering, on condition that these recreations are in themselves irreproachable; that we indulge in them without passion, that we propose a Christian object to ourselves in them, such as a virtuous amusement, or something that will give pleasure to our neighbor; and, lastly, we do not consecrate to such recreations more time than is permitted to us by the duties of our state or the exercises of piety and of charity. Do we make use of these three means for abridging our sufferings?

SECOND POINT

✝ ***Sufferings are, for the Just, the Source of the Greatest Blessings.***

You shall weep, you shall groan, you shall be sorrowful, said Christ to His disciples. Now He, who loved them so much, would not have subjected them to such trials if He had not beheld hidden treasures under them. It is because, in point of fact, suffering detaches the heart from this world, whilst enjoyment attaches it to it. Suffering makes us think of God and of our salvation, whilst prosperity and pleasures make us forget Him; suffering is an expiation of the past a thousand times sweeter than purgatory, reserved for those who, before death, have not performed sufficient penance. Suffering is a preservative against the future faults into which we should be drawn by our nature, which is predisposed to the satisfaction of our sensualities and our attachments. Suffering, lastly, is a presage of predestination, because of the resemblance it gives us to Jesus Christ's suffering (Rom. 8:17). Thanks, then, to the cross, thanks to the sufferings which procure for us such great blessings. If we do not feel in us this love for the cross, let us ask it of Our Lord; it is an eminently Christian feeling.

THIRD POINT

✝ ***Sufferings, borne in a Christian Manner, are Preferable to the Vain Joys of the World.***

All the pleasures of the world cannot content the heart. It is only seeming happiness, under which are hidden sorrow and remorse; and, besides, at the hour of death this false joy will be converted into terrible sorrow. Then the past will present to the soul all the sins committed, all the time lost, all the opportunities of doing good passed by; the present will tear the heart with the necessity of leaving, of quitting all that it has loved; and the future will cast it into indescribable fear by showing it the judgment which awaits it, followed by an everlasting hell. The just, on the contrary, amidst the sufferings inseparable to the present life are consoled, first, by hopes of the future life; St. Cyprian says that, standing on the fragments of a world in ruins, we are calm, patient, always the same; adversities do not cast us down or sicknesses make us murmur, because we know that the infinite felicity which awaits us is well worth the trouble of being bought by crosses here below. They are consoled, second, by the sweetness of grace and the testimony of a good conscience, which made St. Bernard say: The worldly-minded see the cross; but they do not see the unction which renders it delicious. Then, lastly, at the hour of death their sorrow is changed into immense and eternal joy (John 16:20,22). Who, therefore, would not love suffering, or at least accept it with resignation? *Resolutions and spiritual nosegay as above.*

Monday in the Third Week after Easter

SUMMARY OF TOMORROW'S MEDITATION

Having seen in our meditations of last week that we ought to know and imitate Jesus Christ, we will tomorrow study His interior life, which the human eye has not seen, but which ought equally to form the subject of our meditations. The author of the Imitation teaches us in few words what the interior life is. It consists, he says, in keeping the heart: First, recollected in God, and second, disengaged from all other attachments (2 Imit. 5:4). We shall see how the holy soul of Jesus Christ satisfied these two conditions. Our resolution shall be: First, to apply ourselves with our whole heart to a life of recollection and of union with God; second, to repress the license of the senses and of the imagination which is at the bottom of a life of forgetfulness of God. Our spiritual nosegay shall be these two words, God alone, which are the epitome of the two points of our meditation.

MEDITATION FOR THE MORNING

Let us adore the holy soul of Our Lord entirely recollected in God; to adore Him, to love Him, to bless Him, to follow in all things His good pleasure, and to pray to Him for our guilty human race, therein consisted the whole of His life. In this holy soul there was no frivolity; no wandering thoughts; God alone was everything for it. Let us render to Him in this sublime state our homage of adoration and of praise.

FIRST POINT

✝ *The Holy Soul of Jesus Christ Maintained Itself always in a State of Recollection in God.*

The interior of Jesus, always recollected in the Divinity which inhabited it substantially, was a marvelous spectacle in the eyes of God and of His angels. I am not alone, He often said: My Father is with Me (John 8:16). I am in My Father, and My Father is in Me, directing all My movements and all My acts (Ibid. 14:10), inspiring all My words (Ibid. 12:49), presiding over all My undertakings (Ibid. 8:28; 5:17). There was nothing, not even the very slightest acts of His understanding or the least of the judgments of His mind, which did not proceed from this sacred union (John viii. 16). This holy soul also kept itself continually united with God in all its thoughts and all its affections, esteeming and loving God only, without anything being able to distract it from this holy union: neither the events or revolutions of the earth nor the various affairs of this lower world, which it beheld from a height far above it, and which it dominated from the region which it in habited, which was the bosom of God, in which its whole life was passed. Let us draw near to this divine model. Alas! How greatly do the wanderings of our imagination and of our mind, the attachments of our hearts and the dissipation of our senses, cast us far away from this life of recollection in God! We dwell on nothing but the trifles of this world, on all its affairs, on all the daydreams which pass through our heads, and we forget God, who never forgets us, and who is in us. Let us be humbled and confounded at such forgetfulness.

SECOND POINT

✝ ***The Holy Soul of the Savior Lived in Perfect Detachment from all which is not God.***

This admirable soul, seeing on the one hand the infinite perfections of God and on the other the nothingness of the creature, perceived nothing outside God which could captivate or interest its heart. Enjoyment or privation, honor or obscurity, praise or contempt, all was the same to it: God alone was everything to it. In it there was no attachment to anything whatever, no desires, no self-will. I do not live for Myself but for My Father (John 6:58), it said. I do not seek what pleases Me, but solely that which pleases Him (Ibid. 5:30); His most holy will is My life, My food (Ibid. 4:34); His good pleasure is the rule of all My acts (Ibid. 29); whatever it may cost Me, may nothing ever be done as I will it should be (Matt. 26:39); so that, O divine life! O holiness which must have delighted the heart of God! Our Savior, during His whole life never said a word or performed an act excepting by the direction of the Divinity which was in Him. There was, it is true, in His sacred Person a human will and a divine will, but the one united itself lovingly with the other by a single act distinct and created; the human will lost itself in the love of the divine will in such a manner that from two distinct causes there resulted one same effect equally desired, without there ever being any self-seeking or any admixture of seeking after creatures. Is it thus that we belong entirely to God? What matter for self-examination is there here! *Resolutions and spiritual nosegay as above.*

Tuesday in the Third Week after Easter

SUMMARY OF TOMORROW'S MEDITATION

e will continue to study the interior life of Jesus Christ, and we will consider it in its two fundamental principles, which are: First, the spirit of prayer; second, the spirit of sacrifice. We will then make the resolution: First, to be exact in making our meditation every morning before performing any other action; to make sacrifices willingly, be they great or small, with which grace inspires us, or which events demand of us. Our spiritual nosegay shall be the words of St. Paul: "Walk worthy of God, in all things pleasing." (Coloss. 1:10)

MEDITATION FOR THE MORNING

Let us penetrate with religious respect into the holy soul of Jesus. Let us honor it as the source and the model of the interior life (John 1:4), as the sweet light which rejoices the eyes of God amidst the darkness of the world (Ibid. 5), as an ocean of graces the fullness of which overflows upon us (Ibid. 16).

FIRST POINT

✝ ***Prayer: the First Principle of the Interior Life of Jesus Christ.***

The soul of Jesus Christ, by means of the intuitive vision which it enjoyed, did not limit itself to being always in the presence of God; it spoke to Him in prayer and maintained a holy intercourse with Him. This prayer began from the very first moment of the incarnation in the rapture of ecstasy, was continued through His life, and will last throughout eternity. If during His mortal life He spent whole nights in prayer (Luke 5:12), if He betook Himself to the mountains or the desert that He might give Himself up to this holy exercise (Ibid. 5:16), it was only to preach to all coming ages, by His example, the necessity of prayer. For in His case, His prayer knew no interruption; day and night He lived in the profound abasement of His whole being in presence of the infinite excellence of the Divine Being, of His littleness in presence of the immensity of God, of His dependence in presence of the sovereignty of God, of His lowness in presence of the Divine Majesty. There issued from His heart adorations and praises which ravished the whole of the celestial court, happy to acquiesce in them by an eternal amen; there were burning affections, there were effusions of love, to which God responded by a love which was always new ; there was fervent prayer which embraced and still embraces all the interests of the world. Jesus hears, on the one hand, the voice of our crimes, crying aloud to heaven for vengeance, and He stifles it by the more powerful voice of His prayer which makes the thunder to fall from the hands of God; on the other hand, He receives the homage and the prayers of all Christians, clothes them with His merits, and thus being rendered divine, He offers them to His Father. Oh, how admirable is the prayer of the holy soul of Jesus Christ! How it maintains and perfects without ceasing interior life and union with God! O prayer, treasure of the soul, bond of union between heaven and earth, thou art a foretaste of Paradise. Do we hold it in the esteem we ought to?

SECOND POINT

✝ ***The Spirit of Sacrifice: the Second Principle of the Interior Life of Jesus Christ.***

Devoid of the spirit of sacrifice, nature which seeks itself, exterior objects which distract us, attachments which drag us earthwards, desires which take us captive all these things tend to make us live in a state of eternal dissipation; now interior life is not possible except on the condition of sacrifice. Jesus Christ began to immolate Himself when He began to live; from that moment He looked upon Himself as a victim destined to sacrifice; and He kept Himself before God in the habitual disposition of a holocaust; happy to obtain, by one and the same act, infinite glory for God, salvation for the world, and an example for all future ages. Following this heavenly model, we ought interiorly to renounce all right over our body and our senses, our mind and our heart, and still more over external goods, and make of all these things a complete sacrifice to God, without any "robbery in the holocaust" (Is. 61:8). We ought no longer to use them except with a view to God, and according to God, and we ought often to say to ourselves: All this does not belong to me, it all belongs to God; it is for God to dispose of it as pleases Him; it is for me to feel that all He wills is good, to do always that which seems to me to be most conformable to His good pleasure, and to maintain myself in His presence in a state of perpetual dependence, of sacrifice, and of a holocaust. It is only in this manner that the interior life is formed and perfected in the soul. Let us ask God to enable us to understand these truths. *Resolutions and spiritual nosegay as above.*

Wednesday in the Third Week after Easter

SUMMARY OF TOMORROW'S MEDITATION

After having learned from the example set us by the Savior, in what the interior life consists, we shall see that this life is: First, a duty of reason; second, a duty of faith. We will then make the resolution: First, to avoid all which tends to dissipation of thought, and to recall the presence of God to ourselves, from time to time, by a moment of recollection and of reflection; second, to mingle with our different occupations the frequent use of ejaculatory prayers, and, above all, the practice of offering to God every one of our actions. Our spiritual nosegay shall be the words of Jacob: "Indeed the Lord is here and I knew it not." (Gen. 28:16)

MEDITATION FOR THE MORNING

Let us adore the holy soul of Jesus Christ, always perfectly recollected in God, always praising, glorifying, and loving His adorable perfections, and let us offer Him all the homage of which we are capable. Let us beg of Him to enable us to enter into His sentiments and into His practice.

FIRST POINT

✝ *Reason Makes the Interior Life a Law for us*

On the sole account that reason shows to us God present in the bottom of our heart as well as in the splendors of the saints, it thereby imposes on us the duty of thinking of Him. Of respecting His presence, of speaking to Him, of adoring Him, of praising Him, of thanking Him, of asking of Him grace, and soliciting pardon for our sins; it prescribes us to listen with holy recollection to His interior word, which excites so many good thoughts and good sentiments in whoever will listen to it; it tells us, lastly, to please Him by the offering of our actions, by the sacrifice of our wills, of our tastes, and of all that we are, by the practice of virtues, above all of the humility which abases us in the presence of His greatness, and by the divine love which raises us to Him, so that from thenceforth His heart and our own are but one. We are astonished that anchorites should have thus spent the half of a century in a cavern, deprived of intercourse with men; but if we knew of what value is the society of God, with whom they kept company night and day in the bottom of their hearts, and how creatures are as nothing to a soul which has the Creator with it, we should be much more astonished to see man think so much of creatures and so little of his God, who accompanies him everywhere, occupy himself so greedily and so continually with what is worth nothing, so rarely and so coldly with Him who is everything. Oh, how sin must have obscured the senses in order to make us forget, as we do, the great God whose presence invests and penetrates us, and to prefer to Him the thought of the miserable things of this lower world, and even the phantoms of our imagination !

SECOND POINT

✝ *Faith Makes the Interior Life a Law for us.*

In the same way, says Jesus Christ, that the shoot draws its life from the vine, by receiving from it what is most interior in it, which is the sap, the juice by which it itself lives, so you cannot live spiritually excepting in so far as you remain united to Me. If you do not remain in Me, He continues, you shall be cast out like the dry and sterile shoot which is cast into the fire. (John 15:4-6) In conformity with this doctrine, the apostle St. Paul says to us: "Let this mind be in you which was also in Christ Jesus." (Philipp. 2:5) "Though our outward man is corrupted, yet the inward man is renewed day by day." (2 Cor. 4:16) "I bow my knees to the Father of Our Lord Jesus Christ" he says to the Ephesians, "that He would grant you, according to the riches of His glory, to be strengthened by His Spirit with might unto the inward man, that Christ may dwell by faith in your hearts, being rooted and founded in charity." (Eph. 3: 14,16,17) "If any man have not the Spirit of Christ, he is none of His." (Rom. 8:9) There is, indeed, no Christian action except that which is performed in the spirit of Jesus Christ, after the pattern set us by Jesus Christ and in union with Jesus Christ. Now, when the interior life is neglected, actions are performed without being inspired by faith, without any thought of Jesus Christ, and outside Jesus Christ, even as though He did not exist. Is it not too often that we thus act? *Resolutions and spiritual nosegay as above.*

Thursday in the Third Week after Easter

SUMMARY OF TOMORROW'S MEDITATION

We will meditate tomorrow: First, upon the excellence of the interior life; and, in order that we may understand it, we will compare it with the exterior life, which is the life of the world; second, we shall see that it raises the Christian to the height of the divine life in Jesus Christ. We will then make the resolution: first, to avoid all that dissipates us, or to which we have an attachment, such as certain kinds of society and certain conversations. Second, to enter into the spirit of Christ by often asking ourselves: Is it thus that Jesus Christ would speak or act? Is this the spirit or the intention which would direct His words or His acts? Our spiritual nosegay shall be the words of St. John: "God Hath sent His only begotten Son into the world that we may live by Him." (1 John 4:9)

MEDITATION FOR THE MORNING.

Let us prostrate ourselves in spirit before Jesus Christ; let us adore Him as the Author, the Founder, and the Model of the interior life, of that life which begins here below by grace and which is consummated in heaven by glory. Let us make a sacrifice at His feet of our want of recollection, that great enemy of the life of Jesus Christ in us; let us beg of Him to correct us of it, so that hence forth we may live only by His life.

FIRST POINT

✝ ***The Comparison between the Interior Life with the wholly Exterior Life of the World.***

What is the exterior life? It is the life which St. Paul calls the old man, the man of sin, the animal man, the old Adam, entirely filled with the spirit and the inclinations of his miserable father. A slave, like him, to his senses, the exterior man thinks only of the things of this world, and not of those of heaven. Sensible things attract him, distract him, and dissipate him to such a degree that he finds it difficult to enter into himself, that he may understand what has respect to God and to his salvation; he is wholly occupied with the lower things of earth, and scarcely ever with the greater things of heaven; he is entirely taken up with the present and with what passes away, scarcely ever with eternity and with what endures forever. It is quite otherwise with the man who leads an interior life. By means of this most blessed life, the Christian becomes a man of heaven, because his thoughts, his desires, and his affections, instead of groveling upon the earth, rise to heaven. By it he becomes the spiritual man, because, leaving beneath him, as things that are unworthy of him, the inclinations of corrupt nature, he treads his passions under foot, and if they rebel he crushes them; he attaches himself to God alone, he desires God only, and he places all his happiness in thinking of God. What a difference between these two lives! The first is wholly terrestrial and animal: it is nothing but self-love, pride, vanity, impatience, idleness, love of pleasure, enjoyments of the flesh, and, after that, death (Rom. 8:13). The second is celestial and angelic; it withdraws us from sensible objects, recalls us within ourselves to occupy us with God, and fills our minds with the illuminations of faith, our hearts with the fervor of devotion. It is the life of the predestinate and of the children of God; it has been the life of all the saints since the birth of the Church, and it is still the life of the elect souls which are the honor of religion. Let us aspire to so beautiful a life, and let us labor to form it in ourselves.

SECOND POINT

✝ ***The Interior Life Raises the Christian to the Height of the Divine Life in Jesus Christ.***

St. Paul describes to us admirably the divine life which the practice of the interior life realizes in us. It is no longer I who live, he says, it is Jesus Christ who liveth in me (Gal. 2:20). It is no longer I, that is to say, it is no longer the child of Adam, the old man whose life is wholly exterior, with low and terrestrial inclinations, but it is Jesus Christ who lives in me; His thoughts are my thoughts, His heart is my heart, in the sense that I love what He loves, I only will what He wills. Jesus Christ is my life (Philipp. 1:21), and He ought to be yours (Coloss. 3:4), He says to the faithful; that is to say, that as the soul is the life of the body, all of whose senses it puts into motion, the eyes to see, the tongue to speak, the hands to act, the feet to walk so Jesus Christ, our life, ought to do in us all that pleases Him without finding any resistance on our part; He ought to regulate the movements of our bodies by keeping them within the bounds of modesty and of decorum, to govern our tongue that it may say nothing which is evil, our hands, that they may be occupied in good works, our mind that it may be filled with nothing but good thoughts, our heart that it may have no other sentiments but His (Philipp. 2:5). We are grafted upon Jesus Christ, says the same apostle (Rom. 6:5). Now the graft becomes one and the same thing as the tree upon which it is grafted; it lives the same life; the same sap nourishes it. It is thus that we ought to live one same life with Jesus Christ, to have with Him only one common principle regulating our acts and our wills, the same objects, the same intentions, the same sentiments in all and for all. Lastly, continues St. Paul, Jesus Christ is out head, and we are His members (Eph. 5:23,30). Now the head and the members ought to live the same life, and as it is from the head that life flows down upon all the inferior members, so the divine life ought to flow down from Jesus upon us. As we form with Him one sole body, we ought to form with Him one sole spirit, and one and the same heart; one sole body and two different spirits would be a monstrosity. We ought then to think in all things like Jesus Christ, love what He loved, nothing more and nothing less; inspire ourselves with the whole of His sentiments, animate all our acts with the same intentions, and keep our interior as He kept His, always recollected in God. Such is the grand Christian life, which, according to St. John, was the object of the Incarnation of the Word (I. John 4:9), and whoever does not live this life is not a Christian (Rom. 8:9). How beautiful it is, this divine life, and how worthy it is of our ambition, of our efforts, and of our prayers! *Resolutions and spiritual nosegay as above.*

Friday in the Third Week after Easter

SUMMARY OF TOMORROW'S MEDITATION

In order that we may penetrate still more deeply into the excellence of the interior life, we will consider tomorrow its influence upon our happiness even in this world, and we shall see: First, the happiness of the soul which lives an interior life; second, the unhappiness of the soul which does not live this divine life. We will then make the resolution: First, to watch over our senses, our imagination, and our useless thoughts, so as not to allow ourselves to be dragged in to dissipation; second, to accustom ourselves to the use of ejaculatory prayers, which unite the soul to God. Our spiritual nosegay shall be the words of the Patriarch, "The Lord liveth, before whom I stand." (3 Kings 17:1)

MEDITATION FOR THE MORNING

Let us adore the interior of Jesus Christ as the sanctuary of God, as the temple wherein the Divinity continually receives homage worthy of it, and where man always finds protection, defense, salvation, and happiness. Let us offer Him all our homage of admiration, of praise, of thanksgiving, and of love.

FIRST POINT

✝ *The Happiness of the Soul which Leads an Interior Life*

There is a foretaste of heaven, like an anticipated Paradise, in the divine union which permits he interior man to say: I am in the company of God, of the God who loves me, who protects me, who is attentive to the slightest good that I do, to recompense me eternally, to the least sigh of my heart, to render me love for love. A quarter of an hour of this life is worth more than all the pleasures of this world put together. Therefore the Apostle invites all just souls to rejoice in the Lord (Philipp. 4:4), and he declares that peace and joy are the fruit of the Holy Spirit reigning in the soul (Gal. 5:22). Filled with the same sentiment, David said: In my troubles I remembered God and I was consoled (Ps. 76:4). I said to myself, the Lord is at my right hand to sustain me, and this thought thrilled me with gladness (Ps. 15:8,9). Let the just thrill with gladness and rejoice in the presence of God (Ps. 67:4). The author of the Imitation admirably describes to us this happiness of the interior life. The interior man, he says (2 Imit. 1:1), often receives a visit from God, which gives him a delightful feeling, an exquisite enjoyment of His presence. God speaks to his heart, and he speaks to God. It is an amiable exchange, a sweet intercourse consisting in intimate communications between the Creator and the creature. It is an ineffable consolation in his trials. It is calm amidst the agitations of the world, it is peace in the midst of tumult; the soul feels itself to be therein in its element, in its true bed of rest, and nothing can trouble it there, because God alone suffices it, God alone is everything to it. Then there takes place between God and the soul, as between two hearts which understand and which love each other, a more than astonishing familiarity, and the familiarity of a child with its father and of a father with his child. If God, in order to try it, is sometimes silent, and seems to abandon it, it complains lovingly to Him, without being cast down; it sees in this temporary abandonment a lesson of humility which teaches it that in itself it is nothing; a lesson of love which makes it feel how good God is to love such a poor creature; it blesses Him for this double lesson, but without on that account, in any way, diminishing its exactness in serving Him, and soon grace reappears and consoles it. Let us encourage ourselves by means of these considerations to practice an interior life.

SECOND POINT

✚ *The Unhappiness of the Soul which does not Lead an Interior Life*

The soul devoid of an interior life is essentially dissipated; its mind being unoccupied within and empty of all that could interest it, it wanders and employs itself with all kinds of exterior things; its heart is attached to what passes away, its will follows its caprices, its self-love is fed upon praise and esteem. Now in such a state as this, it is essentially unhappy. The heart drawn upwards by grace and downwards by nature suffers a kind of torture. Each deception of vanity, each contrariety of the will, is as a sword which pierces it; the imagination, always wandering, transforms exercises of piety into insipid practices, prayer into distractions and fatigue; it makes solitude a weariness, the whole life nothing but disgust. It feels nothing any longer of the cross than its nails and its thorns, nothing of the yoke of Jesus Christ but its weight, nothing of His chalice but its bitterness. Then are accomplished the words of St. Augustine: Thou hast made us for Thyself, Lord, and as long as our heart does not repose in Thee, it cannot enjoy either repose or happiness. Let us examine whence come our disgust, our weariness, and our troubles, and we shall see that the absence of the interior life, that is to say, our dissipation and our attachments, are the principal cause of them. *Resolutions and spiritual nosegay as above.*

Saturday in the Third Week after Easter

SUMMARY OF TOMORROW'S MEDITATION

We will terminate our meditations upon the interior life by considering three means of acquiring and perfecting it in us: First, by a well-regulated life; second, by keeping a restraint over the senses; third, by the frequent use of ejaculatory prayers. We will then make the resolution: First, not to leave the employment of our time to caprice, but to follow a rule of life which assigns to each moment its own proper duty; second, to keep ourselves on our guard against useless thoughts and against the curiosity which desires to see and know all that is going on; to exercise ourselves, day and night, in the practice of ejaculatory prayers. Our spiritual nosegay shall be the words of the canticle: "Let us serve God in holiness and justice before Him all our days." (Luke 1:74,75)

MEDITATION FOR THE MORNING

Let us adore the holy soul of Jesus Christ in the depth of the recollection of His interior life, conversing with His Father in the secret of His heart, and following in all the details of His life the good pleasure of His adorable Father, without ever yielding to caprice or to useless thoughts. Let us thank Him for the beautiful example which He gives us, and let us render our homage to Him.

FIRST POINT

✝ *A Well-regulated Life the First Means of Acquiring and Perfecting the Interior Life within us*

Two things are both necessary and efficacious to the leading of an interior life: First, there must be order in the employment of time. Exterior disorder makes the interior to be ill-regulated, it disorganizes it, dissipates it, and makes it fail to perform, either through forgetfulness or a bad arrangement of its time, its essential duties, even as, on the other hand, a well-regulated exterior makes the soul recollected, keeps it steadfast to its rule, and renders life in God and for God easy. Second, there must be fidelity in regard to certain pious exercises, which are as necessary to the soul as the soul is to the body; these exercises maintain within the soul views of faith, good thoughts, pious sentiments. With these exercises all goes on well; without them all proceeds badly; the soul dries up, and is disgusted with its duties, with God, even with its own interior, where it cannot any longer bear itself to be, having no pleasure beyond that of giving itself up to outside things. Now a well-regulated life is the sole means of being orderly and faithful to the practice of pious exercises. Where there is no rule there is no order. We live by caprice and fancies; we do everything at a wrong season; each day differs from the one which precedes it; there is a continual variation in the employment of our time. With a rule of life, on the contrary, all is done in an orderly manner; each duty has its proper time set apart for it; nothing is forgotten; nothing is done in advance or retarded; nothing is done in haste or with slowness. Thanks to a rule of life, all is done well; and that which is true in regard to order is equally so in regard to practices of piety; with a rule of life they are done with exactitude; without a rule they have no fixed hour, we defer them, then we again defer them, and we finish by omitting them entirely. Let us examine our conscience, and we shall see how true this is.

SECOND POINT

✝ *Restraint kept over the Senses: another Means of Acquiring and Perfecting the Interior Life within us*

Eyes which will see everything, even things which they have no need to see, are like the windows of the soul by which the resemblances of exterior objects enter, and sometimes even spiritual death, but at least interior dissipation and forgetfulness of God. The ears which are insatiable in hearing, people the interior with a world of matters which distract it; the tongue which has not learnt to restrain itself empties the heart of all piety, to such an extent that never has a great talker, says St. Augustine, been a man of God; whence it follows that no one can be an interior man, excepting in so far as he maintains a restraint over his eyes, is sober in regard to questions excited by curiosity and useless conversations, and is reserved in his words. To maintain the interior senses in restraint is not less important. If we allow ourselves to indulge in vain and useless thoughts, there will be within us a tumult, less violent indeed than that of the world, but not less tending to dissipation, where the past, the present, and the future, persons and places, seasons and things have their place of meeting; the past, in order to remind us of what we have seen or heard, done or felt; the future to ask us what we will do, and how we will do it; persons to hold intercourse with us, although they are absent; places where we have been to go over them afresh. Now with this agitation reigning within us, the interior life is as incompatible as peace is with war, silence with tumult, and the day with darkness. Let us ask our conscience if that be not true.

THIRD POINT

✝ *The Frequent Use of Ejaculatory Prayers; the Third Means of Acquiring and Perfecting the Interior Life within us*

Bourdaloue gives this practice as being one of the best means of becoming an interior man. Ejaculatory prayers are to the interior life what wood is to fire; the more wood that is thrown on the fire the more lively does the flame become; in the same way the oftener ejaculatory prayers are offered the more the heart is warmed, and the more recollected is the interior. This exercise, which is so useful, is all the more easy because the whole creation gives matter for ejaculatory prayers. The sky has not a star, the earth a plant or a flower, the universe a creature of any kind, which does not invite us to it. The examples set us by the good lead us to it; even the sins of the wicked may be, if we so will, a means for raising ourselves up to God, in order to afford Him reparation and honorable amends. *Resolutions and spiritual nosegay as above.*

Fourth Sunday after Easter

THE GOSPEL ACCORDING TO ST. JOHN, 16:5-15

"Jesus said to His disciples: Now I go to Him that sent Me, and none of you asks Me: Whither goest Thou? But because I have spoken these things to you, sorrow hath filled your heart. But I tell you the truth: it is expedient to you that I go: for if I go not, the Paraclete will not come to you: but if I go, I will send Him to you. And when He is come, He will convince the world of sin, of justice, and of judgment. Of sin: because they believed not in Me. And of justice: because I go to the Father; and you shall see Me no longer. And of judgment: because the prince of this world is already judged. I have yet many things to say to you: but you cannot bear them now. But when He, the Spirit of Truth, is come, He will teach you all truth. For He shall not speak of Himself: but what things so ever He shall hear, He shall speak, and the things that are to come He shall show you. He shall glorify Me; because He shall receive of Mine and shall show it to you."

SUMMARY OF TOMORROW'S MEDITATION

We will meditate tomorrow upon a sentence in the gospel of the day: "It is expedient to you that I go" and in order to understand it we will consider: First, what are the spiritual aridities which are useful to the soul; second, what we must do in these states of aridity. Our resolution shall be: First, not to retrench anything from our exercises of piety, or our duties, whether they be small or great, even when we feel nothing but disgust for them; second, not to allow ourselves to be cast down or discouraged by these trials, but to continue to serve God in peace and humility. Our spiritual nosegay shall be the words of St. Paul: "Let us be fervent, because it is the Lord whom we serve." (Rom. 12:11)

MEDITATION FOR THE MORNING

Let us adore Jesus Christ addressing these strange words to His apostles: "It is expedient to you that I go." How, Lord, can it be useful to Thy apostles to be separated from Thee, who art their light, their strength, their consolation? Was it not, on the contrary, to lose all? No! Thou dost affirm it will be very useful to them; they have too natural an attachment to my humanity, they are too fond of the sensible consolations which My presence makes them enjoy; they must learn to love the God of consolations more than the consolations of God. The heart which desires to belong to God must be detached from all ties to the creature, however excellent the creature, may be. That is why it is useful for them that I go away. I thank Thee, O Lord, for so useful an explanation; help me to understand it thoroughly and to profit by it well.

FIRST POINT

✝ *What are the Aridities which are Useful to the Soul?*

By aridities are understood a withdrawal of the light of God which illumines the soul, or of His unction which touches it; in such a manner that exercises of piety are thereby divested of attraction, the service of God of enjoyment, duty of its pleasure. These aridities are of two kinds: the one kind is a trial with which God visits fervent souls; the other is an effect or chastisement of tepidity. Let us meditate upon the three features by which they are distinguished: First, the fervent soul which is tried by aridity sighs, in the presence of God, over the state of misery and powerlessness in which it languishes; it humbles itself for it, and would like to set the whole universe on fire in order to compensate the coldness of its heart. The tepid soul, on the contrary, does not sigh over its state of languor; it does not care for it, and does not even feel it. Second, the soul which is tried is in a violent crisis, out of which it constantly endeavors to come forth; thinking of the evil which in its weakness it commits; of the good which it ought to perform and which it does not do; comparing itself with fervent souls and seeing how far away it is from them, it experiences that fear and trembling with which the Apostle desires that our salvation should be worked out. Confounded at having done so little for God, it is inspired with an immense desire to do better, and it animates itself to lead a better life. The tepid soul, on the contrary, feels itself to be at ease as it is. Considering the evil which it does not do, and the small amount of good which it does perform, comparing itself with persons who are lax, to whom it prefers itself; and also making a profession of not aspiring to a lofty degree of perfection, but to keep itself in a state of mediocrity, it lives in a state of tranquility and presumptuousness, without having any fear of God, without aspiring to become better. Third, the fervent soul, in spite of its aridities, is not any the less exact in all its exercises, which it performs as well as it can; in the performance of all its duties, to which it willingly sacrifices its comfort and its pleasures; to all its pious practices, which it feels to be all the more necessary precisely on account of the state in which it finds itself. The tepid soul, on the contrary, performs its exercises badly, abridges them or omits them entirely; will not submit to anything which restrains it, is a weariness to it, or displeases it; it makes no account of the little things which are not to its taste, and will not understand that there is anything that can be called little in the service of God, that great things are maintained only by little ones, and that it is a very great thing to be faithful even in the smallest things. Let us judge by these characteristics whether our aridities are a trial sent by God or an effect of our tepidity.

SECOND POINT

✝ ***What we ought to do in Aridities.***

First, if aridities evidently come from our tepidity we must issue promptly from this state, which the Holy Ghost declares to be worse than a mortal sin (Apoc. 3:15), and which He even calls a beginning of reprobation (Ibid. 16), and in order to issue from it we must correct the three characteristics of tepidity on which we have been meditating. Second, if our aridities are only a trial, we must accept them without being discouraged or distressed; we must offer to God our heart as being dry ground, which is exhausted and which thirsts for grace and for His holy love. This thirst will, of itself, speak to God, this humble exposure of our wretchedness will say everything to Him; and whilst waiting for Him to hear us, let us continue to serve Him in peace. Second, let us watch over ourselves vigilantly, in order not to pass from aridity to tepidity; nothing is more easy than this passage, and, at the same time, nothing is more dangerous, because we tranquillize ourselves when we are in this state, as though it were one of the trials to which God makes His best friends submit; and seduced by this illusion, we fall into a terrible sleep which leads to death. *Resolutions and spiritual nosegay as above.*

Monday in the Fourth Week after Easter

SUMMARY OF TOMORROW'S MEDITATION

We will meditate tomorrow: First, upon the most ordinary causes of spiritual aridities, and, second, upon the means of preventing them. We will then make the resolution: First, to maintain ourselves in a spirit of recollection by frequent ejaculatory prayers and the offering of our actions to God; second, to combat dissipation, which is the principal cause of our aridities, by means of the mortification of the exterior and interior senses. Our spiritual nosegay shall be the advice of St. Paul to Timothy: "Take heed to thyself." (1 Tim. 4:16)

MEDITATION FOR THE MORNING

Let us adore God making us enjoy, from time to time, in order to sustain our weakness, the sweets of His service and the milk of His consolations. Let us humble ourselves in His presence, that we so often, says St. Bernard, allow this precious milk to escape by the opening of our dissipated senses. Let us ask of Him grace to correct this great evil within us.

FIRST POINT

✝ *The most Ordinary Causes of our Aridities.*

There is amongst Christians an illusion which is too common; it is that which casts all interior troubles upon God and upon virtue, as though God called man to His service only to render him unhappy; as though virtue were a land which devoured all its inhabitants, and Christian perfection a state in which only bitterness is to be found. Doubtless God sometimes sends aridities to the best amongst souls, in order to sanctify them, to purify them and increase their merits. But most frequently the aridities and difficulties which we experience in prayer and meditation have their cause in ourselves. The general cause is tepidity, as we have already seen, but this cause is divided into several branches, with which it is important we should be acquainted. These branches are the passions, which throw us into a state of disorder; self-love, which causes distractions in our thoughts, desires which fill our minds, curiosity, which, filling our minds with worldly matters and exterior objects, deprives the soul of being able to fix its thoughts upon God; they are, also, negligence in ruling our vagabond will, in repressing our self-will, in detaching our heart from all that ties it down to earth. Strange contradiction! We want to be recollected in prayer, and everywhere else we allow ourselves to indulge in dissipation of thought; we would like to possess within us the unction of piety, and we allow ourselves to entertain a thousand vain thoughts, attachments, and desires, which, like a sponge, draw all unction out of the heart, dry it up and exhaust it, until they leave it devoid of all taste or feeling for divine things. A thousand times in meditation, at Holy Communion, in visits to the Blessed Sacrament, God gives us a feeling of fervor, a spiritual consolation, which is intended by Him to sustain our weakness; and immediately afterwards we allow our eyes to wander wherever curiosity attracts them; we yield to a fancy or to a caprice; we take too large a share in frivolous conversation, in worldly affairs; we lose our time in vain thoughts, in useless imaginations; and directly all the sweetness of piety vanishes, and we become cold, weary, and disgusted. Do not let us be surprised: "God is a jealous God" (Exod. 34:14); Deut. 4:24). We leave Him for the creature; He leaves us in His turn. The spirit of grace and of prayer cannot ally itself with the license of the mind, which occupies itself with outward things; of the heart, which permits itself attachments; with the imagination, which flies from one thing to another. We ought, therefore, to impute to ourselves the greater portion of our aridities, and, instead of laying the blame of them on God and on virtue, seek the cause of them in ourselves, cut off this cause, and bear, in a spirit of penance, the state in which we find ourselves to be, and which is a just chastisement of our fault.

SECOND POINT

✝ ***Means for Preventing the Greater Portion of our Aridities.***

Doubtless we cannot forestall the aridities which come from God, because they enter into the plan of our salvation; but we can forestall those which have their origin in ourselves. We can do so, first, by recollection, making of the bottom of our heart, as it were, a sanctuary, where we shall be alone with God only. We must, with sweet and peaceful attention, stand, like sentinels, at the door of this sanctuary, to keep the entrance closed against wandering thoughts and useless desires; and soon heavenly consolations will make in us a new Tabor, of which we shall be able to say, with St. Peter: How good it is to be here (Matt. 17:4); how good to pray here, to adore and to love! We can, second, forestall aridities by mortification, which separates the soul from creatures, at the same time that recollection unites it to God. A little sacrifice made for God brings down grace upon us and fills the heart with a delightful feeling. We are glad to have done something for a God so good, so amiable, and so great. It is then that we pray aright, that we perform all our exercises well, and that the unction of piety renders them easy; whilst, if we refuse God the sacrifice He asks of us, we are discontented with ourselves, the heart dries up, and is covered with an inexplicably black and somber shadow, which takes away all taste for prayer and the things of God. Let us have courage to give ourselves up to recollection and mortification, and soon God will make us sensible of the sweetness of serving Him. *Resolutions and spiritual nosegay as above.*

SUMMARY OF TOMORROW'S MEDITATION

e will meditate tomorrow upon the conduct to be observed in states of aridity, and we shall see that we must keep ourselves: First, from the discouragement which leads to laxity; second, from the trouble which takes peace away from the soul. Our resolution shall be: First, to accept cheerfully the disgust, the weariness, and the aridities we may meet with in the accomplishment of our duties; Second, to keep ourselves calm and patient, in spite of our interior troubles. Our spiritual nosegay shall be the words of the Psalmist: "In a desert land, and where there is no way, and no water, so in the sanctuary have I come before Thee." (Ps. 62:3)

MEDITATION FOR THE MORNING

Let us adore Jesus Christ afflicted upon the cross by the abandonment of His Father. "My God, My God," He exclaims, "why hast Thou forsaken Me?" (Mark 15:34) Let us bless Him for having willed to pass through this state of abandonment and aridity to encourage us to bear it ourselves.

FIRST POINT

✠ ***In Times of Aridity we must Keep Ourselves on our Guard against Discouragement.***

To serve God when we find pleasure in doing so is an easy thing, but to bear the cross without feeling the unction of it, to drag, as though it were a burden, a cold and insensible heart to prayer, to meditate without feeling any taste for it, to communicate without being sensible of any attraction towards it, to fulfill our duties without enjoying any consolation, in a word, to be like a stupid creature, a beast of labor, in our relations with God (Ps. 72:23), this is what often discourages and engenders in us feelings of sadness and of melancholy, which renders us insupportable to ourselves and to each other. In these states, it is greatly to be feared that we shall end by abandoning everything, for then we have no longer hearts for anything. To so dangerous a temptation as this we must oppose: First, the rights of God. God has a right to require from us even things in which we find no pleasure. Never was a servant authorized not to serve his master for the reason that what he was commanded to do wearied him or gave him no pleasure; now God is our master, and He has an undeniable right over all our actions, independent of our tastes as well as of our repugnances. We must combat this temptation with, second, the law of penance. We have sinned greatly, we still sin every day. Now the best penance for so many sins is to serve God, spite of the disgust and repugnance (1 Kings 3:18) of discouraged nature. This is why the saints, when they received sensible consolations and, as it were, the caresses of grace, said: O God, this is not suitable for a sinner like me; and when they experienced interior troubles: Now, Lord, this is exactly how I ought to be treated. My daily infidelities deserve this chastisement and greater chastisement still. We must combat it, third, with the hope of heaven. Is it just to desire to be paid at the time for all we do for God, and not to be willing to await the recompense which will be given us in Paradise, or give credit to God until then? Oh, how badly we understand our own interests! If we are not remunerated here below by sensible consolations, we shall have a double recompense in heaven the recompense of the action performed purely for God, and the recompense of the courage which overcame the repugnance: and this double recompense will be eternal. Let us know, then, how to wait: upon earth patience, in heaven enjoyment, but a better kind of enjoyment and an enjoyment which will never end. Let us penetrate ourselves deeply with these truths.

SECOND POINT

✝ *In Seasons of Aridity we must be on our Guard against Agitation and Keep our Soul at Peace.*

The soul when it is in a state of aridity and in sensibility sometimes imagines itself to be abandoned by God and to be no longer loved by Him because it receives from Him nothing but severity, and no longer to love Him because it feels itself to be cold and tepid. If God ceases to caress it as a mother does her child, it believes all to be lost, is discouraged and depressed. Agitated and ill at ease, it does not know itself any longer, it does not see itself, it does not know whence it comes or whither it goes. Distracted by its troubles, it does not any longer hear the voice of the Holy Spirit speaking within it; it no longer maintains that sweet and peaceful attention to itself which follows all the movements of the heart, which gives facility to prayer, wisdom for counseling it, and which makes it advance in virtue. O my soul, wherefore dost thou thus trouble thyself and lose thy peace? (Ps. 42:5) Wherefore, because thou art displeased with thyself dost thou fear that thou dost displease God? True piety does not consist in tastes and in feelings, but only in the firm determination to serve God. Sensible fervor is a gift which God bestows when it so pleases Him; it is not a service which He requires, since it is a thing which does not depend upon ourselves. If He refuses us this favor, which He alone can give, He will not revenge His withholding it upon us. Insensibility is so far from being an evil that all the saints have been subject to it (2 Imit. 9:1, 4). The holy man Job is a proof of it, when He said to God: Lord, Thou dost visit me in the morning with Thy consolations, and in the evening Thou dost try me by Thy absence (Job 7:18). Whence the pious author of the Imitation draws this conclusion: If it has been thus with the greatest saints, why should we who are poor and miserable be grieved because we are treated in the same way? (2 Imit 9:5.) Do we follow these holy maxims? *Resolutions and spiritual nosegay as above.*

Wednesday in the Fourth Week after Easter

SUMMARY OF TOMORROW'S MEDITATION

We will continue to meditate upon the conduct to be observed in states of aridity, and we shall then see that we must be: First, more faithful in performing our exercises of piety; second, we must keep ourselves united to God. We will then make the resolution: First, not to curtail any of our pious exercises, spite of the small amount of taste we have for them; second, to persevere, although we have no attraction thereto, in a spirit of recollection and of union with God. Our spiritual nosegay shall be the words of St. Augustine: "It is a great thing to be faithful to God in little things."

MEDITATION FOR THE MORNING

Let us adore Jesus Christ in the Garden of Olives recommending His Apostles to watch and to pray on the approach of temptation (Matt. 26:41). They were overcome by sleep; they had no taste for prayer. In spite of that, Our Lord says to them: "Watch ye and pray." Taste is not necessary, but prayer is indispensable. Let us thank Him for so useful a counsel.

FIRST POINT

✝ ***In States of Aridity we must Remain Faithful to our Exercises of Piety.***

Pious exercises are the food of the soul. By retrenching any portion of them we weaken our souls, even as the body is weakened by diminishing its nourishment; and this weakness is all the more dangerous in states of aridity, when the soul is already weakened by the subtraction of graces. With the withdrawal of light night begins in us; the suppression of pious exercises finishes it, and casts the soul into utter darkness. Aridities place the soul on the edge of the precipice; pious exercises are the branch which sustains it and prevents it from falling: without them we become wholly earthly and wholly sensual; we have no longer any zeal for our salvation, and the soul is in the greatest peril. At such a time we ought to be more than ever exact in performing our spiritual exercises, give the usual time to prayer, maintain ourselves in the same religious attitude, observe the same rule of life, the same restraint over the senses, in a word, cut off nothing from what we did formerly, it signifying little whether we have a taste for it or experience nothing but disgust. The exercises which we perform without feeling any taste for them will save us all the more surely because they will be more meritorious and will better prove our love to God. Have we followed these rules?

SECOND POINT

✝ ***In States of Aridity we must Maintain our Union with God.***

As in a state of aridity we find no consolation in ourselves, we are led to seek for it in outside things. He who yields to this temptation aggravates the evil. It is precisely then that we must all the more occupy ourselves with God in our interior, keep ourselves on our guard against useless thoughts and imaginations which render us unaware of His presence, moderate our impulsiveness and our preoccupations, curiosity in looking at what passes around us, intemperance in our language, and levity in our deportment and manners, all of which things make us forget God. When God beholds in a soul courage to maintain itself constantly, although without taste, recollected both within and without, living in the arid desert of its heart with the same fidelity as in seasons of sensible devotion, He is touched by such holy dispositions, and hardly ever delays to visit it with His grace, at least in the ordinary course of His providence. Soon He makes His manna to fall in the desert, and He makes heavenly consolations issue out of the hard heart like water from the rock (Ps. 147:18). Let us believe the words of the King Prophet when He said, "My soul refused to be comforted, I remembered God and was delighted." (Ps. 76:3, 4) What strong consolation for us in our days of trial! *Resolutions and spiritual nosegay as above.*

Thursday in the Fourth Week after Easter

SUMMARY OF TOMORROW'S MEDITATION

e will meditate tomorrow upon the advantages to be derived from states of aridity, and we shall see that we can obtain from them: First, the greatest merits; second, the most solid virtues. We will then make the resolution: First, in states of aridity to be as exact in the performance of our duties as we are in times of consolation; second, to be glad to profit by these days of trial in order to form ourselves by means of renunciation in solid virtues. Our spiritual nosegay shall be the words of the Gospel: "The kingdom of heaven suffereth violence, and the violent bear it away." (Matt. 11:12)

MEDITATION FOR THE MORNING

Let us adore Jesus Christ submitting in the Garden of Olives to the trial of aridity and of weariness (Mark 14:33) that we may thereby encourage ourselves to bear similar trials, and to teach us that the weariness which saddens the soul, far from being an evil, may, on the contrary, be the means of acquiring the greatest merits and the most solid virtues. Let us thank Him for the example He has given us and ask of Him grace to profit by it.

FIRST POINT

✝ ***Seasons of Aridity are for the Faithful Soul for Acquiring the Greatest Merit.***

It is a great delusion to imagine that everything we do for which we have no taste is on that very account without merit and but little pleasing to God. God does not ask of us to serve Him with a taste for doing so, but to serve Him faithfully in spite of all the weariness we may feel in doing so. He takes pleasure in the generosity of the faithful soul, which, a prey to disgust and cast down as it were under the weight of repugnances, rises as Jesus Christ did in the Garden of Olives, saying, "Rise, let us go," (Matt. 26:46) let us go, even though it be to death. The more disgust a servant feels towards what is commanded him, the more he is worthy of the favor of his master when, spite of his dislike, he performs with exactitude all he is told to do. It is the same with the service of God. Never does this good Master better appreciate what is done for Him; never do we acquire more merits than when we triumph over repugnances to follow at every instant the voice of duty. To perform the good which is pleasing to us is a thing of mediocre merit; sometimes even, it is to be feared, that, performing the duty for the sake of the pleasure we find in it, and not for the sake of God, we thereby lose all merit, and that God may say, "They have received their reward" (Matt. 6:2); but to perform our duty by overcoming the repugnances of nature, behold, herein lies the supreme merit to which is assured the most beautiful of crowns. Far, then, from works performed with aridity and with weariness being less meritorious, they are richer in merit, and they receive a recompense in proportion to the difficulty they cost us. Consequently, far from neglecting them in these circumstances, we ought to set to work with all the more energy, because it is better to enjoy less happiness here below in order to have more enjoyment in eternity.

SECOND POINT

✝ ***Seasons of Aridity are for the Faithful Soul for Increasing in Solid Virtue.***

Virtue which requires the milk of consolations is still in its infancy. It does not require a great effort to be pious, says the author of the Imitation, when the unction of the Holy Spirit attracts is to be so, to run when the grace of God impels us, to bear the burden when the hand of the Almighty sustains us (2 Imit. 9:1). The only solid virtue is that of the mature man who, being weaned from these sweetnesses, eats the substantial bread of tribulation and trial. It is with the soul as it is with the body. In proportion as we leave childhood behind us, we cease to give the body those tender and delicate attentions which were lavished upon it at our entrance into life; it is subjected to painful exercises, which, whilst fatiguing it, strengthen it. In the same way, God withdraws from the soul the sensible joys, which, by weakening it, would prevent its vigor from being developed. He exercises it by trials of aridity, which fashion it to abnegation, to patience, to love of the cross, and render it more vigorous and capable of great sacrifices. It is thus that strong souls are formed and solid virtues implanted in the heart. Whoever is able amidst weariness and aridities to perform his duty constantly and perfectly, will be capable of the most difficult things, and his robust energy will be superior to all obstacles. May we appreciate this useful lesson! *Resolutions and spiritual nosegay as above.*

SUMMARY OF TOMORROW'S MEDITATION

e will consider tomorrow aridities from a new point of view: First, as a corrective of false love; second, as a lesson of humility. We will then make the resolution: First, to humble ourselves before God on account of these aridities in our spiritual exercises; second, to humiliate ourselves before men by esteeming others better than ourselves, by not taking any praise to ourselves, and by accepting any kind of contempt and want of consideration. Our spiritual nosegay shall be the words of Our Lord in Isaias: "To whom shall I have respect but to hint that is poor and little and of contrite spirit?" (Is. 66:2)

MEDITATION FOR THE MORNING

Let us adore the immense love which Jesus Christ has for us. By the very subtraction of His graces, He teaches us to derive from it the precious grace of humility, as formerly He made water issue from the rock that He might slake the thirst of His people, excellent honey from holes in the stone, and delicious oils from out the hardest rocks (Deut. 32:13). Let us bless Him for showing us so much love.

FIRST POINT

✝ *Aridities are a Corrective of Self-love*

Man has a natural tendency towards pride, into which everything that raises him exposes him to fall; all that sanctifies him, as soon as he perceives it, exposes him to sin, and even the graces of God themselves become in his case the most subtle of temptations. Let him be but inundated with sensible fervor; let grace, flowing in upon him on all sides, make his soul to be overwhelmed with joy and delight, and immediately his soul whispers to him that this fervor is of his own accomplishing; that God ought to be pleased with him; that he is making progress in virtue; that he is worth more than so many others whose exterior seems to indicate a cold and dissipated interior. This is what explains the sensitive self-love of certain souls, otherwise pious, and the fall of more than one solitary of the desert after eighty years of fervor. Self-love, then, feeds on all which we believe to be love of God. We are so contented with ourselves that we never for a moment think of despising ourselves and taking the lowest place. But let consolations be withdrawn, let aridities take their place; there is then no longer any self-love, no longer any temptation to believe ourselves to be better than others; then humility is easy, and the small degree of virtue which there is in us is more secure. Never is a treasure more safe than when it is in obscurity; never does beauty better keep its luster than when it is beneath a veil. This is why the author of the Imitation addresses to us these beautiful words: "When you receive consolations from God understand that they are not due to any merit on your side, but that they are a gift of God. Do not be lifted up by them, do not rejoice too much, and do not allow yourselves to be tempted to indulge in vain presumption, but be all the more humble and keep yourselves on your guard." (2 Imit. 9:4) To God alone be honor and glory; to us, shame and confusion. Is this the fruit we derive from our aridities, our distractions, and our powerlessness in prayer? Do we come forth from it less susceptible, less full of ourselves, more disposed to despise ourselves and to esteem ourselves to be less than others? This is the design God has in permitting these aridities. Let us respond to it.

SECOND POINT

✝ *Aridities are a Powerful Means of Teaching us Humility*

We often behold around us holy souls which pray with all their hearts, and which seem to breathe nothing but holy love; whilst we, on our side, are as cold as ice, and can draw nothing out of our poor heart God permits this contrast, to show us plainly that we are nothing and worth nothing; that, far from possessing any title to esteem, there is no one more miserable than we are; that all self-esteem is nothing but a lie, and that we deserve to be trodden under foot by everyone. Oh, how excellent are these darknesses wherein self-love is lost! How precious this in sensibility in which self-esteem finds its death! It is then that the soul, confounded by its powerlessness, casts itself humbly before the throne of God, adores Him by the confession of its own nothingness, is astonished to be allowed to appear in His presence, and abases itself utterly in presence of His eternal majesty. In the confusion into which it is thrown by its insensibility, it does not expect a return of consolations, for the delights of piety, it says, are suitable only to saints; as for me, sinner that I am, unworthy of His love, unworthy of His eyes being cast upon me, and of His thoughts, it is only too much honor for me to be here at His feet in order to satisfy His justice by privations, by aridities, and by struggles, and to say to Him, whilst exhibiting myself to Him in all my poverty: "O God, I am indeed nothing! Yes, verily, I am altogether evil, and Thou art altogether good; I am nothing but darkness and Thou art altogether light; insensibility, and Thou art all consolation; poverty, and Thou art all riches. The portion which is my share is humiliating to me, but to Thee it is glorious, and I rejoice at it. It is a consolation that my miseries make Thy greatness show forth and serve Thy glory. I take pleasure in my nothingness and my ignorance, content that Thou alone shouldst be praised and glorified." Oh, if we but knew how to make this use of our aridities, how they would make us increase in humility, and would attract the complaisant notice of Him who has said: "To whom shall I have respect but to him that is poor and little and of contrite spirit?" (Is. 66:2) Then will the truth of these words be realized, that the best prayer is that which makes us most humble. *Resolutions and spiritual nosegay as above.*

Saturday in the Fourth Week after Easter

SUMMARY OF TOMORROW'S MEDITATION

e will tomorrow consider aridities as a means of increasing in love towards God: First, because they make His goodness show itself forth; second, because they dispose the soul to love Him with a more ardent love; third, because they make us love Him with a purer love. We will then make the resolution: First, to bless God in the midst of aridities, and to exalt His love, which condescends to our misery; second, to call upon Him to visit us by holy desires often repeated: Come to me, Jesus, come to my help, make me to love Thee. These words shall serve as our spiritual nosegay.

MEDITATION FOR THE MORNING

Let us adore Jesus withdrawing Himself from Mary and Joseph in the journey He made from Jerusalem at the age of twelve. His parents sought Him in their distress and found Him at the end of three days. He often hides Himself thus from the soul; it seeks Him and finds Him and loves Him all the more. It was what He desired, for all is love in God s guidance of souls. Let us bless Him for this proof of His goodness, and let us beg of Him to increase our love, even by aridities.

FIRST POINT

✝ *In Aridities the Faithful Soul Better Appreciates the Love of God.*

There is no one who does not understand that love is all the more appreciated when it has an elevated origin and descends from thence; that the more extreme is any one's poverty, the more astonishing would it be for a monarch to lower his affections to him. Now, it is in aridity that the soul sees itself to be miserable, poor, vile, and abject; it is then, consequently, that it better appreciates the goodness of God. How is it, it says to itself, that the great God of eternity does indeed will to love me; that not only does He not forsake me who am so unworthy of His notice, but that He comes to me by His grace; that He deigns at this very moment even to show me my wretchedness, that without His aid I should not have seen; that He unites Himself to me by communion, that He overwhelms me with His bounties, both in the natural and the super natural order? O inconceivable love! That He should love the seraphim, that He should love holy souls burning with love to Him, is of itself a great marvel, because inasmuch as being creatures they are at an infinite distance from His supreme greatness; but that a God should love me, I who am so cold, so tepid, so devoid of anything that is good, that a God who is so great should let His heart descend to such profound misery, that such infinite elevation should unite itself to such a bottomless abyss, that is indeed love carried to its highest point! Divine goodness alone could bring together such extremes; and the whole of eternity will not be long enough to sing such ineffable mercies. (Ps. 88:2) It is thus that aridities make us better appreciate the love of God. And we, when we are in those states which might be so profitable to us in this point of view, we do not give the matter a thought what harm we do to our soul!

SECOND POINT

✝ *In Aridities the Faithful Soul Seeks God with a more Ardent Love*

The absence of a beloved person renders him dearer to us when we see him once more, and the heart feels itself to be filled with more ardent love towards him. As long as a child sees its mother, it seems to forget her, and thinks only of its own amusements; but as soon as she disappears for a moment, it weeps, it calls out for her; and as soon as it has found her, it embraces her, and loves her more than before. It is because privation makes it feel the value of its mother, and so redoubles its love for her. In the same way, when God hides Himself in the night of aridities and privations, it is only to make the soul desire Him still more, in order to make it better appreciate the value of His possession, and to teach it to exercise more vigilance when it has the happiness of possessing Him. When the spouse in the Canticle lost him whom her soul loved, she sought him in his dwelling, she sought him in the streets of the city, and she inquired about him of all whom she met. She did not find him (Cant. 3:2). She sought him again, she found him at last; and her love, become more ardent through privation, made her exclaim: "I have found him whom my soul loveth: I held him and will not let him go." (Ibid. 4) Oh, why do we not appreciate in the same manner the happiness of possessing God? His absence in aridities would then make us desire Him more earnestly, seek for Him with more ardor, find Him with more love, and keep Him in us more watchfully.

THIRD POINT

✝ ***In Aridities the Faithful Soul Loves God with a Purer Love.***

We often seek ourselves in piety; we desire to love God, but on the condition of finding pleasure in our love. We seek the God of consolations less than the consolations of God. We amuse ourselves with interior enjoyments; and in the love of God it is ourselves whom we love. But aridities purify this mixture of our own interests, and perfect the purity of our intentions. The soul which then loves, loves God for Himself alone, with a disinterested love, which has no other aid except faith. Oh, how agreeable to God is the soul which is in this state! God alone suffices and contents it: God alone in the understanding, without any ray of light; God alone in the will, without any flame of fervor; God alone in the heart, without any sweetness of consolation. Therein is merit; therein is perfection. Let us aspire to this state and ask it from God. *Resolutions and spiritual nosegay as above.*

Fifth Sunday after Easter

THE GOSPEL ACCORDING TO ST. JOHN 16:23-30

"Amen, amen, I say to you: if you ask the Father anything in My name, He will give it you. Hitherto you have not asked anything in My name. Ask and you shall receive: that your joy may be full. These things I have spoken to you in proverbs. The hour cometh when I will no more speak to you in proverbs, but will show you plainly of the Father. In that day you shall ask in My name; and I say not to you, that I will ask the Father for you; for the Father Himself loveth you: because you have loved Me and have believed that I came out from God. I came forth from the Father, and am come into the world: again I leave the world, and I go to the Father. His disciples say to Him: Behold now Thou speakest plainly, and speakest no proverb. Now we know that Thou knowest all things, and Thou needest not that any man should ask Thee. By this we believe that Thou earnest forth from God."

SUMMARY OF TOMORROW'S MEDITATION

s the gospel of tomorrow recalls to us the duty of prayer, and as the three following days are called days of rogation or of prayer, we will meditate tomorrow on the humility and respect which ought to be associated with all our prayers. We will then make the resolution: First, always when praying to maintain a deeply reverential deportment; second, to entertain within us the humble sentiments experienced by the publican, who, at the door of the temple, is filled with confusion before God at the remembrance of his sins. We will retain as our spiritual nosegay the words of St. Francis of Assisi: "Who art Thou, Lord, and who am I?"

MEDITATION FOR THE MORNING

Let us prostrate ourselves with profound humility and with deep reverence before the Divine Majesty, saying to Him as did St. Francis of Assisi: "Who art Thou, Lord, and who am I who come and present myself before Thee?" Or like the holy patriarch Abraham: Shall I dare to speak to my Lord, who am but dust and ashes? (Gen. 18:27) Let us beg Him to inspire us in the bottom of our hearts with the humility and reverence which are the two first conditions of a good prayer.

FIRST POINT

✝ *The Humility which ought to be Associated with our Prayers*

God loves truth and takes pleasure in truth; wherever He sees it His heart expands, and He sheds His graces there. He hates lies and injustice, and wherever He discovers them His heart turns away and His ear closes. Two results flow from these clear facts: the first is that humility is the best means of obtaining from God the things which we ask. If we present ourselves before Him inspired with a profound feeling of our misery, humbly exposing our sad state to Him, as a poor man does to one who is rich, and saying to Him: "Lord behold my indigence, I hunger and thirst for Thy graces; I am devoid of all that is good and of all virtue; I have asked every creature for something to feed my soul, to cover my nakedness, and they have all replied that they have nothing to give me, that from Thee only comes every good and perfect gift," God will infallibly answer us; for it Is written that "the prayer of him that humbleth himself shall pierce the clouds" (Ecclus. 35:21), and opens to us the bosom of divine mercies; that the Almighty hath regard to the prayer of the humble" (Ps. 101:18), that He never forsakes the humble heart (Ps. 1:19), that He feels a special tenderness for the poor who, feeling themselves to be really poor in His presence, sigh beneath the weight of their wretchedness (Ps. 101:20,21; 108:31). David is heard because he presents himself before God as a poor man and a beggar (Ps. 39:18; 108:22), and as one who is sick and covered with wounds (Ps. 40:5; 37:4). The publican is justified because he prays with humility at the door of the temple. The second consequence which results from the preceding statement is that where there is not humility our prayers cannot be pleasing to God. If we entertain, when we come before His throne, any secret esteem of our virtues and our merits; if we do not feel our nothingness in approaching the Being whence all beings come, our lowness in presence of His supreme greatness, our misery in presence of His infinite holiness, we shall only be in His eyes like the poor proud Pharisee whom He holds in horror (Ecclus. 25:3,4); our prayer will incur the malediction reserved for liars, since the truth is that we are poor beyond all power of speech, that we are nothing (Gal. 6:3), that we have nothing of ourselves (1 Cor. 4:7), that we can do nothing (2 Cor. 3:5), and, therefore, why should God give His graces to the heart which is not humble? It would only be furnishing it with food for its pride, which would attribute to itself the gifts of God; it would be to yield up His possessions to a thief. Who is there amongst us who would give alms to a poor man filled with pride and who would not allow that he was miserable? We do not obtain assistance from our fellows except in touching their hearts by the humble exposure of our miseries. God follows the same rule. Let us here examine our conscience. Do we associate with our prayers the profound humility which is at once the warrant and condition of our success?

SECOND POINT

✝ *The Deep Reverence which ought to be Associated with our Prayers*

In order to understand this, it is enough to consider, with a little faith, to whom we address ourselves when we pray. We speak to the great God before whom the pillars of heaven shake, before whom the twenty four elders of the Apocalypse fall in adoration with their faces prostrate on the ground, and the seraphim cover themselves with their wings. Now, when all heaven annihilates itself, how could I, a poor sinner, not be filled with reverence and overwhelmed with veneration? How could I omit to observe, during this divine interview, a profoundly religious demeanor, a perfect recollection in my senses, and above all in my eyes; in a word, the utter modesty imposed upon us by the majesty of God? O supreme God! How differently we treat Thee! When we have to speak to a king, if it be but a single word, it is always with great respect; and yet in Thy presence, O eternal Majesty, how often do habit, routine, and want of attention make us lose all external and internal respect, so that we do not even think of what we are saying to Thee, and we even forget that if we had but a single word to say to Thee we ought always to treat Thee as a God, that is to say, with the utmost reverence! Let us here examine ourselves; let us humble ourselves, let us ask pardon and be converted. *Resolutions and spiritual nosegay as above.*

Monday in Rogation Week

SUMMARY OF TOMORROW'S MEDITATION

e will tomorrow consider the confidence which ought to be associated with our prayers; and we will meditate upon three reasons for having this confidence, that is to say: First, the excellence of the divine perfections, which require it; second, the precept which God has laid down for it; third, the promises which are attached to it. We will then make the resolution: First, to address our prayers to God with the confidence of a child speaking to its father; second, often to ask God to increase this confidence in us. Our spiritual nosegay shall be the prayer which the apostles addressed to Our Lord, "Increase our faith." (Luke 17:5)

MEDITATION FOR THE MORNING

Let us adore the infinite goodness of God binding Himself by an oath to answer our prayers if we pray as we ought: "Amen, amen, I say to you, whatsoever you shall ask the Father in My name, that will I do." (John 14:13) What mercy and love are contained in these words, and how exceedingly just it is to thank Our Lord for them with all our heart and soul!

FIRST POINT

✝ ***The Consideration of the Divine Perfections ought, in Prayer, to Fill our Hearts with Confidence.***

In fact, O my God, dost Thou not know all my needs since nothing escapes Thy infinite knowledge? Canst not Thou relieve them since Thou art the Almighty? Canst not Thou solace them since Thou art the infinitely good God, who so delights to communicate Himself that it might be said that Thou hast, as it were, a need to give Thyself equal to the need we have to receive? "Thou hast," says St. Augustine, "placed mercy at the door of Thy palace, with the mission to receive all those who present themselves there, and to blame and invite all those who delay to come. You have asked for nothing yet, Thou dost exclaim to them; ask and you shall receive; knock and it shall be opened to you. My angels are there, not to close the door against you, but to open it to you; not to repel you, but to bring you in; not to put away your requests, but to present them and give them their support. Come then, knock with confidence; I will not allow the just who is at my door to perish with hunger." "I believe it, O my God," the holy doctor says elsewhere; "for Thy door likes to see a crowd of suppliants knocking at it, crying out and being importunate. Thy treasures suffer and are afflicted at not being asked for and being spread abroad." Also, Thou prefers to be called by the name of Father, rather than by that of Judge and of Lord, in order to show us that, having the love of a father for us, Thou desirest that we should feel towards Thee the confidence of a child. And why should I not have it, Lord? If men, wicked as they are, do not give their children a stone instead of a piece of bread, a serpent instead of a fish, a scorpion instead of an egg; how couldst Thou, who art the most tender of fathers, refuse us Thy spirit and Thy graces, Thou whose knowledge is acquainted with all: things, whose power can do all things, and whose goodness desires to do us so much good?: O God my Father, I will henceforth say with David: I have placed my confidence in Thee. I am an orphan who has no other help but Thee (Ps. 10:14). I appeal to Thy heart, and it seems to me that I hear Thee say: Confide in Me, I am the Father of the orphan (Ps. 67:6). Is it with this filial confidence that we speak to God in prayer?

SECOND POINT

✝ *Confidence in the Virtue of Prayer is a Divine Precept*

God so rigorously demands of us this confidence, which is indeed so perfectly due to His infinite perfections, that without it all prayer is powerless. If anyone, says St. James, desires to pray to God, let him address Him with confidence, that is to say, with a firm persuasion that he will be heard, because if he hesitates, if he doubts, his prayer will be cast away on the wind like the waves of the sea tossed by the tempest, and he will not be able to hope for anything from it (James 1:6, 7). Prayer without confidence is a dead and sterile prayer, says St. Augustine. He who doubts the goodness of God in granting his prayer, says St. Cassian (Col. 9:34), may be sure that he will not be heard. Thus before giving sight to two blind men who asked Him to cure them, Jesus Christ obliged them to make an act of faith. Have you confidence in My power? He asked them, Yea, Lord, they replied. Then be ye cured; be it done unto you according to your faith (Matt. 9:29). The reason why our prayers are so seldom heard is because we most frequently pray without confidence; we mistrust God and His word. Let us ask of our consciences if this be not true.

THIRD POINT

✝ *Promises Attached to Confidence*

Believe, says Jesus Christ, that all which you ask the Father in My name you shall receive (Mark 11:24). If you can have confidence in Me, He says to an afflicted father who asks Him to cure his son, all is possible to him who believeth (Ibid. 21). With faith, He says also to His apostles, you shall say to this mountain: Cast thyself into the sea, and it will do so (Ibid. 23). Such is the law made by God; He will give His graces in proportion to the confidence with which they are asked for. The saints had full confidence and they obtained miracles. If we had confidence like them, we should like them obtain an answer to our prayers; or if what we asked were contrary either to our own interests, or to the general welfare, or to the aims of Providence, which are higher than ours, God, in place of what we had asked, would give us something better; or if He judges it to be more expedient for us to receive at a later period what we ask, He defers the answer to our prayers from love towards us. God often makes use of these delays: First, to render our confidence more heroic in itself, more honor able to Him, and more meritorious for us; second, to increase our fervor: He allows us to go on knocking at the door, in order that we may knock all the louder; He allows us to go on crying, that we may cry all the louder. Third, to force us to persevere in prayer, and thereby to keep ourselves more constantly united to Him. Thus God, even when He refuses or defers, is always love and goodness, always worthy of our confidence. Let us thoroughly understand these truths, and hence forth may the delays inflicted on us by God excite us to pray more and to pray better. *Resolutions and spiritual nosegay as above.*

Tuesday in Rogation Week

SUMMARY OF TOMORROW'S MEDITATION

We will meditate on two other conditions of a prayer, which are: First, fervor; second, perseverance. Our resolution shall be: First, better to appreciate the excellence of the spiritual graces we ask God for, and consequently to infuse into our prayers a greater desire of being heard; second, to persevere in prayer even when we have no taste for it, and even when we do not obtain what we ask for. Our spiritual nosegay shall be the words of the Psalmist, "The Lord hath heard the desire of the poor." (Ps. 10:17

MEDITATION FOR THE MORNING

Let us adore the Spirit of God inspiring David with so great fervor in his prayers, that in order to express the vehemence of it the holy king calls it a great cry which comes from the bottom of the heart to go right to the heart of God (Ps. 129:1; 101:2). Now the cry of the heart, says St. Augustine, is the ardor of love, it is the fervor of desire, and it is that which gives wings to prayer and raises it up to heaven; if the heart is cold, it is mute, and cannot say anything to God (St. Augustine, on Ps. 37); in order that the incense of prayer may reach God, it must be burnt within with the flames of holy desires. Penetrate me, O Lord, with so important a truth.

FIRST POINT

✝ ***Fervor in Prayer***

Fervor in prayer is nothing more than the ardent desires to be heard, which are exhaled in pious sighs, by means of which, under the inspiration of the Holy Spirit, we pray to God, like a child in its extreme distress prays and solicits its father (Rom. 8:25,26). These were the holy desires which made the prayer of Daniel to be granted. "Because thou art a man of desires" the angel says to him, "I am come" (Dan. 9:23); and that of David, in accordance with what he tells us himself: "I opened my mouth and panted, because I longed for Thy commandments." (Ps. 118:131). "Lord, all my desire is before Thee, and my groaning is not hid from Thee." (Ps. 37:10) In order to understand how fervent should be these desires which ought to be associated with prayer, it is sufficient to consider the greatness, whether it be of the graces we beg God to grant us, or of the evils from which we pray Him to preserve us. First, we ask Him to put us into possession of His paradise, of His glory, of His riches, of His own happiness, of the eternal possession of Himself. We ask Him for the gifts of His Holy Spirit; His graces, of which the least is worth more than all empires; His virtues, the least participation in which is greater than all imaginable treasures. We ask Him for the adorable blood of His Son, His merits, His humility, His charity, His meekness, all His perfections. Now, is it not evident that such great blessings ought to be greatly desired; that to ask for them with indifference or with very little ardor is to misconceive the excellence of them and to render ourselves unworthy of them? Great things ought to be asked for with a great affection for them, and the vehemence of the desire ought to be in proportion to their excellence. Let us examine if it be thus that we ask God for His graces. Alas! Where is our reason, where is our faith? We often ask God for His paradise and His graces with less desire than a thirsty man would ask for a glass of water. How could God grant our prayers? Second, in prayer we ask God to preserve us from hell, into which we may fall at any moment, and into which no one can tell whether he may not any day fall. Now, is it requisite to tell a traveler who is threatened by a tempest to beg ardently for the helpful hand which is capable of saving him? Oh, how earnestly he prays for it, how ardently he calls on all who may be able to come to his aid! And we, men of little faith that we are, we sail upon a stormy sea, fruitful in shipwrecks, of which the consequences are eternal; and we pray so little, we pray so coldly, with so little desire of escaping hell! Ah, it is not thus that we ought to beg of God to be preserved from so terrible a misfortune. Let us, then, better understand what ought to be the fervor which should mark our prayers.

SECOND POINT

✝ ***Perseverance in Prayer.***

To pray for a moment, and to expect an immediate answer, is to be wanting in respect towards God; it is to forget that He is master of His gifts, and that He has the right to choose the moment for granting them; it is to misconceive the excellence of these same gifts, which are well worth the trouble of being asked for several times. A poor man is not tired of asking several times for alms. Lastly, it is to forget that our dearest interests are implicated in our being obliged to persevere in prayer: First, because delay in our being granted the graces we ask of God makes us better appreciate their greatness (Euseb. Em. Horn, 2); second, because it is essential to our salvation to habituate ourselves to a life of prayer. Prayer is our spiritual food, and the soul cannot any more cease to pray often than can the body to eat often; otherwise it falls into a state of weakness, and dies (Ps. 101:5). It is our armor in temptations and trials; it is in regard to conquering our enemies like the golden sword given from heaven to Judas Maccabees (2 Mach. 15:16). If we give it up, we are vanquished. It is the mysterious ladder of Jacob, by which the angels ascend to heaven to carry thither our petitions, and descend to bring us the gifts of God. It is the key of graces; to abandon it is to renounce the assistance of God, and condemn us to be powerless in conquering our passions and triumphing over our miseries. It is, lastly, the means of maintaining within us faith, hope, charity, thoughts of heaven and of the future life, love of our duties and courage to fulfill them; so true are the words of the Lord: We must pray always, and never cease (Luke 18:1). Is it thus that we appreciate the necessity under which God lays us to pray perseveringly and continually? What reproaches have we not to address to ourselves on this point! *Resolutions and spiritual nosegay as above.*

SUMMARY OF TOMORROW'S MEDITATION

fter having meditated on the qualities of good prayer, we will meditate tomorrow on the defects which vitiate it and render it inefficacious. St. Augustine points them out in these words: We do not ask God what we ought to ask; we ask Him badly; we ask it in a bad frame of mind. We will then make the resolution: First, to prepare ourselves better for our prayers, by recollecting ourselves before beginning them, and impressing ourselves with the greatness of the action we are about to perform; second, to pray much more for our spiritual and eternal than for our temporal interests. Our spiritual nosegay shall be the words of our meditation: "We do not ask what we ought to ask for; we ask for it badly; we ask for it in a bad frame of mind."

MEDITATION FOR THE MORNING

Let us adore Jesus Christ in prayer, embracing in His meditation heaven and earth: heaven, for saints and angels offer their adorations through Him alone; earth, because it presents its prayers and homage through Him alone. It is of a truth He who always asks His Father everything that is best, who asks for it as He ought, and with holy dispositions. Let us thank Him for the great service and the great example we derive from His prayer.

FIRST POINT

✝ *We often Ask God what we ought not to Ask of Him*

First, we often ask God for temporal advantages, begging Him to order events in accordance with our pride or our ambition, our vanity or our sensuality, to keep from us all kinds of crosses, all kinds of sicknesses, the death of persons who are dear to us, lastly, all temporal calamities. It is not that these requests are wrong in themselves, provided we add, "My God, not my will be done, but Thine; if Thou sees it is better that my desires should not be granted, do not grant them;" otherwise they would be wrong. For we are no longer under the mosaic law, which had for its sanction earthly blessings and evils; but under the reign of Him whose kingdom is not of this world, under the law of the Gospel, which preaches to us detachment from earthly possessions, and draws up towards heaven and eternal blessings all the aspirations of our heart. Second, whilst asking of God spiritual blessings we do not ask what we ought, excepting in so far as we leave to Him the time and manner of granting them to us; for sometimes we are not prepared to receive usefully what we ask; sometimes it is better for us to have time to appreciate our wretchedness, and to ask during a longer period, that our merits may be increased and our desires may be inflamed by delay. To desire to receive too quickly the best things is not to ask as we ought. Do we observe these rules, both as regards the natural and the spiritual order?

SECOND POINT

✝ *We often Ask badly what we Ask for*

First, we often, indeed, treat God in prayer in a strange manner. If we speak to the most ordinary of men, we think of what we are saying to him; and in speaking to God, alas! We often do not think of the sense of our words. Now, how could God grant a prayer offered in such a manner? How could He possibly listen to anyone who does not listen to himself? "You ask, and you receive not, because you ask amiss," says the Holy Spirit (James 4:3). In order that our prayer may be granted, we must be recollected within that portion of ourselves, that inner temple where we confer with God alone, far from all thoughts of this world. It is there that God loves to listen to prayer. If our heart escapes us, spite of ourselves, we must recall the fugitive, and deplore its wanderings, like David, who exclaimed, "My heart hath forsaken me" (Ps. 39:13); and when we have found it again we must rejoice like the holy king, and return to our prayer with our whole soul (2 Kings 7:27). Lastly, we must imitate St. Hilarion, of whom history tells us that he recited the psalms of the holy office as though he had God present to him, listening to what he said (Lesson of the Office). Alas, how rarely we pray in this manner!

THIRD POINT

✝ *Our Bad Frame of Mind often Vitiates our Prayer*

To pray to God in a bad frame of mind is to present Him with a heart which has neither any regret for past wrong-doing, nor any real desire to reform, nor any courage for overcoming frivolity and distastes, nor any habit of recollection, nor any energetic efforts to please God. Now, possessing such a frame of mind as this, how can we expect our prayers to be heard? The habit of dissipation of thought, the cowardice and effeminacy which will not allow of any restraint, the attachments which take possession of the heart, are as a cloud placed between God and ourselves, which hinders our prayer from reaching Him (Lam. 3:44). Let us here enter into ourselves, and see if we do not vitiate our prayers in one or other of these ways. *Resolutions and spiritual nosegay as above.*

SUMMARY OF TOMORROW'S MEDITATION

In the great solemnity of tomorrow we will select for the two points of our meditation two articles of the Creed: First, Jesus Christ has ascended into heaven; second, He is seated at the right hand of God, the Father Almighty; and we shall see that in both these mysteries Jesus Christ is, as always, full of love for us. We will then make the resolution: First, to raise our thoughts and our affections to heaven, where is Jesus Christ, our advocate, our High Priest, our Head; not to have any longer any attachment to this world, and henceforth to live only for heaven; second, to place all our confidence in our Mediator who is in heaven. We'll retain as our spiritual nose gay the words of the Church, "Lift up your hearts!" and these other words of the Apostle: "I am straitened between two: having a desire to be dissolved and to be with Christ." (Philipp. 1:23)

MEDITATION FOR THE MORNING

Let us transport ourselves in spirit to the Mount of Olives, there to assist in thought at the triumphant ascension of the Savior. Let us adore Him not ascending to heaven like Elias upon a chariot of fire, but raising Himself by the sole means of His virtue, followed by all the just of the Old Law, whom He has liberated from their prison. Let us admire Him received by all the heavenly court, in the midst of a thousand canticles of adoration, of admiration, of praise, and of love. Let us unite our homage with that of all the princes of heaven.

FIRST POINT

✝ ***Jesus Christ has Ascended to Heaven.***

Jesus Christ ascended to heaven by means of the same principle which had made Him descend from it; He had descended through love for us, and He ascended also through love. He desired to go: First, in order to open the gates of heaven; second, to prepare a place for us there; third, to shed upon us from thence His blessings. Until the ascension, the doors of heaven had been closed against all the children of Adam, and neither the innocence of Abel, nor the faith of Abraham, nor the zeal of Moses, nor the holiness of the prophets and the patriarchs had been able to open the entrance to it. All, after their death, were relegated to limbo, without possessing any other consolation than that of hope; but today, O day of happiness! Jesus makes them leave their prison, and takes them with Him to heaven; He opens the doors of it to them, and He enters first through the merits of the blood which He has shed; and thus are accomplished the types of the ancient law. It no longer exists, that mysterious sanctuary, which was wont to remain closed during the whole year, that Holy of holies wherein the high priest alone could enter once a year, bearing in his hands the blood of the victims. Jesus Christ, the sole true Pontiff, has entered this day, not into the sanctuary made by the hands of man, which was only a figure of the true sanctuary, but into heaven itself, the true sanctuary inhabited by God; He has entered there, not with the blood of others, but with His own blood; He has torn and made the veil to disappear which hid from the people the Holy of holies and symbolized the doors of heaven closed until then to man through sin. O Jesus, a thousand times amiable, it is thus that Thou dost open to us heaven today; we have nothing to do but to enter into it. What gratitude do we not owe Thee! But Thou didst not stop even there. Like a good father who occupies himself in finding a suitable place for his son, Thou dost Thyself say to us: "I go to prepare a place for you." (John 14:2) I will that you should be where I am, and that My throne should be yours (John 17:24; Apoc. 3:21). O adorable Savior! Thou dost us too much honor. What! I shall be seated upon Thy own throne! My nature so poor and miserable in itself shall be raised in heaven above even the angels, up to the throne of a God! Oh, what a beautiful place Thou art gone to prepare for us, and how precious is Thy ascension to me! How it excites my admiration, my gratitude, and my love! It is not even yet all! From the highest heaven Thou dost bless us, says the Gospel (Luke 24:50). O beloved blessing, which helps our weakness to rise where Thou dost call us! O Savior, bless us always, and attract our hearts to Thee, in order that henceforth we may live only for heaven (Cant. 1:3).

SECOND POINT

✝ *Jesus, on the Day of His Ascension, is Seated at the Right Hand of the Father*

What does that mean, Lord? It means that Thou dost today enter into the divine and eternal repose which was so well earned by Thee after so many labors; it means that Thou dost take possession of Thy throne as King of kings, of Thy tribunal as Judge of the living and the dead; it means that in heaven Thou art equal to God, being God Thyself. And, oh, how admirable it is! In this lofty position Thou dost not forget the man with whose nature Thou didst clothe Thyself. Lest our fragility should make us lose the place Thou hast prepared for us, Thou dost constitute Thyself in the presence of Thy Father as our advocate, our pontiff, our head. As our advocate Thou dost ceaselessly plead our cause by the voice of all Thy wounds, by all the beatings of Thy heart (Heb. 7:25); ceaselessly dost Thou present us before the face of God (Ibid. 9:24). When weakness has drawn us away into sin, Thou dost interfere to take our defense upon Thee; of our cause Thou dost make Thy own, and Thou dost prove, by Thy blood, which was shed and which speaks better than that of Abel, what mercy ought to be shown to us (1 John 2:1,2). As our pontiff, Thou dost offer Thyself for us constantly in sacrifice (Heb. 8:1; 4:14). Lastly, as our head, Thou dost draw us after Thee, for the members are obliged to follow their head; Thou art our precursor (Heb. 6:20), and wouldst Thou be if we do not follow Thee? Thou art that mysterious eagle which flies above its little ones to excite them by its example to take their flight towards the sun (Deut. 32:11). Lord, attract me to Thee by Thy graces, by Thy charms, by Thy beauty, and Thy perfections, which ravish the angels. Oh, how I long to see Thee in the splendor of Thy glory, and to enter that beautiful heaven where we can no longer offend Thee, and where we shall love Thee always! *Resolutions and spiritual nosegay as above.*

Friday after the Ascension

SUMMARY OF TOMORROW'S MEDITATION

After having meditated yesterday on what Jesus Christ did for us in the mystery of the Ascension, we will meditate tomorrow on what we ought to do for Him, and we shall see that this mystery: First, preaches to us universal detachment; second, that it calls us to holiness. We will then make the resolution: First, often to raise our eyes to heaven, to give us encouragement to sanctify ourselves by detachment from creatures, and by being determined to become saints; second, by means of loving ejaculations and holy desires to keep ourselves always united to Jesus Christ reigning in heaven. Our spiritual nosegay shall be the words of the Psalmist: "I shall be satisfied when Thy glory shall appear." (Ps. 16:15)

MEDITATION FOR THE MORNING

Let us adore Jesus Christ in the glory of His Ascension and of His enthronization at the right hand of His Father. O Sovereign Lord! Thou only art the Most High! Thou only art holy with the Holy Ghost in the glory of Thy Father! Oh, how ravished I shall be to contemplate Thee in this glory, and in Thee to behold human nature elevated to the right hand of God! I submit myself now and forever, and with all the affection of my heart, to Thy sweet empire.

FIRST POINT

✝ *The Mystery of the Ascension Preaches to us Universal Detachment*

How would it be possible for us to attach ourselves to anything here below when we see Jesus, Our Lord, take flight to heaven? What affection is there of our hearts which would not follow Him there? Seek the things that are on high, says St. Paul, because there is Jesus Christ (Coloss. 3:1,2). My great desire, says the same apostle, is to die, that I may be with Jesus Christ (Philipp. 1:23); and, seeing my Savior ascend to heaven, I understand that we are all of; us only pilgrims here below. Exiles, we travel towards our country, sighing in the expectation of that beautiful heaven where our adoption as children of God will be perfected (Rom. 8:23). Filled with the same thought, St. Peter said to the faithful: I conjure you to abstain from all attachments to things which pass away, and to look upon yourselves here below as travelers on a journey, who pitch their tents in the evening and raise them the next morning (1 Pet. 2:11). Now, it is at the spectacle of Jesus ascending to heaven and showing Himself to us in His glory that these lofty sentiments ought to be awakened in us. Called to such sublime destinies, we could not any longer attach ourselves to the possessions of this world, which are so small, so miserable, and so soon pass away. Called to infinite felicity, we ought to disdain the false enjoyments which self-love, the satisfaction of the senses, and the use of temporal goods present to us. Called to in comparable glory, we ought to count as nothing the false glory of the world, the opinion of men, the splendor of honors, and say with St. Ignatius: "Oh, how vile earth seems to me when I look up to heaven;" and with St. Paul: All is nothing to me, provided that I gain Jesus Christ. (Philipp. 3:8)

SECOND POINT

✝ *The Mystery of the Ascension Calls us to Holiness.*

When I consider Jesus Christ ascending to heaven and opening to me its doors, showing me the place He has prepared for me, I understand two things: First, that I must be a saint, for the heaven to which Jesus Christ calls me is made only for saints; and how could I hope to go and take my place amongst the saints on high if I were not a saint here below; if I did not often say to myself during my life: In what way would the saints utter this prayer and perform this action? So that I might be encouraged to pray and to act as they did? I understand, second, that nothing ought to cost me too much in order to become a saint, for we do not obtain heaven without making generous efforts (Matt. 11:12); we cannot enter therein without a struggle (Luke 13:24); but also does not heaven well deserve the pain to which these sacrifices expose us? The pain lasts but for a moment, the glory is eternal (2 Cor. 4:7); and all that we can do or suffer here below has no proportion with the greatness of the recompense (Rom. 8:18). Let us enter with our whole heart into these two dispositions: the first, to determine to be a saint; the second, to be decided to become one, no matter at what sacrifice. *Resolutions and spiritual nosegay as above.*

Saturday after the Ascension

SUMMARY OF TOMORROW'S MEDITATION

It is the practice of pious souls to spend in retreat the season between the Ascension and Pentecost, in order to prepare themselves to receive the Holy Ghost, following in this the counsel given by Jesus Christ to the apostles: Remain in retreat at Jerusalem till you be endued with power from on high (Luke 24:49). We will consequently meditate: First, in what this retreat or solitude consists; second, how necessary it is in order to receive the Holy Spirit on the day of Pentecost. We will then make the resolution: First, to pass all our days until Pentecost in a spirit of recollection and of prayer; second, to be specially faithful during the whole time to our exercises of piety; third, to avoid all that might tend to dissipate us, such as certain kinds of society or conversation. Our spiritual nosegay shall be the words which have come down to us from heaven: "Fix your soul in the recollection of retreat until the descent of the Holy Ghost."

MEDITATION FOR THE MORNING

Let us adore Jesus Christ giving to His apostles the counsel to pass in solitude the ten days intervening between the Ascension and Pentecost, to dispose us to receive the Holy Ghost. Let us apply to ourselves so useful a counsel; let us thank Our Lord for giving it to us; let us beg Him to enable us thoroughly to understand it.

FIRST POINT

✝ *In what the Solitude Preparatory to the Reception of the Holy Ghost Consists*

This solitude consists not in leaving this world, in the midst of which Providence has placed us, but in maintaining a spirit of recollection within ourselves, and making within our soul a kind of interior solitude wherein we live with God alone, disengaged from everything that may tend to dissipate, trouble, or bind us. In the ordinary course of our lives, our soul is invaded by a thousand foreign thoughts, a thousand preoccupations or imaginations, which render us incapable of prayer and recollection, and hinder the whole action of the Holy Spirit within us. It is a little world of affairs, of events, often even of nothings and chimeras; it is a theatre less noisy indeed than the great world, but often not less tumultuous, wherein all past, present, and future events, all the reveries of the mind and the imagination, pass across the scene, sometimes one after the other, sometimes confusedly. Hence dissipation in our conduct, distractions in prayer, and of God in our daily life; hence an ill-regulated interior, a soul in a state of complete disorder, upset, overwhelmed by exterior things, and incapable of all recollection. The solitude of which we speak consists in remedying so deplorable a state of things, in separating ourselves interiorly from the little world which troubles and agitates itself, in making within ourselves a sanctuary for God, where we can remain in tranquility, alone with God only. The little world of thoughts and wandering imaginations may indeed make a noise around us; but we do not let them penetrate within us. Within is the sanctuary of God; to allow worldly thoughts to enter into it would be to profane it. We do, of course, give a moderate attention to exterior things which enter into the order of our duties; but we do not allow ourselves to be dominated by them, much less to be absorbed by them, and we do not, on account of them, remain less solitary with God in the deepest part of our interior. There we occupy ourselves with the God whom we love, His beauty and His infinite amiability; we speak to Him with the simplicity of confidence and love; we offer Him all our actions, our words, and our thoughts; we beg of Him to send us His adorable Spirit to enlighten us, to touch us, and to inflame us; and in order not to trouble His divine operations, we keep ourselves on our guard against haste and hurry, against the little passions which disorder the interior, hold intercourse with us, and make us lose our time; against the attachments which trouble and distress us; against the desires which calculate beforehand the probabilities and the results of means; against the spirit of curiosity, always in search of news, always wanting to know about everything that takes place, to hear everything that is said, and introduce into the soul a thousand vain and superfluous thoughts, a hundred chimerical designs, to the great prejudice of the soul's peace. The author of the Imitation sums up admirably the idea of interior solitude in these few words: "Empty your mind and your heart of all things created; unite yourself alone with God alone; open your heart to Jesus Christ and close it to all beside." (2 Imit. 8:5; 1:2) Oh, how far we are from this happy solitude, how distracted is our interior, how disordered, how little recollected, how full of the world and of all that takes place in it!

SECOND POINT

✝ ***How Necessary Interior Solitude is to Prepare us for Pentecost.***

First, the Holy Spirit is a jealous God who will not share a divided heart (Ex. 10:5); and this divine jealousy extends to the point of cooling His friendship and withdrawing it from the soul; it takes from us His grace, sometimes only because of a simple opening in the heart left for the admittance of created objects; a willing look cast upon things we have no need to see, a deliberate attachment, a useless thought. It is true that God, in His goodness, seems sometimes to forget His severe jealousy, as far as to recall the soul that has been voluntarily unfaithful to Him; but these are exceptions which we must not take into account. In the ordinary course of things, the Holy Spirit does not communicate Himself fully except to the soul which, from respect to the sensitiveness of His love, giving itself fully to Him, avoids the bestowing of itself upon outside things. It is indeed true that the imagination has its inexplicable frivolities, which it does not depend upon us to foresee: with these He does not reproach us but what He does will is that we do not entertain ourselves knowingly with these imaginations; that we should not recall them when they leave us, and that we should not give ourselves up to new ones at our own will and pleasure; that we should stand like a sentinel at the door of our interior, to arrest immediately any strange thought or image which tries to enter within us. Is it thus that we act? Second, the Holy Spirit is a God of peace who will not have anything to do with a heart which is troubled (3 Kings 19:11); and there where the little world of vain thoughts and imaginations enters there is necessarily trouble, tumult, agitation of the mind which is a cause of dissipation of thought, an upheaval of the heart which is preoccupied, consequently incompatibility with the Holy Spirit. Third, in vain God might favor with His gifts the soul which does not know how to maintain interior solitude: it would soon lose them. A conversation, a piece of news, an affair, would be sufficient to plunge the soul once more into darkness, the heart into languor and dissipation. The habit of occupying itself with outward things would make it forget its best resolutions, would dry up the waters of grace, and paralyze the most holy dispositions, and, like seed cast on the wayside, the good inspirations of the Holy Spirit would soon be trodden under foot by the thousand thoughts and imaginations which come and go in the dissipated soul. *Resolutions and spiritual nosegay as above.*

Sunday in the Octave of the Ascension

SUMMARY OF TOMORROW'S MEDITATION

We will continue tomorrow our meditation upon interior solitude, and we will consider three principal advantages of it: it glorifies God; it sanctifies us; it forms our happiness. We will then make the resolution: First, to unite heartily and frequently during the whole week with Mary and the apostles in retreat at the cenacle; second, to watch over all the ill-regulated movements of our imagination, in order to repress them firmly and resolutely; and to examine our soul at certain fixed times, to see if God only dwells and reigns completely within it. Our spiritual nosegay shall be the words of the Imitation: "Empty thy heart in order to live alone with God alone." (2 Imit. 8:5)

MEDITATION FOR THE MORNING

Let us transport ourselves in spirit to the cenacle, and, uniting our meditation with that of Mary and the apostles assembled together there, let us render to Jesus Christ, seated at the right hand of His Father, our homage of adoration, of admiration, of praise, and of love. Let us beg of Him to make us thoroughly understand the advantages of interior solitude, and to give us the love and the practice of it.

FIRST POINT

✝ *Interior Solitude Glorifies God*

The soul which has the courage to be isolated within itself from all that is not God, that it may be given up wholly to God alone, thereby tells Him that He alone is all, that everything else is nothing; that the world and all the creatures in it do not deserve a thought of its mind or an affection of its heart; that to God alone it belongs and will always belong; that He only is sufficient to it, because He alone is all good (Ex. 33:19). Now is there any homage more worthy of the Divine Majesty? What can we take from within ourselves which will glorify Him more and better testify to Him that esteem of supreme deference due to Him on so many accounts? Have we the heart to glorify God in this way? Let us question our conscience.

SECOND POINT

✝ *Interior Solitude Sanctifies us*

The whole of Christian perfection reduces itself to these two points; To separate ourselves from creatures, and to unite ourselves to God. Now, both the one and the other are admirably accomplished in the interior solitude. There we learn to separate ourselves from the world and from ourselves; from the world, because we clearly see the nothingness and the folly of it; from our selves, because our eyes being always kept open and beholding our own heart, we see all its miseries, and we clearly recognize how vile and despicable it is. Oh, how all creatures seem but as nothing when we consider them in the interior solitude, and how willingly then does the heart detach itself from them! But at the same time how truly God appears as He really is, that is to say, as the great All; the one alone amiable, the one alone perfect! Listen, O my soul! Listen in the bottom of thy heart; not in that part where the imagination creates its phantoms, but in that deeper portion where truth makes itself to be heard; where pure and simple ideas collect together; and there in the secret of thy heart will noiselessly resound those divine words: God alone is all, God alone is just; all which is not God is nothing. At these words, ravished by the beauties of this Supreme Being, thou wilt take to Him all thy love, and immediately thou wilt find Him approaching towards thee with in comparable goodness, according to the words of the Apostle: "Draw nigh to God, and He will draw nigh to you." (James 4:8) Thus, in the interior solitude is consummated the divine union. The soul, ravished at such a blissful meeting, cries out then with the spouse of the Canticles: "I found Him whom my soul loveth, I held Him and will not let Him go." (Cant. 3:4) I will keep Him in the solitude of my heart, and I will remain there alone with Him, alone without any other desire than that of His presence, alone without any other love than His alone, without any other will than His good pleasure. Oh, what rapid progress do we then make in virtue! We find nothing difficult, because we have the strong God with us; nothing painful, because we have with us the God of all consolation. We are no longer tempted to pause in our career, because it is God Himself who bears us along it; to be attached to creatures, because this union, contracted in the shadow of the internal solitude, consumes the soul with charity and makes it in a manner divine even in this life.

THIRD POINT

✝ ***Interior Solitude Forms our Happiness.***

The interior solitude is the delightful place of meeting given by the Creator to His creature. There we love God, we enjoy His presence; and the soul, rendered happy and tranquil, exclaims, like the apostles upon Tabor: "It is good to be here." (Matt. 17:4) There we lead a hidden life, but it is hidden in God and in the society of Jesus Christ (Coloss. 3:3). What more do we want in order to be happy? There we converse delightfully with God; and, in comparison with a word uttered by God, what are all the speeches of men? (Ps. 118:85.) There things belonging to the world do not enter, but things belonging to heaven descend into it every day; every day God reveals to the soul beauties unperceived until then, and the soul is completely ravished by them (Cant. 5:6). There the vain joys of the world are put outside the door, but Jesus Christ compensates for them by the unction of His consolations, the abundance of His peace. Oh, what do we not gain by the exchange even as regards pleasure and happiness! O solitude, says St. Jerome, paradise on earth, road to heaven! O desert, where we enjoy familiarity with God! O Christian soul, what dost thou in the world, thou who art greater than the world! (Hier. ad Hel.) There, lastly, is the tabernacle where the faithful soul hides itself as in the face of God, far from the tumult of men and the contradiction of tongues; the strong tower where reigns a continual calm, an uninterrupted peace, because man, the enemy, cannot reach it (Ps. 60:4); and it is there that it is good to dwell from the rising to the setting of the sun, and during the night as often as sleep withdraws from the eyelids. It is there that it is good to work and to repose, to pray and to converse; finally, to do all things. How are we situated in regard to this interior solitude? Have we formed it in ourselves, and do we maintain it by the practice of recollection? *Resolutions and spiritual nosegay as above.*

Monday before Pentecost

SUMMARY OF TOMORROW'S MEDITATION

In order that we may be inspired to prepare ourselves rightly for Pentecost, we will meditate during the following days on the seven gifts which the Holy Spirit brings with Him to the soul, as so many inestimable treasures wherewith to ornament and enrich it. We will therefore meditate tomorrow: First, on the gift of understanding, which makes us know God and all the titles which He possesses to our love; second, the gift of knowledge, which makes us comprehend the nothingness of all created things and the use we ought to make of them to raise ourselves to God. We will then make the resolution: First, often to call down upon us, by means of ejaculatory prayers, the gifts of understanding and knowledge; second, to cultivate recollection as a means of attracting the Holy Spirit towards us, and vigilance to avoid the numerous sins which might make Him depart from us. Our spiritual nosegay shall be the words of the Gospel: "Blessed are the clean of heart, for they shall see God." (Matt. 5:8)

MEDITATION FOR THE MORNING

Let us adore the Holy Spirit as the eternal and personal love of God. Let us offer Him our homage of love, begging of Him to enable us to understand the excellence of His gifts, and to prepare us Himself for the great feast which is drawing nigh.

FIRST POINT

✝ *Of the Gift of Understanding*

The gift of understanding is a supernatural light which the Holy Spirit diffuses in the soul in order to enable it the better to know God: First, in His ineffable perfections; second, in the riches of love enclosed in the mysteries; third, in His word contained in the Holy Scriptures; fourth, in the religion so marvelous in its wisdom, which He has revealed to us; and, fifth, in the Providence which presides over all the events of our lives. Oh, how desirable this gift is, and with what fervor ought we not to ask for it! The ideas of reason on these lofty truths are so confined, even the ideas engendered by faith are so dark! As yet it is only twilight; but the gift of understanding is the broad daylight, by the aid of which we see so clearly into the depths of all things, that the intelligere is really the intus legere, and that the soul is thrown into a state of real astonishment at there being men who take offence at all these holy truths, or who hesitate to believe them. Devoid of this gift, God, His perfections, His mysteries, His religion, His providence, say nothing to the mind or to the heart. Possessed of this gift, the ravished soul discovers in God beauty which transports it, in the mysteries in expressible charms, in religion so magnificent a whole that the heart is filled with love for it, and in Providence designs so worthy of God that it cannot contain its admiration and praise. Without this gift, the Holy Scriptures are as a dead letter for us; we read them, we recite the psalms, we utter Paters and sacred canticles with a want of understanding which does not arouse even our attention. But with this gift, the Holy Scriptures ravish us; each time we read them we discover in them new meanings; piety finds therein delicious nourishment, and its happiness consists in reading or reciting them. It was this gift which David celebrated when he exclaimed: "The uncertain and hidden things of Thy wisdom Thou hast made manifest to me." (Ps. 1. 8) It was this gift which St. Augustine received when he penetrated so deeply into the counsels and the guidance of God in relation to the whole universe and to himself, that he never wearied of contemplating them. It was through this gift that St. Antony felt to be all too short whole nights added to days for the contemplation of the divine marvels, and that St. Bernard complained of not being able to suffice for the abundance of thoughts and of illuminations which inundated his soul every time that he meditated on the life or death of Jesus Christ! Let us ask God for this gift with all the fervor of our desires, and let us recall to ourselves that it is promised solely to perfect purity of heart. "Blessed are the clean of heart, for they shall see God." (Matt. 5:8)

SECOND POINT

✝ *Of the Gift of Knowledge*

If the gift of understanding enables us to know God, as we have just seen in our meditation, the gift of knowledge teaches us to know creatures; and this knowledge is not less necessary to our salvation than is even the knowledge of God. By this gift the Holy Spirit renders three great services to the soul: First, He shows it all created things in their true light; He divests riches, honors, pleasures, all earthly goods, of the seductive charm which surrounds them, and points out how fragile they are, how vain, of how short duration, how incapable of making us happy, how hurtful and dangerous they are to Our salvation. The soul, surprised at the light appearing to it, feels nothing now but horror for them, as being despicable things supremely unworthy of it; and this it is which peoples cloisters, and which gives to the world so many generous, charitable, and devoted Christians. Second, the Holy Spirit, by the gift of knowledge, teaches us to use all visible beings as so many steps to raise us up to God, who has created them for us; to make of the whole of nature, as it were, a great book full of the divinity, in which everything speaks of God, everything preaches love; lastly, to see in all that exists a mirror in which are reflected from all sides the goodness, the wisdom, the power, the providence of God, or a harmonious concert calling upon all hearts to love the Supreme Good. Therein consists the knowledge of the saints. Third, by the gift of knowledge the Holy Spirit teaches preachers the great art of worthily announcing the word of God, and directors of consciences the art of directing souls, of strengthening them in their weaknesses, of consoling them in their sorrows, of making them walk in the way where God wills them to be, of correcting their defects, and raising them to the practice of virtues. Oh, how precious this gift is! How we ought to desire it and to prepare ourselves to receive it! Have we ever known up to the present moment what it really is? We have misconceived it, we have been ignorant of it, we have neither desired nor asked it of God. Let us remedy this forgetfulness. *Resolutions and spiritual nosegay as above.*

Tuesday before Pentecost

SUMMARY OF TOMORROW'S MEDITATION

We will continue to meditate upon the gifts of the Holy Spirit, and taking as the subject for our meditation the gift of counsel, we shall see: First, the excellence of the gift; second, the conditions on which it is communicated; third, the obstacles which keep it at a distance from the soul. We will then make the resolution: First, to mistrust our own selves, and to put our confidence in the Spirit of God in regard to everything which we have to do, whether in the spiritual or the temporal order; second, to call to our aid, by frequent and fervent ejaculations, the Holy Spirit; third, not to anticipate by haste, nor retard by slowness, the action of the Holy Spirit in us. Our spiritual nosegay shall be the words of the Psalmist: "Thy good spirit shall lead me into the right land." (Ps. 142:10)

MEDITATION FOR THE MORNING

Let us adore the Holy Spirit communicating Himself to the soul to direct it, like a faithful friend, in the pathway of life; to show it the end whither it ought to tend, and to reveal to it the means of reaching it. Let us thank Him for so much goodness, and let us beg of Him to animate our will to follow in all things His holy inspirations.

FIRST POINT

✝ *The Excellence of the Gift of Counsel*

The gift of counsel is given to the soul to direct it in its acts, and it is in regard to the supernatural order what prudence is in the natural order. It shows us what we must do, or not do; say, or not say, according to persons, times, and seasons; it aids the wisdom of reason by the better lights of the wisdom which comes down from on high, in all our enterprises, actions, and words. It teaches us how to derive benefit from everything as a means towards our salvation, towards the sanctification of others, and towards the advancement of the work of God; and it even teaches us to derive advantage from sin, as St. Paul and

St. Augustine say. This single idea reveals to us the excellence of the gift of counsel; for what can there be more difficult than always to do and to say what is right without passing the limits of perfect discretion? It is but little to know that a thing is good in itself; all that is good is not always expedient, and the best things are often accompanied by serious inconveniences. The essential thing is to know what is proper and suitable in present circumstances, and it is this secret which is taught by the gift of counsel. By this gift we learn to know men and the way of treating them to choose favorable times and circumstances, to say nothing and do nothing which may shock them, to act always with discretion, to humor all which requires humoring, and to avoid all false steps. Before receiving this gift, the apostles called down fire from heaven upon Samaria, which refused to welcome the Savior; after having received it, they endured all kinds of rebuffs in patience and with meekness. One amongst them, St. Paul, confounds the Sadducees and Pharisees by making them contradict each other, and appeals from the tribunal of Festus to that of Caesar. By virtue of the same spirit, Jesus Christ confounds the accusers of the woman taken in adultery as well as those who reproach Him with not having paid tribute to Caesar. Oh, how excellent is this gift, how many imprudent and uncharitable words it prevents us from uttering, what indiscreet actions it teaches us to avoid, what difficulties in which we should not know how to conduct ourselves does it enlighten and resolve with human prudence alone for our guide, we sail along only with difficulty, and by using our oars diligently, like the ship which has both wind and tide against her; but with this gift we go on our way quickly, like the ship which has all her sails set and which has the wind in her favor. Let us recognize the many faults into which we have fallen for want of this gift, and how important it is for us to obtain it, by dint of prayers and holy desires.

SECOND POINT

✝ *Means for Obtaining the Gift of Counsel*

We must, first, renounce the spirit of the world; for it is evident that the person who is guided ought to tend to the same end and walk in the same path as his guide; now the spirit of the world is opposed to the spirit of God, both in its end and in its path. The spirit of the world only regards happiness in the present life, the spirit of God tends to lead the soul to eternal hypocritical and politic ways and is content to deceive others by appearances; the spirit of God follows direct and open ways; it wills that we should be what we ought to be, and should not only appear so. We must, second, consult the Spirit of God, and call Him to our aid by a humble and confiding prayer, saying to Him from the bottom of our hearts: My God, have pity on my misery; I am blind, make me to see (Luke 118:41); I am ignorant, "enlighten my darkness" (Ps. 17:29); I am incapable of guiding myself, "conduct me" (Ps. 85: 11); and we must say this prayer every morning for all the actions of the day; repeat it each time that we are called upon to take a part, to make an answer; finally, every time we have to act or to speak. We must, third, habitually offer ourselves to the Holy Spirit in a disposition of recollection, that we may listen to Him, and of generosity, to do all that He may tell us, at whatever cost.

THIRD POINT

✝ *Obstacles to the Gift of Counsel*

The first obstacle is presumption. It is written, "God resists the proud" (James 4:6), consequently there is no gift of counsel for the presumptuous, who, full of self-sufficiency, thinks he has no need of help. Why, besides, should God speak to him? He pays no attention to His Word; he does not listen to or respect Him because he does not think he has any need of Him. The second obstacle is haste. If we follow the eagerness of natural activity, God, who never hurries, allows the imprudent man to walk under the guidance of his own spirit, as inconsiderate in words as he is bold in projects and showing want of reflection in all that he does; "He that is hasty with his feet shall stumble" (Prov. 19:2), says the Holy Scripture. Lastly, slowness forms the third obstacle. If after having maturely taken a resolution we delay in executing it, circumstances change, the opportunity is lost, and the Spirit of God leaves in his indolence the man who keeps behindhand. Have we not placed these three obstacles in the way of the action of the Holy Spirit within us? *Resolutions and spiritual nosegay as above.*

Wednesday before Pentecost

SUMMARY OF TOMORROW'S MEDITATION

ontinuing to study the gifts of the Holy Spirit, we will meditate tomorrow upon the gift of wisdom, and we shall see: First what the gift of wisdom is; Second, what the excellence of it is. We will then make the resolution: First, frequently during the day to invoke the Spirit of wisdom that He may direct our acts, our thoughts, our words; second, to watch over our heart that it may not be seduced by the false maxims of the world in respect to enjoyments, riches, honors, and the desire to attract notice. We will retain as our spiritual nosegay the maxim of the Holy

Ghost: "Wisdom is better than all the most precious things; and whatsoever may be desired cannot be compared to it." (Prov. 8:11)

MEDITATION FOR THE MORNING

Let us return to the cenacle, let us represent to ourselves Mary and the apostles at prayer, and ourselves in the midst of them. What an admirable prayer was theirs! And ours what is ours going to be? Let us recollect ourselves; let us conceive a great desire to make of our prayer today the best prayer of our life, and to attract within us the gift of wisdom, on which we are about to meditate.

FIRST POINT

✝ *What is the Gift of Wisdom?*

Wisdom, according to St. Bernard, is disgust for the things of this world and taste for the things of God. The soul which has received this divine taste finds an inexpressible pleasure in thinking of God, in enjoying the things which belong to God, His greatness, His beauty, His perfections, His mysteries: so infinitely adorable, so infinitely amiable does it find them to be. All the goods of this world, its praises and its honors, its riches and its pleasures, are supremely insipid to it. It has tasted God; it cannot henceforth enjoy anything else. Thanks to this gift of wisdom, it knows no other pleasure in this world than that of prayer, of meditation, of spiritual reading, of good works, of exercises of piety, no other attraction than that of the divine pleasure, so that it is more delighted to perform the meanest things for the love of God than to bear scepters and wear crowns, as St. Teresa said of herself. Poverty seems to it to be a treasure, austerities an enjoyment, contempt an inestimable blessing; sufferings are happiness, humiliations a glory, prison and scourges a privilege (Acts 5:41). The whole earth is as nothing to it, it esteems heaven alone. Time appears to it but as a shadow, eternity alone is worthy of occupying its thoughts. Oh, what great need have we of this gift! For without it we have no taste for the things of God; we neither desire nor seek for them, we end by neglecting them because everything about them seems to us dry and insipid, and even the most touching prayers and the most pious exercises say nothing to our hearts. Without this gift, we allow ourselves to be seduced by the folly of the world, which places its last end in the creature and not in God; it's content in things which pass away, and not in eternal things; in things which dazzle, which flatter vanity or give pleasure, and not in humiliation, poverty, the cross, all of which things are so much loved by Jesus Christ and the saints. Let us here examine ourselves; have we the gift of wisdom, or do we not give ourselves up to worldly folly? We shall discover this by examining what are our tastes and our dislikes, whether with regard to God and divine things, or with regard to creatures and earthly things; what gives us pleasure and what gives us pain, what gives rest to our heart and what makes it discontented; in a word, whether we have no taste except for that for which the saints and Our Lord had a taste, that is to say, poverty, abjection, the cross.

SECOND POINT

✝ *What is the Excellence of the Gift of Wisdom?*

First, it is the specific remedy for the corruption left within us by original sin. Such, in point of fact, is our evil nature, that we have a taste for everything which amuses and gives us pleasure, for all that flatters self-love and vanity, for all that attracts towards us praise and esteem, in a word, for the world and its false treasures. Whilst, on the contrary, we have but little taste for spiritual things, for exercises of piety, for the practice of virtues. We even often feel an aversion and a disgust towards everything which belongs to duty, so that it is sometimes sufficient that a thing should be commanded in order to make it displeasing to us; that it should be forbidden in order that it should become attractive to us. Now the gift of wisdom is precisely that which corrects these depraved tastes. It shows us in all its nakedness the falsity of everything which the world esteems, and inspires us with disgust for it, the real merit of all which sanctifies, and inspires us with a love for it. Second, the gift of wisdom renders all virtues easy to us, and makes us run with dilated heart in the ways of perfection. It makes us enjoy God and spiritual things, the cross and privations, recollection in God, charity and devotedness towards our neighbor, humility and self-sacrifice; and with these supernatural tastes, there is nothing in regard to our salvation which costs us anything. We do all things well, because we do them with a taste for them; we perform them courageously and without weariness, because they are a pleasure to us; we perform them lovingly, because we find happiness in them, even in this present life. Let us ask and entreat with all our hearts for so precious a gift. *Resolutions and spiritual nosegay as above.*

SUMMARY OF TOMORROW'S MEDITATION

e will continue our meditations upon the seven gifts of the Holy Spirit, and will meditate tomorrow on the gift of piety. We shall see: First, what this gift is in regard to God; second, what it is with regard to our neighbor. We will then make the resolution: First, to spend in a special state of recollection the three days which separate us from Pentecost, in order that on that great day the Holy Spirit may find our souls well prepared; second, always to see in God a Father full of tenderness, and to apply ourselves to love Him rather than to fear Him. Third, to see in our neighbor a child of God, a brother of Jesus Christ, and on account of these titles, to treat him with tender respect. Our spiritual nosegay shall be the words of St. Paul: "God hath sent the Spirit of His Son into your hearts, crying, Abba (Father)." (Gal. 4:6).

MEDITATION FOR THE MORNING

Let us adore the Holy Spirit shedding on the souls of men the gift of piety, that precious gift which softens the natural hardness of the heart and fills it with tenderness towards God and towards our neighbor. Let us thank Him for this ineffable gift; let us beg of Him to communicate it to us, and to make us rightly understand its excellence.

FIRST POINT

✝ *What the Gift of Piety is in Regard to God*

Very different from the virtue of religion, which honors God as the Creator and supreme Master, the gift of piety teaches us to honor Him as our Father, and produces with regard to Him, in the soul, a wholly filial affection, full of unction, of tenderness and suavity, which places its whole happiness in occupying itself with God and the things belonging to God, and with doing all things with the desire of pleasing Him. By means of this gift we no longer see in God the Judge whose severity makes us tremble; we only see a tender Father whose kindness consoles us; a Father who looks lovingly upon us, and on whom we look in the same manner. We no longer think of fearing Him, we only think of loving Him. To love Him is everything, and the more we love the more we still desire to love. This affection and this tenderness kindle in the heart an ardent desire to please Him at all costs. If we fall into a fault, we are not troubled. God is a Father; we cast ourselves into His arms to ask pardon, with humble confidence, as a child who has fallen casts itself into the arms of its mother, and the soul is allowed to make amends for its fault by more love, by better behavior, and it resumes its manner of life in peace with renewed fervor. There is no anxiety, no scruple to be entertained in the service of so good a Father; all is love in it, and our heart is always at ease, like that of a child in the society of its good father. Whatever events may happen, we abandon ourselves lovingly to all that comes from His paternal hand. "It is my Father who permits it so to be, we say to ourselves from the bottom of our hearts; "it is His heart so full of goodness that has ordered it thus: may His good pleasure be accomplished! I will all that He wills, and nothing but what He wills." From these holy dispositions proceed out of the soul a great zeal for the glory of God, an inexpressible displeasure at seeing Him offended, the displeasure of a child at seeing the best of fathers insulted; from thence, also, a tender love for the divine word contained in the Holy Scriptures; it is the word of a father, always dear to the heart of a son; from thence a special affection for the Church triumphant, that is to say, for Mary, the angels, and the saints, because they are those who have the most loved God, and we owe them infinite gratitude for it; hence a very hearty devotion towards the Church suffering in purgatory, because therein are the just souls whom God desires to receive into His paradise, and whom we can enable to enter therein by means of our prayers and our merits; from thence, finally, a lively interest in the Church militant upon earth, because it has laid upon it the duty of proclaiming the glory of God; and its misfortunes tear our heart as much as its success ravishes it. Let us here examine ourselves: have we this gift of piety? If we have it not, let us ask it of God with our whole heart.

SECOND POINT

✝ *What the Gift of Piety is in Regard to our Neighbor.*

As all men are the images and the adopted children of God, the brothers and co-heirs of Jesus Christ, the gift of piety puts into the heart, with regard to them, a real fraternal love, a benevolent inclination, an abundance of delectation and of sweetness, which is as a ray of the goodness of God, a participation in His charity, an emanation of His mercy, whence result towards all men a frank and gracious manner of acting, an always frank expression of countenance, an always affable intercourse, which is composed of kind and amiable words. We behave towards them with the simplicity of a child towards its superiors, the cordiality of a brother towards his equals; we have entrails of compassion for all who suffer, accompanied with a tender inclination to help them. We are afflicted with those who sorrow, we weep with those who weep, we rejoice with those who rejoice. We bear with cheerfulness the infirmities of the weak, the defects of the imperfect; we make ourselves all things to all, by being serious and reserved with those who are so, prompt and fervent with prompt and fervent minds, merry with those who are merry, without ever exceeding the limits of modesty; and we bring to the practice of virtue, in so far as virtue permits, the condescendence and the attention which the characters of those with whom we have to deal call for. Let us here examine ourselves: instead of the tender sympathies which the gift of piety inspires, have we not often that unfortunate hardness of heart which, being attentive only to that which touches ourselves, prevents us from knowing either how to pity the wretchedness of our neighbor, or to put ourselves out of our way in order to oblige others, or to bear defects and injuries, or to moderate hatred and desires of vengeance, or the bitterness and antipathy which is not afraid of displeasing our neighbor? Do we not belong to those who style solidity of mind and firmness of character this antichristian hardness? *Resolutions and spiritual nosegay as above.*

Friday before Pentecost

SUMMARY OF TOMORROW'S MEDITATION

e will meditate tomorrow on the gift of fear, and we shall see: First, what is the excellence of this gift, which is so little understood; second, the unhappiness of those who are deprived of it. We will then make the resolution: First, frequently to ask, during today, the Holy Spirit to grant us the gift of fear, which will make us practice all the other virtues. Second, to maintain a reverential attitude towards God in prayer, at church, and everywhere. We will retain as our spiritual nose gay the words of David: "Blessed is the man that feareth the Lord."(Ps. 109:1)

MEDITATION FOR THE MORNING

Let us recollect ourselves profoundly in the presence of God; let us thank Him for having enriched the Church with the gift of fear; let us beg of Him to grant us the understanding of it and esteem for it.

FIRST POINT

✝ ***Excellence of the Gift of Fear***

Fear, in so far as it is one of the gifts of the Holy Spirit, has nothing in common either with the fear which seizes us in the presence of danger, or with the apprehension of sin which torments the scrupulous soul, or even with the

Christian fear of the torments of hell. The fear of which we speak is a gentle fear, inspired by love and reverence for the eyes of God which are fixed upon us. For the sole reason that we love God, we are afraid, but without being troubled by it, that something may displease Him, either in our acts or our words, the thoughts of our mind or the slightest movements of our heart, upon which we know that His eyes are constantly intent; and this fear renders us circumspect in the whole of our conduct, careful in doing all things well, attentive to give to every one of our actions all the perfection of which it is capable. "A wise man," says Solomon, "feareth and declineth from evil; the fool leapeth over and is confident." (Prov. 14:16). For the sole reason that we feel ourselves to be in the presence of God, we are filled with supreme reverence in the presence of so lofty a majesty, we revere Him with sentiments so humble and so profound, that we are, as it were, annihilated by the mere remembrance that He is beholding us, and we dare not permit anything but what is holy and perfect to present itself in presence of a God so just. Such is the fear which is one of the seven gifts of the Holy Spirit, and it would be impossible to express how many are the blessings it confers on the soul. It preserves it in a state of eminent purity, by giving it a supreme horror of committing the least offence against God, an inexpressible apprehension of the least sin, to such an extent that it would love a thousand times better to throw itself into the midst of flames and into torments such as those of hell rather than commit the slightest sin. This fear fills it in prayer with a deep piety which banishes from it all languor and all pusillanimity, and which fixes the frivolity of mind in a state of recollection. It inspires it at church with a reverential attitude, restraint with regard to the eyes, a silence of adoration; everywhere, in private as in public, with exemplary modesty and perfect restraint, because everywhere it keeps it in a reverential attitude as being in the presence of God. Finally, the soul favored by the gift of fear has towards God confidence of strength, says the Holy Spirit (Prov. 14:26), and at the same time a love always increasing in proportion as it is inspired with a more lofty sentiment of the incomparable grandeur of the divine perfections. Let us hence judge how excellent this gift is, and with what fervent prayers we ought to ask that it may be bestowed upon us during these holy days.

SECOND POINT

✝ *Unhappiness of the Soul which does not Possess the Gift of Fear*

Such a soul is most unhappy and in great peril of being lost. As it is not kept in restraint by fear, it allows itself to be given up to the love of its own ease, its caprices, and its liberty, which become the sole rule of its conduct.

There is no order in the regulation of its life or of its time, no exactitude in its exercises of piety, and, even when it does perform them, it is with a thousand distractions, and even without the exterior religious demeanor which ought always to accompany them. There is no modesty, no decency, or seriousness in the whole of its behavior; it is frivolous, inconsiderate, carried away by its impetuosities and its impulses, or by the ill-regulated movements of its exterior, which are the sign of a person who is without reflection. If it acts, it is without thinking of making all it does supernatural by performing it for the sake of God and of His love, and in this way it loses all merit. If it speaks, it follows its natural inclinations in speaking and replying, and how many words deserving of regret escape it! If it prays, it is without love, without respect, without attention to what it says. And thus its prayer, which ought to save it, ruins it, since it is converted into sin. Lastly, in the whole of its life it makes small account of little faults, of negligence which it does not believe to be a mortal sin: a sad symptom, which characterizes tepidity, that dreadful evil which angers the heart of God, and which leads to mortal sin without our being aware of it. Can there be anything more wretched than a soul which is in this state? How greatly ought this consideration to excite us to spend in a holy manner the next two days, in order to dispose our hearts for the coming of the Holy Ghost! *Resolutions and spiritual nosegay as above.*

Saturday before Pentecost

SUMMARY OF TOMORROW'S MEDITATION

We will meditate tomorrow upon the gift of fortitude, the last and the complement of the gifts of the Holy Spirit on which we have to meditate, and we shall see: First, what man is without this gift; second, what he becomes by this gift. We will then make the resolution: First, to pass in a very holy manner the eve of Pentecost, in order to attract the Holy Spirit to come and dwell within us; second, often to call to our aid the gift of fortitude, and not to permit ourselves to give way to any pusillanimity today or to make any concession to our evil nature. We will retain as our spiritual nosegay the prayer of Holy Church: "Holy Spirit, give Thy seven gifts to the faithful who call upon Thee with confidence." (Hymn of Pentecost)

MEDITATION FOR THE MORNING

Having reached the eve of the great day on which the Holy Spirit is coming to dwell in souls that are well disposed to receive Him, as He formerly descended upon the apostles, let us recollect ourselves, and prepare ourselves. Let us adore the Spirit of fortitude in the heights of heaven, and let us beg of Him to descend into our hearts.

FIRST POINT

✝ *What Man is without the Gift of Fortitude*

The gift of fortitude is a supernatural energy which strengthens us against pusillanimity or cowardice in the service of God, against our own weakness, against the difficulties, dangers, and trials we may meet with in the accomplishment of our duties. More excellent than the virtue of strength, which only supposes an ordinary grace, the gift of fortitude is an interior vigor, a divine courage, which, raising man above himself renders possible, and even easy, things which appear to be impossible. Unless this gift is added to virtue, we are incapable of fulfilling all our duties; ordinary strength is not sufficient to sustain nature, which is sometimes afraid at certain great sacrifices which duty imposes; sometimes wearied by the continual violence which we must do ourselves in order never to fall; sometimes discouraged by its own weakness, which, as regards what is good, can do nothing, not even to the producing of a thought which would be useful to our salvation, and which, in regard to all that is evil, is capable of everything if not restrained by grace. What strength does it not indeed require to keep firm against a heart in which are the germs of all the vices; which is besieged by temptations and solicited by passions; which is cast down by adversities and is attached to prosperity; which is frightened at obstacles and discouraged by sorrows; which human respect enchains through the wretched fear of raillery, of a look or a sign of want of approbation! Without the extraordinary vigor which is communicated by the gift of fortitude, the weakness of the will paralyzes the best resolutions and extinguishes all spirit of prayer and of mortification. Hence the fall of persons we thought to be firm as pillars, and who have bent like reeds. O weakness! O misery of poor humanity! What good reason had the Apostle to say: "He that thinks himself to stand, let him take heed lest he fall." (1 Cor. 10:12). The gift of fortitude is, above all, necessary to those who are in authority; for then, from want of this gift, is added to personal evil public evil. Through an unworthy timidity, a cowardly and pusillanimous condescension, evil is permitted to be committed, from want of speaking and reproving it. Hence the lowering of characters, the triumph of the wicked, the reign of evil, to which weakness gives the reins: a weakness which is deplorable at all times, but, above all, in these evil days, wherein the genius of evil makes such furious war against all that is good. Let us recognize how greatly we ourselves stand in need of this gift, in whatever position we may be; let us therefore prepare ourselves to receive it into our hearts on this holy day.

SECOND POINT

✝ *What Man Becomes through the Gift of Fortitude*

One of the greatest beauties which characterizes the Church is the transformation of souls by the gift of fortitude. The apostles, as soon as they had received it, became strong, intrepid, and magnanimous. He who had trembled at the voice of a servant dared to denounce the whole nation on account of the deicide it had committed. "You denied the Holy One and the Just," he said to them; "you desired a murderer to be granted unto you, but the Author of life you killed." (Acts 3:14, 15) The preacher was arrested for having dared to speak in such a manner. Preach no more in His name, the judges say to him. You ask of us what is impossible, answered the intrepid apostle. "We cannot but speak of the things which we have seen and heard." (Acts 4:20). He does not say, remarks St. John Chrysostom, we will not; the will of man is subject to change; the judges might have hoped that they could conquer it, but, we cannot. We can suffer, we can die, but we cannot, through unworthy weaknesses, betray our ministry. By means of this gift of fortitude, the Ambroses, the Basils, the Athanasiuses, become heroes, their courage raises them above all the evils with which they are threatened as well as all the favors which are promised them. Let bad fortune of all kinds fall upon them, let calumny attack them, let them be surrounded by misfortunes; they are firm and calm as is a rock attacked by a tempest; they pass through all these trials with the generosity of a heart which loves God above all else (3 Imit. 5:4,5). Even death does not terrify them (Cant. 8:6). Patient in waiting for, or in doing what is good, as well as in suffering evil, they are always the same. St. John Chrysostom causes it to be said of him, "This man fears nothing but sin," and St. Francis Xavier, in the midst of a thousand perils of death, exclaims, "The surest remedy is to fear nothing, leaning upon confidence in God, and the greatest evil would be to fear the enemies of God whilst upholding the cause of God." Thus, by means of the gift of fortitude, the saints do and suffer all things, expose themselves to the greatest dangers, overcome the most painful labors, support the most severe anguish. Happy, then, the soul which, mistrusting itself, through a deep feeling of its weakness, calls to its aid the Spirit of fortitude and puts all its confidence in Him! It is capable of all virtue. Is anything more required to make us desire it and earnestly ask it of God? *Resolutions and spiritual nosegay as above.*

The Holy Feast of Pentecost

THE GOSPEL ACCORDING TO ST. JOHN 14:23-31

"At that time, Jesus said to His disciples: If anyone love Me, he will keep My word, and My Father will love him, and We will come to him, and will make Our abode with him. He that loveth Me not, keepeth not My word; and the word which you have heard is not Mine, but the Father's who sent Me. These things have I spoken to you, abiding with you; but the Paraclete, the Holy Ghost, whom the Father will send in My name, will teach you all things, and bring all things to your mind whatsoever I shall have said to you. Peace I leave with you, my peace I give unto you; not as the world giveth do I give unto you. Let not your heart be troubled, nor let it be afraid. You have heard that I said to you, I go away, and I come unto you. If you loved Me, you would indeed be glad because I go to the Father; for the Father is greater than I. And now I have told you before it came to pass, that when it shall come to pass you may believe. I will not now speak many things with you; for the prince of this world cometh, and in Me he hath not anything. But that the world may know that I love the Father, and as the Father hath given Me commandment, so do I."

SUMMARY OF TOMORROW'S MEDITATION

e will transport ourselves tomorrow in thought to the cenacle, where the Holy Spirit descends upon the apostles; and we will consider: First, the reasons of His coming into the world; second, the wonders of His divine operations in heaven and upon earth. We will then make the resolution: First with all our hearts to thank the Holy Spirit for all that He does for the good of the Church and for our own salvation; second, to offer ourselves to Him, to obey in all things His holy inspirations. Our spiritual nosegay shall be the words of the Psalmist: "Thou shall send forth Thy Spirit, and Thou shall renew the face of the Earth." (Ps. 103:30)

MEDITATION FOR THE MORNING

Let us transport ourselves in spirit to the cenacle, where the Blessed Virgin and the apostles are assembled, awaiting in the fervor of prayer the descent of the Holy Ghost. Let us represent to ourselves the marvelous descent, the tongues of fire which rest on the head of every one of them, a symbol of the invisible transformation which takes place within, of the sacred flames of love and of zeal which fill the whole of their interior and change them into other men. Let us ardently desire to be ourselves kindled with the sacred fire, and let us call to us the Divine Spirit, the Author of all these wonders.

FIRST POINT

✝ *Why the Holy Ghost Descends upon Earth on this Day*

If the Holy Ghost descends upon earth today, it is not to make us a passing visit; it is to remain there always with us throughout all ages; it is to found there, and there to govern, the holy Church; to preserve it always one, holy, catholic, and apostolic; to maintain it in the truth against all the attacks of impiety and of heresy; to assist it in its teaching, in such a manner that it shall always be able to say: "It has seemed good to the Holy Ghost and to us." (Acts 15:98) It is to render it eternally fruitful and forever to engender in it saints and children of God, apostles to carry it over the whole earth, martyrs to confirm it by the testimony of their blood, doctors to enlighten it by their science, elect souls to edify it by their virtues. What a great and beautiful mission! It is only a God who could fulfill it. And this mission is the work of the Holy Ghost rather than that of the two other Divine Persons: First, because God, having already sent us His word, His thought, His intellectual image, He wills that His love should still come and visit us, in order that we may thoroughly understand that everything in the Trinity consists of love for us; power creates and preserves us, wisdom redeems us, and love sanctifies us. Second, because the sending of the Holy Ghost characterizes and shows forth the spirit of the New Law. Jesus Christ does not will that we should suffer fear and servitude; He says to the substantial love which unites the Father and the Son, and who is God equal to both the one and the other, "O Spirit of love, go and teach them to serve Me by love; shed in their hearts the spirit of adoption of children, whereby they will call God their Father; the spirit of charity, the spirit of love." Such, in fact, since Pentecost, has been the true character of religion. All in it is love; love is the whole of the Gospel; love flowing in every direction through the heart as the fountain of life, there is the whole of Christianity. Is this the idea we form of it? Do we endeavor to realize it in the whole of our conduct, above all in our exercises of piety and in the reception of the sacraments? Is it love which rules and inspires us? Is our life a life of love?

SECOND POINT

✝ *The Marvelous Operations of the Holy Spirit in Heaven and on Earth*

We may consider these operations as a whole or in their details. First, if we consider them as a whole, they present a magnificent spectacle to us. They begin in the bosom of the Father, where the Divine Spirit alone perfectly loves the divine greatness, even as the Father alone is perfectly acquainted with them and the Word alone praises them worthily. This love ravishes the Father and the Son; it is their eternal felicity. If, from the bosom of the Father, we pass on to Mary, to the angels and the saints, we behold the Divine Spirit which moves and animates them all, which vivifies the whole of heaven, sets it on fire and makes it sing its magnificent canticles to the honor of God. If from thence we descend to the earth, we still see there the same Divine Spirit inspiring all holy souls, inspiring their hearts with innumerable noble sentiments, praises and love which rise ceaselessly to heaven; so that it is one and the same Spirit which makes all the saints pray in heaven and upon earth, which animates God Himself and His fragile creature, and forms, as it were, a magnificent concert, a sublime harmony to the glory of the three Divine Persons; a sweet truth, which ought to lead us to do everything, to say everything, and to think everything in union with the Holy Ghost and by His movements. Second, the operations of the Holy Ghost, considered in their details, are not less admirable. What a marvel it is to see the eternal God occupied every day with the soul of every one of us, in order to sanctify it, knocking at the door of every heart when we will not open it to Him (Apoc. 3:20), knocking at it whole years long without allowing His love to be discouraged by rebuffs; and when we receive Him, enlightening our intelligence, inflaming our will, reproving or encouraging it, sometimes attracting it by the sweetness of His unction, sometimes perfecting it by means of a seeming severity, but always at work to form Jesus Christ in us (Gal. 4:19). Oh, how greatly do these marvels deserve all our praise, all our gratitude, and all our love, above all on the great feast of Pentecost! *Resolutions and spiritual nosegay as above.*

SUMMARY OF TOMORROW'S MEDITATION

We will meditate tomorrow: First, on the homage of adoration and thanksgiving which we owe to the Holy Ghost; second, the homage of honorable reparation for the past and of solicitations for the future which are equally due to Him. We will make the resolution: First, to receive, with great piety, as being the word of God, the good thoughts and inspirations of the Holy Ghost; second, to mature them by reflection and to put them thoroughly into practice. Our spiritual nosegay shall be the words of the Apostle: "The Spirit of God dwells in you." (1 Cor. 3:16)

MEDITATION FOR THE MORNING

Let us adore the Holy Spirit pouring Himself out, upon the day of Pentecost, on the apostles, and at all times upon the faithful who are well disposed (Acts 2:4). Let us thank Him for His divine operations in our souls, and let us beg of Him to make us share in His gifts.

FIRST POINT

✝ *The Adoration and Thanksgiving we owe to the Holy Ghost*

If adoration is an homage exclusively due to God, it is eminently so to the Holy Spirit (Symb. Nic.), because everywhere in Holy Writ He is spoken of under the title and possessing the attributes of God, like the Father and the Son. From the first day of the world, He covers the waters with His creative heat to make them fruitful (Gen. 1:21); He adorns the heavens and gives life to all (Job 26:13; Ps. 103:30). Elsewhere we see Him inspiring the prophets, and revealing through them all the secrets of the future (Symb. Nic.), forming in the womb of Mary the body of the Word (Matt. 1:20), leading Jesus into the desert and directing all His acts, working miracles by the apostles, and by all such among Christians as receive the gifts of performing them in confirmation, having His temple in us (1 Cor. 4:19), where He is our Sanctifier by the same title that the Father is our Creator and the Son our Redeemer. There He consumes sin in us by means of the fire of holy love, infusing the life of sanctity which He draws from the bosom of the Father and of the Son. Oh, how worthy is He then of our adoration, He who is the author of these marvels! And yet I think of Him so little! I live as though there were nothing in me but myself! I bear within me a God, and I adore Him so rarely, and I do not allow myself to have the honor of being led by Him, by His good pleasure and His divine attractions! To adoration I ought to unite thanksgiving, for if the Holy Spirit labors ceaselessly within me for the good of my soul, is it not just to thank Him continually for being so good as to communicate to us so many gifts and graces, and, notwithstanding the contempt we show for them, to continue His divine operations spite of rebuffs? Eternity would not be long enough worthily to thank this Divine Spirit for one good thought; for the good thought is worth the blood of Jesus Christ, which is the price of it, it is worth heaven, which will be its recompense if I make a proper use of it; therefore it is of infinite value, and if it be thus with one single good thought, what do we not owe to the Holy Spirit for all those which He has given us since we had the use of reason? O sanctifying God, never can I thank Thee enough!

SECOND POINT

✝ *Honorable Reparation and Solicitations Due to the Holy Spirit*

What reproaches have I not here to address to myself, and how many reparations do I not owe to the Holy Spirit? I have so many times made no account of His graces! He has inspired me to do what was good, and I have closed my ears to His voice; He has insisted, and I have still offered Him resistance. O insolence! O baseness! I should not turn my back to a venerable man who might speak to me, and be so utterly wanting in respect to him as to take no heed of his pressing recommendations. It is only towards Thee, O adorable Spirit! O adorable Third Person of the Most Holy Trinity, that I dare permit myself to commit such an act of rudeness. I disobey Thy inspirations; I do not yield to Thy counsels. Ah! I feel today how great is my fault, and I ask forgiveness for it, with "a humble spirit and a contrite heart." I offer to Thee reparation and honorable amends. Pardon, my God! A thousand times pardon. Forget the past, and let me beg of Thee for the future new graces by which I will better profit. I am a poor man who has nothing, and, impelled by the feeling of my wretchedness and that of Thy mercy, I come to ask of Thee, Divine Spirit, the alms of Thy grace, without which I can do nothing; (1 Cor. 12:3), the alms of good thoughts, of good desires, of pious movements, of the strong resolutions by which saints are formed. I open to Thee the mouth of my heart by the fervor of my prayers (Ps. 118:131). Come, Father of the poor, Light of hearts; O blessed light, come to me! May the light of Thy grace illumine my understanding; may the fire of Thy love inflame my heart (Hymn of Pentecost). In order to be saved, I do not count upon myself, but upon Thee, who dost communicate Thyself to those who have recourse to Thee. (Luke 11:43) *Resolutions and spiritual nosegay as above.*

SUMMARY OF TOMORROW'S MEDITATION

We will meditate tomorrow on the marvelous action of the Holy Spirit upon the primitive Christians at Jerusalem, and we shall see that He made of them models: First, of detachment; second, of piety; third, of charity. We will then make the resolution: First, to practice during the day an act of mortification or of detachment; second, to observe, in the whole of our behavior, a great modesty, as a means whereby to form within us a spirit of recollection; third, to exercise the most perfect charity towards all with whom we have any relations. Our spiritual nosegay shall be the beautiful eulogium which the Holy Spirit pronounced on the primitive Christians: "The multitude of believers had but one heart and one soul." (Acts 4:32)

MEDITATION FOR THE MORNING

Let us adore the Holy Spirit forming in the primitive Christians the most accomplished models of holiness; let us praise Him for this masterpiece of His power and His love, and offer Him for it all our thanksgivings.

FIRST POINT

✝ *Detachment of the Primitive Christians*

The Holy Spirit, having descended upon them, showed them the vanity of all things here below, the nothingness of all that passes away, and repeated to them in the bottom of their hearts the words of the Savior: He who does not renounce himself wholly, cannot be My disciple. Go, sell what thou hast, and give to the poor. Immediately, docile to the interior voice, these generous Christians renounce everything. They renounce worldly possessions, for Holy Writ says that they sold their possessions and laid the price of them at the feet of the apostles, who divided them amongst all, according as everyone had need (Acts 2:45; 4:31 et seq.). They renounced honors, glory, the esteem of men, for, in public opinion, they were looked upon as apostates from a religion which was certainly divine, as madmen who adored a man crucified, and as disciples of poor fishermen. They renounced their friends and their relations, who wept over their desertion, and would not any longer hold intercourse with them. They renounced themselves and placed their wills in the hands of the apostles, whom they obeyed in perfect simplicity of spirit. Thus, freed from all attachments, they enjoyed perfect liberty of mind, and an unchangeable tranquility of soul, by means of which they served God without hindrance, prayed to Him with love, and enjoyed Him with delight. Let us examine what is the point we have reached in regard to this complete detachment, and what are the fibers which still attach us to earth.

SECOND POINT

✝ *Piety of the Primitive Christians*

Every day they met together in the temple, says Holy Writ, in the union of one same spirit, persevering in prayer and in communion, which they received praising and glorifying God with joy and simplicity of heart (Acts. 2:42 et seq.). Let us admire the spirit of prayer which animated these primitive Christians; they had rightly understood the words which Jesus had spoken to His disciples: "We ought always to pray and never to faint" (Luke 18:1), and those of God to Abraham, "Walk before Me and be perfect." (Gen. 17:1) For not only were they recollected, but it was in a proper manner; their recollection had nothing in it which was sorrowful or severe, nothing constrained or affected; it was, on the contrary, accompanied by great simplicity of heart and that wholly joyful gladness which divine love brings with it into the soul (Acts. 2:46,47); a beautiful model, which teaches us to communicate often and to make the spirit of prayer and recollection precede and follow communion; because if communion accompanied by the spirit of recollection is the most nourishing aliment of piety and virtue, communion allied with a dissipated life and devoid of the spirit of prayer would redound to our loss. Let us here examine our selves.

THIRD POINT

✝ *Charity of the Primitive Christians*

They were, says the book of the Acts, all united together as one and the same family all of whose members are united together by strict charity. Between them there was no mine and thine; all they had was in common (Acts 2:41), and the multitude of the believers formed but one heart and one soul (Ibid. 4:32). Although they were an assemblage of persons belonging to various countries, and who were of different positions, differing in character, and who had diverse interests, charity made of all these members one sole body, of all these hearts one sole heart, of all these souls one single soul. Sweet and happy union, fore taste of Paradise, of which we might say with the Psalmist: "Behold, how good and pleasant it is for brethren to dwell together in unity!" (Ps. 132:1) This beautiful spectacle was the admiration of all who were witnesses of it (Acts 5:13), a great number were converted by means of it (Ibid. 14), and even those who were not converted were obliged to praise and bless the Christians (Ibid. 2:47). Let us hence learn to love one another, not with the icy love which confines itself to not hating or wishing evil to anyone, but with the sincere love which has its root in the heart, which wills all possible good to its brethren, and shares their troubles as well as their joys; that tender love which has a wholly cordial manner of acting, and which avoids even the slightest words or actions capable of giving pain; that generous love which, forgetting itself in order to give pleasure to others, accommodates itself to all characters, makes all kinds of sacrifices, and is full of delicate attentions for everyone. *Resolutions and spiritual nosegay as above.*

Wednesday after Pentecost

SUMMARY OF TOMORROW'S MEDITATION

We will tomorrow continue our meditations upon the Holy Spirit; we will study His actions in the soul, and we shall see: First, how He illumines our understanding; second, how He raises our hearts; third, how He perfects our acts. We will then make the resolution: First, often to ask ourselves during the course of the day: Is it indeed the Spirit of God who animates me at this moment, who makes me perform this action, say these words, makes me dwell on this thought? Is there nothing human in my intentions and aims? Second, we will make the resolution to keep ourselves on our guard against being occupied with desire or attachment which would prevent us from listening to the Holy Spirit. Our spiritual nosegay shall be the prayer of the Church: "Come, Holy Spirit, and visit the soul of those who belong to Thee."

MEDITATION FOR THE MORNING

Let us adore the Spirit of God as the supreme and universal Director of souls. He fills heaven and earth with His holy inspirations, and there is not a single soul which escapes His action, excepting in so far as it wills to do so (Ps. 17:7). Oh, how greatly does He merit through this title all our praise and all our love!

FIRST POINT

✝ *The Holy Spirit Illumines the Understanding*

It is the Spirit of God, it is written, "who teaches all truth;" (John 16:13) it is His unction "which instructs the soul in everything." (1 John 2:27) The purely natural knowledge of God leaves us insensible and says nothing to the heart, but let the Holy Spirit only shed His light and His unction upon this knowledge, and we are immediately ravished; we are overwhelmed with admiration and love, and certain souls have been known to spend whole hours in dwelling with ecstasy on one sole word, My God. It is the same with all religious truths, to such a point that the proofs of faith, even those which are the most victorious of them, never decided a man to believe, unless the Holy Spirit, the great Enlightener of the understanding, did not Himself show them to him; so that even the beginning of faith is a grace, as the Church has defined it. It is the same with ourselves and with all things. Without the Spirit of God we are blind, we know nothing; hence our pride and our presumption; we do not see the nothingness, the falsity, and the danger of the seeming goods of this world; hence our attachments and our passions; we know neither what we ought to do nor what we ought to say; hence imprudences and daily faults. But with Thee, O Divine Spirit! O most blessed Light! We see our nothingness and our misery, our malice and our ignorance, all the reasons there are for despising ourselves, for keeping ourselves always very humble, for mistrusting ourselves, for flying from occasions of evil, and for praying to Thee without ceasing: "Come then to our aid, O Holy Spirit; send down from heaven a ray of Thy light."

SECOND POINT

✝ *The Holy Spirit Raises the Heart*

The Spirit of God, when He possesses a heart, raises it above all the things of this world; riches, for such a great heart, lose their splendor, pleasures their tastes, honors their false brilliancy, the what will they say its empire. It exclaims, with St. Ignatius, What nothingness the earth seems to him who looks up to heaven! If it has to suffer, it rejoices; it is glory and honor. "They went away rejoicing that they were accounted worthy to suffer for Jesus Christ," (Acts 5:41) it is said of the apostles. And this it is which has determined during the last nineteen centuries, and which still continues to determine so many souls, placed in brilliant positions, to abandon everything and to devote themselves to the austere and obscure life of the cloister. It is thus that the man who has the Spirit of God raises himself above all that passes away; he raises himself even up to God, and unites himself with Him in prayer. Oh, how well he prays! How recollected, touched, and impressed he is! It might be said of him that he is already in heaven, amongst the saints and angels. How he makes to ascend to the heart of God those ineffable sighs which alone the Holy Spirit can bring forth in the soul (Rom. 8:26), those tender effusions of a wholly filial piety which makes it cry out to heaven, "Abba, (Father)" (Rom. 8:15). How, lastly, is contracted that love of prayer and of union with God which becomes the happiness of life (Acts 6:4), a wonderful effect of the charity of God which the Holy Spirit infuses into all the powers of the soul! It is thus that are formed noble hearts and great souls capable of all kinds of sacrifices, ready for all holy works. O Holy Spirit, Author of all that is good, come and take possession of my poor heart; come and create within me a new heart, a generous heart, a heart which no longer beats except with love for Thee, and for my brethren through love for Thee and with the desire to please Thee.

THIRD POINT

✝ *The Spirit of God Perfects our Acts*

When we possess the Spirit of God, we do all things well, for we perform them not through fear and servitude, but in love and by love. Then nothing costs us aught, or, if it does cost us sacrifices, it is an enjoyment. Then we no longer act mechanically and without an object, from habit and routine, still less from humor and caprice, from frivolity and want of reflection, or from the false wisdom of the world; but we always propose to ourselves the elevated aims of faith; and, in order the better to attain to them, we reflect before we act; we consult the light of prayer, rather than the calculations of human wisdom; and in the course of acting we proceed maturely, without giving way to the impulses or the haste which obscure the understanding and lead to imprudences. We act with humility, gentleness, and patience, aided by wisdom from on high, which guides all to a good end. It is thus that, where the human eye sees only darkness, the light of God shows us what we must do; and with it, there where the wise men of the world go astray, we perform marvels. Witness the Vincent de Pauls, the Ignatiuses, the Francis Xaviers, whose super-eminent wisdom has surpassed the wisdom of the world. It is that, lastly, which makes men of God capable of performing all kinds of good; it is that which perfects all their acts and renders their life holy. Let us aspire with our whole souls to have in all things the Spirit of God, and not the spirit of man. *Resolutions and spiritual nosegay as above.*

SUMMARY OF TOMORROW'S MEDITATION

e will study tomorrow: First, the obligation laid upon every Christian soul to follow the guidance of the Spirit of God; second, what this divine guidance demands from us. We will then make the resolution: First, to keep ourselves during the whole day in a spirit of exterior and interior recollection, in order to observe and to listen to the inspirations of the Spirit of God; second, to obey, with love and promptitude, the Divine Spirit in all things which He may suggest to us. Our spiritual nosegay shall be the words of the Apostle: "Whosoever are led by the Spirit of God, they are the sons of God." (Rom. 8:14)

MEDITATION FOR THE MORNING

Let us adore this Spirit of God laboring, throughout the whole Church, at the sanctification of souls. Let us bless Him for the numerous good thoughts, the pious affections, the fervent prayers, the generous resolutions, with which He inspires them. Let us offer to Him for it glory and thanksgiving.

FIRST POINT

✝ *The Obligation Imposed upon Every Christian Soul to Follow the Guidance of the Spirit of God*

The Spirit of God leads, by His divine inspirations, all the souls who will give themselves up to Him, and we are Christians only in so far as we follow His guidance. "If any man have not the Spirit of Christ" as the director and moderator of his conduct, "he is none of His" says St. Paul (Rom. 8:9). "Grieve not the Holy Spirit," continues the Apostle (Ephes. 4:30) by resisting Him, or by extinguishing in your heart those precious sparks with which He desires to kindle the flame of holy love in it. (1 Thess. 5:19) Filled with these truths, the primitive Christians gave themselves up to grace, to be led by it as a child who gives its hand to its mother, that she may lead it wherever she pleases. (Acts 14:25) When a God is willing to abase Himself to us that He may serve us as a guide through life, to the extent of making us hear His holy inspirations, on account of the loving commiseration He feels for our darkness and our wretchedness, can we do otherwise than listen to His voice, or not resist Him after having heard Him? To go on presuming on our own strength, without having recourse to the Spirit of God, is to prefer to light from on high our own skill; it is Pelagianism in principle. Hence the weakness which casts us down, the weight of nature which drags us along, the vanity which bleeds us, the resolutions which have no effect, the falls, the alternatives of good and evil; hence, lastly, so many failures in good works, because they were directed by human prudence and not by the Spirit of God. Happy the souls which, like the Apostle, being attached to the Holy Spirit (Acts 20:22), remain under His guidance and allow themselves to be led by Him. He says to them: Go, and they go; do, and they do. Is it thus that we allow ourselves to be led?

SECOND POINT

✝ *What the Guidance of the Spirit of God Requires from us*

There must be: First, attention in listening to His voice; second, generosity in obeying Him. Attention in listening to His voice is taught us by these words contained in the Imitation: "Happy the eyes of the soul, which, closed to outside things, are attentive to those which are within. Happy the ears, which, instead of listening to exterior sounds, listen to truth itself teaching within." (3 Imit. 1:1) That is to say, that we must withdraw our soul from dissipation, from frivolity, from the tumult of creatures and of useless thoughts, from passions which agitate us and the imaginations which lead us astray; we must watch over ourselves in order not to trouble the working of God in the soul, not to hinder it, not to interrupt it, not to weaken it, but to allow Him to work as He will, without meeting with any obstacle, and to do all, to read, to speak, to work, with great interior peace, in concert with Him. The Holy Spirit does not act in the midst of trouble (3 Kings 19:11); for why should He speak to anyone who does not listen to Him? In order that He may speak to the soul, the Spirit of God desires that He should find it calm, recollected, attentive in listening with all its powers, prostrate, in a manner, before Him, like Mary, sister of Lazarus, at the feet of Jesus, to receive, with pious reverence, all His good inspirations, and, like Samuel, to say: "Speak, Lord, Thy servant hears" (1 Kings 3:9); or like David: "I will hear what the Lord God will speak in me." (Ps. 84:9) Second, with attention we must unite generosity. The Holy Spirit leaves in their weakness cowardly and pusillanimous souls, who, tend over themselves to the extent of not sacrificing a single wish, resist His inspirations. What would His guidance be worth to those who will not follow it? He requires strong and generous souls, who obey His voice without hesitation, whatever it may cost them; souls which, like those good servants of whom David speaks, keep their eyes constantly fixed on the hands of their master that they may run at the least sign he gives them, or like those mysterious animals of Ezekiel which go wherever the Spirit of God calls them (Ezech. 1:12); and when He finds such souls, oh, what rapid progress He enables them to make towards perfection! What point have we reached in regard to this recollection and this generosity? *Resolutions and spiritual nosegay as above.*

Friday after Pentecost

SUMMARY OF TOMORROW'S MEDITATION

fter having meditated on the marvelous action of the Holy Spirit within us, we will now consider the unhappiness of the soul which does not permit itself to be led by this divine Guide; and, in order to understand it, we shall see: First, what the soul suffers which is indifferent to grace; second, what it loses. We will then make the resolution: First, to obey with love and promptitude all holy inspirations, without resisting a single one of them; second, often to ask the Holy Spirit for His assistance by addressing to Him the invocation of Holy Church, which will serve as our spiritual nosegay: "Come to my help, Father of the poor; come Giver of heavenly gifts; come, Light of the heart."

MEDITATION FOR THE MORNING

Let us adore the Divine Spirit offering Himself to the soul to sanctify it; let us admire His more than paternal goodness; let us ask of Him pardon for our infidelities, pardon for having so often closed our ears to His word and resisted His inspirations; let us beg of Him to enable us to understand the unhappiness of the soul which is unfaithful to Him.

FIRST POINT

✝ *What the Soul Suffers that is Unfaithful to Grace*

A soul such as this has neither peace nor happiness; for, says Job, "who hath resisted God and hath had peace?"(Job 9:4) It has no happiness; for Jesus, after His resurrection, said to faithless Saul: "it is hard for thee to kick against the goad" (Acts 9:5). It suffers, first, at being deprived of the consolations of piety; whilst it was faithful it enjoyed ineffable consolations in prayer, in communion, in visiting the Blessed Sacrament, and other exercises; but after it became faithless it felt itself to be cold, languishing, disgusted. How, indeed, could the Holy Spirit lavish His sweetness and His consolations on the soul which resists Him, which will not listen to or obey Him, which does not know how to sacrifice to Him an attachment, a will, or an inclination? It suffers, second, at seeing its hopes frustrated; it trusted that it would find happiness in the satisfaction of its tastes and its caprices, and God, in order to revenge Himself, sheds bitterness on these false pleasures. It finds greater troubles in them than in those from which it took flight; a somber sadness reigns within it; exteriorly it suffers from contradictions, weariness, and disgust; it turns itself from one side to another seeking repose; and its movements only make the thorn pierce more deeply into the heart. (Ps. 31:4) It suffers, third, from the reproaches of its conscience, which, discontented with itself, cries out to it ceaselessly that it is grateful, wanting in docility, insane, that it is like the sick man, who, stretched on a bed of suffering, sees the remedy that is capable of curing him, and yet refuses to take it. You see clearly what you ought to do," his conscience says to him, "and you will not do it. You are quite aware you are unreasonable, and you continue to be so; grace is standing at the door of your heart, exhorting you, offering to you its charitable hand to lead you, and you take no notice of it, you make it no answer. Where, then, is your religion? Where is your reason?" It suffers, fourth, from God, who persecutes it through love, who renders it unhappy for its own good, lest, feeling tranquil and at ease, spite of its dreadful state, it should per severe in it. This is why it happens that so often when we have refused God the sacrifice of an idle word, of a feeling of curiosity, of an uncharitable remark, we feel ourselves to be sad and discontented, without knowing why, and without taking much account of it.

SECOND POINT

✝ *What the Soul that is Unfaithful to Grace Loses thereby*

To lose a grace, an inspiration of the Holy Spirit, is to lose a thousand times more than if we were to lose all the kingdoms of the world. All good things here below are temporary and of little value, whilst the least grace has eternal consequences, since it is worth the blood of Jesus Christ, at the price of which it was bought for us. To lose a grace is to lose the essential element of our supernatural life; it is to imitate a madman throwing away the bread necessary for his existence. To lose a grace is to lose at once all the graces which would have been the consequence of the first grace put to profit, since fidelity to a first grace attracts a second, and that a third, and the same with the following ones; it is to lose, consequently, the treasures of which God alone knows the worth; and what unhappiness that is for us who are so poor and so indigent! Oh, what do we not lose in this way? Let us regret these losses, and repair them by never again losing a single grace. *Resolutions and spiritual nosegay as above.*

SUMMARY OF TOMORROW'S MEDITATION

e will continue our meditations upon correspondence with grace, and we shall see: First, what the soul loses which is unfaithful to grace; second, what the faithful soul gains. We will then make the resolution: First, during all the day to be attentive to the voice of the Holy Spirit, in order that we may listen to what He desires of us; second, to obey Him in all things with promptitude and generosity. We will retain as our spiritual nosegay the words of the Psalmist: "Today if you shall hear His voice, harden not your hearts". (Ps.94:8)

MEDITATION FOR THE MORNING

Let us adore the Holy Spirit as the most powerful auxiliary of our salvation; let us thank Him for His kind help, and let us beg of Him to make us see how necessary it is for us to be faithful to Him.

FIRST POINT

✝ *What the Soul Risks which is Unfaithful to Grace*

It risks nothing less than its eternal salvation. For as in the physical order certain causes are so linked together that the last is reached only by passing through those which precede it, so also in the supernatural order there is a chain of graces linked to our final perseverance by secret relations of which we are ignorant. To lose one of these graces is to lose the thread which was leading us; it is to expose ourselves to wander away from the path in which we should find our salvation. Who has told us that the grace to which we are unfaithful is not, in the designs of God, one of these decisive graces? St. Teresa saw her place marked out in the bottom of hell, if she had resisted the grace which told her to combat a temptation of self-love; and the young man in the Gospel who had kept all the commandments has left his salvation doubtful for resisting the grace which said to him: " Sell all that thou hast, and give it to the poor." (Matt. 19:21) The subtraction of graces is the ordinary penalty of the abuse made of them. Ye have rejected my grace, said the Lord, "and I have rejected you". (1 Kings 15:26) And is it not just? When the Divine Spirit comes and knocks at the door of the heart, and we refuse to open it, He departs from us; when He speaks and we will not listen to Him, He is silent; when He makes His light shine and we shut our eyes, He withdraws (Apoc. 2:5). What a terrible chastisement! Be afraid, says St. Augustine, of allowing the grace of

Jesus to pass away when it is offered to you. For then the devil, who perceives it, multiplies his attacks: and man, who does not perceive it, languishes in the carelessness of tepidity, which leads him to eternal death. This is what we risk in being faithless to grace. Who would not tremble at it?

SECOND POINT

✝ *What the Soul Gains which is Faithful to Grace*

It gains two things : happiness and holiness, first, it gains happiness. There is an ineffable pleasure in allowing ourselves to be led in all things by the Spirit of God, like the child by the hand of its mother, in saying to Him with love and simplicity, like St. Paul: "Lord, what wilt Thou have me to do?" and as soon as we have heard His voice, obeying Him gladly, running and flying as it were wherever He calls us (3 Imit. 5:4). Then is our heart calm, as it is in the tranquility of order, our intention is pure, our actions are regulated, our passions are kept in subjection, our faith is more lively. If grace demands sacrifices, it is an additional happiness, because it is an opportunity for our showing more love, and it is then we appreciate the words of St. Aloysius, when he said that a sacrifice made for God gives a thousand times more enjoyment to the soul than would have given even the thing sacrificed. Second, the faithful soul gains holiness. "He that shall hear Me" says the Holy Ghost, "shall rest without terror, and shall enjoy abundance without fear of evils". (Prov. 1:33) In the course of a few days we advance more when we perfectly correspond with grace than in whole months of spiritual exercises. The Holy Spirit does not cease to inspire us when we do not cease to respond to His inspirations, and His unction, which "teacheth all things," (1 John 2:27) teaches the soul which renounces itself that it may follow His divine inspirations more than it ever learns from all the precepts and all the lessons of the spiritual life. Hence it comes that we often see simple and upright souls, deprived of all human succor, but attentive and docile to the voice of grace, making astonishing progress in holiness, and raising themselves to the most sublime virtues. Oh if we would but let the Holy Spirit act within us, if we would but let Him model and fashion us, without hindering His divine operations by our dissipations and our cowardice, how He would change and transform us! Let us recognize this truth and correct ourselves. *Resolutions and spiritual nosegay as above.*

THE GOSPEL ACCORDING TO ST. MATT. 28:18-20

"And Jesus coming, spoke to them, saying: All power is given to Me in heaven and on earth. Going, therefore, teach ye all nations, baptizing them in the name of the Father, and of the Son, and of the Holy Ghost; teaching them to observe all things whatsoever I have commanded you. And, behold, I am with you all days, even to the consummation of the world."

SUMMARY OF TOMORROW'S MEDITATION

We will meditate tomorrow upon the mystery of the Most Holy Trinity, and we will consider it as the beauty of faith, because in believing it we render the most magnificent homage: First, to the veracity of God; second, to His greatness. We will then make the resolution: First, to reanimate our faith and our respect towards the Most Holy Trinity, and to honor it by frequent aspirations; second, to perform all our prayers with profound piety, thereby imitating the angels, prostrate in adoration in presence of the Most Holy Trinity. Our spiritual nosegay shall be the words, "Glory be to the Father, and to the Son, and to the Holy Ghost."

MEDITATION FOR THE MORNING

Let us prostrate ourselves in spirit before the throne of the adorable Trinity. Let us adore the Sovereign Majesty in the unity of its nature and the trinity of its persons; let us adore it, not only with all the powers of our mind, but with the united homage of all the blessed spirits over whelmed with the most profound reverence in presence of its grandeur, and let us ask of it permission to unite our adoration with their fervent homage.

FIRST POINT

✝ ***In Believing the Mystery of the Trinity we Render the most Magnificent Homage to the Veracity of Go.***

When I believe upon his word a traveler who tells me facts that are entirely natural respecting a distant country, I honor his veracity in a moderate manner; but if, upon the authority of his word, I accept as indubitable facts so extraordinary that at first sight they seem hardly credible, then I really honor his veracity, and I show that I believe him to be incapable either of deceiving me or of deceiving himself. In the same way, when God, in the Holy Scriptures, shows Himself to me in the highest heaven, governing from thence, as if He were at play, the innumerable worlds amongst which the whole of our globe counts less than a drop of water in the bosom of the sea; raising up or casting down empires at His pleasure; directing the sun and the heavens in their course, I only give Him moderate honor by my having faith in these marvels; because in this, my reason and His word allying themselves sweetly together as rays of one and the same sun, no sacrifice is involved. But when He teaches me the mystery of the Trinity, three distinct persons in one sole nature, indivisible essence in several persons, three persons, each one of which is eternal, almighty, immense, infinite, and yet one sole eternal, one sole almighty, one sole immense, one sole infinite, in a word, three Persons who are but one sole God, then I give to the divine word, in accepting what it tells me, the highest homage which can be rendered to it. For here my reason, not being able to go any farther, not being capable of raising its conceptions any higher, falls down and is overwhelmed by the feeling of its powerlessness to understand what is revealed to it; and delighted to honor God by its own annihilation, prostrates itself with reverence and love before the divine veracity, and exclaims with holy transports God, Thou hast said it; that suffices me, it is thus, I believe it on Thy word. My weak eyes cannot penetrate the inaccessible light where Thou dwell; but what need is there that I should see? Too happy to be enlightened by Thee in regard to what Thou art, I believe Thy word without discussing it. If I were to understand Thee, my faith would do Thee less honor, and would be less meritorious for me, and on that account it would give me less pleasure. Therefore, precisely because I understand nothing in respect to it, I take pleasure in confessing the Trinity, a Father eternally fruitful, Father as soon as He was; a Son engendered by the knowledge which God has of Himself; a Holy Spirit produced by the substantial love which unites the Father and the Son; a Father who is not more than His Son, a Son of the same age as His Father, who receives everything from Him and does not depend upon Him, a Holy Spirit as ancient as the one and the other, although deriving His origin from the one and the other; as rich as the one and the other, although receiving everything from the one and the other; produced like the Son, but having no birth, like Him; similar to the Father in all things, but not His image. O height, O depth, O abyss of light!

SECOND POINT

✝ *In Believing the Mystery of the Trinity we Render the most Magnificent Homage to the Greatness of God*

The more in fact, that revelation teaches me in respect to God high things which are beyond my understanding, the more it raises the conception of Him in my mind. If it told me only things that were perfectly comprehensible, should say: it deceives me, it dwarfs God in my mind, for the Infinite Being cannot be enclosed in the narrow limits of a created intelligence, an intelligence, consequently, which is essentially limited. But when it shows me the mystery of the Holy Trinity, then I cannot prevent myself from exclaiming: O God! this indeed is worthy of Thee, precisely because my intelligence cannot attain to such elevation. Yes, Being of beings, God incomprehensible, the less I conceive Thee, the more I adore Thee! I will not attempt to understand Thee, O Thou whose nature is so rich in marvels; it would be the idea of a child desiring to hold the sea in the hollow of its hand. My reason, on the contrary, delightedly triumphs at not being in any wise able to understand Thy sublime nature, and is enraptured to annihilate itself before Thee; it is the proof of Thy greatness. If I were to understand Thee, then Thou wouldst not be the Infinite, Thou wouldst not be God. O Supreme Lord, I rejoice to see Thee so great that Thou surpasses all understanding, so great that all eternity will not be sufficient to understand Thee. All other mysteries will disappear on entering heaven, like shadows before the light of the sun; but the mystery of Thy Trinity will remain, O my God, for it is the eternal mystery; we shall clearly see it, but we shall not understand it; it will remain, to be the eternal adoration of the blessed, and in order to recall to them continually that Thy greatness is incomprehensible to all save Thyself (Job 32:19). Let us then adhere with a joyful faith to the great mystery of the Trinity; let us delight to profess it by frequent acts of faith, and often to say, I believe in one sole God in three Persons, and in three Persons in one sole God. *Resolutions and spiritual nosegay as above.*

Monday after Trinity Sunday

SUMMARY OF TOMORROW'S MEDITATION

e will consider tomorrow the mystery of the Most Holy Trinity: First, as the delight of hope; second, as the delight of love. We will then make the resolution: First, often, during the day, to repeat this aspiration, "To God alone in three Persons be confidence and love," and to accompany all our prayers with this double sentiment which the Father, the Son, and the Holy Spirit so well deserve; second, to serve God, and to perform all our actions, not in the spirit of fear, which is the portion of slaves, but in the spirit of confidence and love, which is proper for children. Our spiritual nosegay shall be the words of the Apostle: "God hath not given us the spirit of fear but of love".(2 Tim. 1:7)

MEDITATION FOR THE MORNING

Let us raise our thoughts to a height above the splendor of the saints, to an infinite distance above the most lofty intelligences, the purest cherubim. Let us contemplate, adore, and bless the mystery of the divine essence, of the very nature of God, in the deepest secret of His substance, and let us beg of Him to enable us to see in this mystery the delight of our hope and also the delight of our love.

FIRST POINT

✝ *The Mystery of the Holy Trinity the Delight of our Hope*

If we only consider ourselves as we really are, with our powerlessness to do anything that is good, our tendency to evil, and the sins that we have committed, we find therein matter for discouragement; but if we cast our eyes upon the Blessed Trinity, instantly our hope revives and is thrilled with happiness. We see in the first of the divine Persons a Father who loves us to the extent of calling us and really making us His children; (1 John 3:1) in the second, a Mediator who offers His blood in payment of our debts, a Pontiff who prays for us, an Advocate who pleads our cause; and in the third, a Friend, occupied night and day with our sanctification, an Aid in our weakness, a Light in our darkness, a Consoler in our trouble, the Inspirer of all good thoughts, of all pious affections or resolutions, the Author of the graces which touch and convert, which make saints. O sweet names of Father, and Son, and Holy Ghost, what repose do you give to the heart! How you make it swim in hope! How the soul which appreciates you enjoys you and tastes you with delight! It is by these sweet names that baptism regenerates us, that confirmation makes us perfect Christians, that penitence remits our sins, that marriage unites the faithful, and that ordination consecrates priests. It is by these sweet names that the Church blesses her children, that she begins and ends her prayers, that she terminates her psalms and her hymns. It is these sweet names which she teaches first to children when they leave the cradle, and which she repeats to God in favor of the dying on the borders of the tomb (Prayers for the dying). In the mystery of the Trinity the Church thus sees the support, the strength, and the charm of Christian hope! Following the example set us by the Church, let us lovingly confide in the Father, the Son, and the Holy Ghost.

SECOND POINT

✝ *The Mystery of the Most Holy Trinity the Delight of Love*

Nothing is more calculated to dilate the soul with love than the thought of the Father, of the Son, and of the Holy Ghost. Never does God appear to be more beautiful, more God, if I may so speak, than when, penetrating the secret of the Trinity, I contemplate the ineffable operations, the divine greatness, fully known by the Father, praised as it deserves to be by the Word, and worthily loved by the Holy Ghost. Never does charity urge my heart in so lively a manner to exclaim; Yes, verily, God is all love. The Father is love; for, not content to be the Father of the Eternal Word, He wills to be our Father also; Father by creation, since He gave us our being and our life (Deut. 32:6); Father by providence, since He takes such care of His children whom He has placed in the world (Wis. 14:3); Father by predestination, since from all eternity He has conceived us as His adopted children in the same bosom wherein He engendered His Word (Ephes. 1:5); Father by the preaching of His Gospel (James 1:18); Father by the regeneration of baptism (John 3:5); Father by the sanctifying grace which puts into our hearts the spirit of His Son, enabling us to cry out to Him with confidence: "Abba, Father" (Gal. 4); Father, lastly, by a love which no earthly father ever reached an inconceivable love, which goes so far as even to immolate His first-born to save us from death. O God, Thou art then my Father, and I am Thy child ! At such a thought as this, where is the heart which would not melt with love? Who is there that would not have the heart of a child towards so good a Father? And Thou, also, O Eternal Son of God, Thou art all love! For me Thou didst make Thyself man; for me Thou didst sacrifice Thy life, and Thou dost not blush in the presence of Thy Father and of Thy Holy Ghost to call Thyself my brother (Heb. 2:11); to make me sit upon Thy throne (John 17:24; Apoc. 3:21); and, not being able to make of me a God by nature, Thou hast willed that I should be so by grace, by union and consummation in Thee (John 17:21). And Thou, Holy Ghost, Thou art also all love, since Thou art the very love of the Father and of the Son, equal to Thy origin; and it is through Thee that the Son has given Himself to me; it is through Thee that charity is shed in our hearts (Rom. 5:5); it is through Thee that good prayers are uttered (Rom. 8:26). Thou dost live in us as in Thy temple, to correct our faults, to form us to virtue, and of sinners, that we are, to make saints (1 Cor. 3:16). What then, is more amiable than the three Persons of the Most Holy Trinity? And why have we not three hearts to love each one of them? But let us be consoled; in loving one sole God we love all three Persons, since They have but one sole nature. O love, inflame my heart! May I love only for the Father, the Son, and the Holy Ghost! *Resolutions and spiritual nosegay as above.*

SUMMARY OF TOMORROW'S MEDITATION

We will meditate tomorrow upon the worship due to the Most Holy Trinity, and we will consider two acts of worship. The first is a frequent thought, full of reverence and of love, directed towards the three divine Persons; the second is the practice of fervent prayers in their honor. We will then make the resolution: First, often, with reverence and love, to recall to our selves the remembrance of the three divine Persons, and never to permit ourselves in their presence to think of or do anything which is not holy. Second, to offer, as our homage to these three adorable Persons, all our actions and all our troubles, willing only to live, to act, and to suffer for them. Our spiritual nosegay shall be the aspiration of St. Francis Xavier, which we will frequently repeat to ourselves day and night: "O Most Holy Trinity!"

MEDITATION FOR THE MORNING

Let us raise ourselves above all earthly thoughts; let us penetrate, with pious trembling, into the very depths of God; into that unity of nature and that trinity of persons which the angels never weary of adoring and of blessing in their sacred canticle: "Holy, holy, holy, Lord God of Hosts!" Let us repeat the canticle of heaven with the reverence of the seraphim, who veil their faces with their wings, because they dare not fix their eyes on so lofty a majesty; and, as nothing created can approach to what the adorable Trinity merits, let us offer to it the beatitude which it enjoys in itself, in beholding its greatness to be perfectly known by the Father, praised not less perfectly by the Son, and worthily loved by the Holy Ghost.

FIRST POINT

✝ *We owe it to the three Divine Persons to Think of them Frequently with Reverence and Love*

Let us suppose that there is a man whom several great personages, moved by a wholly gratuitous and completely disinterested affection, would do the distinguished honor of accompanying everywhere and always. If this man were wanting in deference to such honorable companions; if he did not show them either respect or love; if he did not even pay any attention to them, or thought of them carelessly and with indifference, would he not be guilty of a strange want of reverence? Now, the Christian is much more reprehensible who does not frequently recall to remembrance, with reverence and love, the three divine Persons. He knows that these three adorable Persons are with him night and day, abroad and at home; that always and everywhere they keep him company; how guilty, then, would he be if he took no account of their august presence, if he hardly ever spoke to them or gave them any evidence of his reverence and love for them? If he had but a little faith, it would be the delight of his heart to look upon himself as being in the society of the good Father who created him, who preserves him and folds him to His bosom with more than maternal love (Acts 17:28); in the society of the beloved Son who redeemed him at the cost of so much suffering, who never ceases to pray for him in heaven and in the tabernacles, in union with the Holy Spirit, who has such good will towards him, and who occupies Himself ceaselessly with his salvation. Such society as this formed the happiness of the anchorites and the hermits. Living apart from the world, they never felt themselves less alone than when they were alone; and far from this seeming isolation giving them either ennui or sadness, they found a paradise in the most savage desert, and heaven in the meanest cell, because, always remembering that they were in the society of the Father, the Son, and the Holy Ghost, they knew how to speak to them, to hearken to them, to enjoy them, and to love them. It was the same with St. Francis Xavier ; in the midst of his immense labors, the remembrance of the Trinity was his strength, his hope, and his consolation; it was everything to his heart; and the cry of love: Most Holy Trinity! was so often upon his lips, that even the heathen acquired the habit of pronouncing it, because, they said, they were words uttered by the man of God. Oh, if, like these saints, we never forget that a Christian is never alone, that he has always with him four persons, the three Persons of the Most Holy Trinity and the person of his angel guardian, how greatly would the recollection console us in our abandonments and our troubles, how it would strengthen us in our weaknesses, revive us in our languors, and render us victorious in temptations! The respect which is inseparable from it would maintain us in modesty, moderation, the horror of evil, and attention to the good performance of all things; it would enable us to suffer all things patiently, to do everything prudently. Let us ask pardon of the three holy Persons for having so greatly for gotten them, and so often thought of them without reverence and love.

SECOND POINT

✝ *We Owe to the three Divine Persons the Homage of Frequent and Fervent Prayer*

The founder of St. Sulpice, M. Olier, under stood this duty so well, that he ordered his priests to begin their morning and evening prayers with these words: "Blessed be now and forever throughout all ages the holy and indivisible Trinity" as well as every day to adore, to thank, and to invoke the three divine Persons; to offer their deeds to the Father, their thoughts and their words to the Son, the affections of their heart to the Holy Ghost; to renounce all confidence in themselves, in order to trust in the strength of the Father; their own intelligence, in order to unite it to the wisdom of the Son; their inclinations, in order to enter into the desires after holiness with which the Divine Spirit inspires docile hearts; lastly, to give themselves to the Father, that He might be the perfection of their souls; to the Son, that He might be their light; to the Holy Spirit, that He might direct all their movements. In the same way, Holy Church begins, continues, and terminates the divine sacrifice by an invocation to the august Trinity, to which alone she makes profession to offer it. "Receive this offering, Holy Trinity; accept, O Holy Trinity, the homage of my dependence". She has nothing more frequently on her lips than those beautiful words: "Glory be to the Father, to the Son, and to the Holy Ghost, as it was in the beginning, is now, and ever shall be, world without end". She repeats them in a thousand different ways, at the end of all her hymns, of all her psalms, of all her canticles; and she grants an indulgence of a hundred days for each time that they are uttered piously, with a plenary indulgence for each month that they have been recited three times a day. It is saying sufficiently to all Christian hearts how great is her desire that they should often address to the Most Holy Trinity this exclamation of love and of praise, this sigh of a zeal which burns to see the Father, the Son, and the Holy Ghost known, blessed, glorified, and served by the whole earth; this canticle of heaven and of eternity which St. John heard in his sub lime ecstasy: "To Him that sitteth upon the Throne, and to the Lamb, benediction, honor, glory, and power forever and ever". (Apoc. 5:13) Oh, what indocile disciples has the Church found in us! Let us sigh over the past and resolve to do better for the future. *Resolutions and spiritual nosegay as above.*

Wednesday after Trinity Sunday

SUMMARY OF TOMORROW'S MEDITATION

We will continue tomorrow our meditations upon the worship due to the Most Holy Trinity, and we will reflect upon two acts of this worship: the first is the sign of the cross; the second is the practice of Christian charity, modeled upon the union of the three divine Persons between themselves. We will then make the resolution: First, henceforth to make the sign of the cross with great reverence, to see in this sign our profession of faith in the mystery of the Trinity, of the Incarnation, and of the Redemption; and through the consideration to love to make it in the morning at our awakening, and in the evening when we lie down, and during the day at our meals and before our principal actions; second, to renew in our selves charity toward our neighbor, by applying ourselves to make all those with whom we are connected happy, and by suffering all things from others and never making any one suffer our selves. Our spiritual nosegay shall be the words of Our Lord: "O Father, that they may be one, as we also are one!" (John 17:22)

MEDITATION FOR THE MORNING

Let us transport ourselves in spirit to the highest heavens. Let us there adore the Most Holy Trinity, let us prostrate ourselves before the darkness which environs it (Ps. 17:12), as well as before the inaccessible light in the depths of which it dwells (1 Tim. 6:16). Let us humbly confess that its knowledge marvelously surpasses the range of our understanding, and that with all our efforts we could not reach it (Ps. 138:6). Let us unite ourselves with the inexhaustible admiration of the blessed throughout eternity; and whilst waiting to share in it, let us meditate on two means of honoring the Most Holy Trinity.

FIRST POINT

✝ *The Sign of the Cross a Means of Honoring the Most Holy Trinity*

The sign of the cross rightly understood, is a magnificent compendium of the whole of Christianity. The words which accompany it proclaim one sole God in three Persons; and the sign itself traced by the hand recalls to mind the sacrifice of Calvary, which was the most sublime homage which could be received by the supreme God. Thus the Most Holy Trinity has always had so much pleasure in this sign, that it has made it the instrument of the greatest miracles. By virtue of this sign, the primitive Christians made the devils keep silence, tremble, or take flight; it delivered the possessed, threw down idols, worked divers marvels; and the Church has always taught that, made with faith and piety, it is a sign which effaces venial sin, makes temptation depart from us, and merits grace for us. In harmony with this doctrine, she never utters a prayer, she never bestows a benediction, without mingling this sign with her holy ceremonies. If, at the present day, the sacred sign is often sterile and inefficacious in our hands, on what must the fault be laid, if it be not that we make it with heart breaking routine, without reverence, without faith; and that we pronounce the adorable names of the three Persons without thinking of them; the mind and the heart have nothing to do with it, the lips and the hands alone are concerned in this pious action. Is it not evident that the Most Holy Trinity cannot either feel itself to be honored by a wholly material worship or recompense those who perform it? As it is spirit and truth it requires a worship of spirit and truth. Let us here examine ourselves; let us be humiliated by so many signs of the cross made through routine, without reverence or attention, and let us understand the necessity of performing in a holy manner a thing so holy.

SECOND POINT

✝ *The Union of the three Divine Persons the Model of Christian Charity*

Children of the Trinity, it becomes us to be its imitators. There is no surer means of pleasing it than to resemble it, by uniting all our hearts together by charity, even as the three divine Persons are united together by nature. Holy Father, grant that they may be all one by charity, as we are one by nature, that their hearts may be but as one heart, that they may be consummated in the unity of mutual love, and that the charity which unites Me to Thee may bind them all together in its sweet bonds (John 17:21,22), that is to say, that as the three divine Persons understand each other perfectly, always love one another tenderly, and are but one sole God, although there are three Persons, so we also ought to cause to disappear from our mutual relations all misunderstanding, all coldness, all division, all sensitiveness, and be united together as one heart and one soul. Such was the marvelous spectacle given to the astonished world by the primitive Christians, which forced the heathen to exclaim: "See how they love one another." Such was the all-powerful charm by which Christianity in its cradle gained all hearts. Oh, how beautiful would be the earth, if now, as then, this doctrine were understood and practiced! Let us examine our conscience upon this important point of Christian morality. *Resolutions and spiritual nosegay as above.*

SUMMARY OF TOMORROW'S MEDITATION

s one sole day is not sufficient for the study of the great mystery of the Eucharist, which is honored on Holy Thursday, the Church consecrates to it another feast with an octave, in which she displays, in honor of this ineffable mystery, all the pomp associated with her ceremonies. In order to enter into her spirit, we will meditate tomorrow first; on the excellence of the gift made to us by Jesus Christ in giving us the Eucharist; second, the perpetuity of this gift. We will then make the resolution: First, to revive in our souls, during the present feast and octave, love towards the Holy Eucharist; second, to perform our communions better and also our visits to the Blessed Sacrament. Our spiritual nosegay shall be the words of St. John: "Jesus having loved His own who were in the world, He loved them unto the end." (John 13:1)

MEDITATION FOR THE MORNING

Let us adore the immense love of Jesus Christ in giving us the Eucharist. He loved us from the beginning of time, in the long premeditations of eternity. He loved us when creating us, when preserving us, when becoming incarnate, at His birth in the crib and at His death on the cross, but He loved us incomparably more when instituting the Eucharist; it is therein, says St. John, that His love reached its extremist limits. (1 John 13:1) Let us adore, let us praise, let us bless, let us love so much love, and let us beg Him to enable us to understand it.

FIRST POINT

✝ *The Excellence of the Gift which Jesus Christ Makes us in Giving us the Eucharist*

The excellence of the gift is shown in the very words of the Savior Himself, "Take and eat," Jesus Christ said, "this is My body;"and what I have just done by words, "do ye" also, my apostles, you and your successors forever (Luke 22:19). Could there be a more excellent gift? Let us meditate upon all the words of this donation: "This is My body," the Savior said; that is to say, the same body which was born in the crib and which died upon the cross; the same which ascended to heaven, and is seated at the right hand of God the Father, where it is the joy of the angels, the glory of Paradise, and the bliss of all the blessed ; and there is here not only the glorious body of Jesus Christ, there is also His blood, His soul, His divinity, which are inseparable from it ; so that, when I communicate, paradise is within me, and the whole of heaven is within my heart. "This is My body" I believe it, Lord, because Thou hast said so, Thou who art the Holy and the True; I believe it as I believe in the existence of God, and I pity the heretic, who, measuring by his own littleness of heart the immense charity of God, is determined to see only the figure of the body there where Thou hast said that it was of a truth Thy body. "Take and eat"; What a new kind of food! To be nourished with a God, to incorporate a God, to become the living tabernacle! "Do what I have just done;" that is to say, take bread, say like Me, This is My body" and at that very moment it will be My body, even as I said at the creation, Let light be, and light was. It will be My body, in the hands of every priest without exception, because the power I confide to you is imperishable; the course of ages cannot exhaust its fecundity. It will be My body in all places: called upon by you into the most humble dwelling, I will descend therein as I will into the most superb basilica; and the very moment which will have seen you pronounce the sacred words will see me in your hands. It will not matter how many millions of priests call upon Me at one and the same moment on all the different points of the globe; I will multiply the miracle by millions, multiplying My presence everywhere, whole and entire upon every altar, whole and entire in every host, whole and entire in every visible particle of each host. O Jesus, how great is Thy love, how ineffable the excellence of Thy gift! And what an evil heart should I have if I did not love Thee with my whole soul.

SECOND POINT

✝ *The Perpetuity of the Gift which Jesus Christ Makes us in Giving us the Eucharist*

All other gifts, even all the other sacraments, are but temporary; the Eucharist alone has the privilege of perpetuity. It is a gift of every moment of the day and of the night; at the moment and in the degree in which the sacrifice ceases on one portion of the globe it begins again in another; whilst our hemisphere is asleep, the other hemisphere is awake, and the priests who are there hold in their hands the Victim of the sins of the world; and when the sun, declining towards the horizon, returns to us, Jesus Christ comes back with it, to immolate Himself upon our altars, so that our heavenly Father always sees the Divine Mediator, suspended, as it were, between heaven and earth to avert the blows of His justice and to call down upon us the effusions of His mercy. More admirable still is the permanence of the Eucharist as a sacrament. The sacrifice having been consummated, Jesus Christ remains with us day and night, always ready to receive us and to bestow on us His graces, always in adoration before His Father, always at prayer for us, always offering Himself in sacrifice for our salvation and for that of the whole world (Offertory of the Mass). Even when we forget Him, He thinks of us; even when we offend Him, He immolates Himself for us; when we have trials, He is in His tabernacle ready to console us; when we are weak, He is there to strengthen us; when our courage gives way and we are cast down, He is there to raise us up again; He cries to us without ceasing: "Come to Me, all you that labor and are burdened, and I will refresh you." (Matt. 11:28) O ineffable love! How just and right it is that I should live only by love for Thee! *Resolutions and spiritual nosegay as above.*

Friday after Corpus Christi

SUMMARY OF TOMORROW'S MEDITATION

We will tomorrow consider the Eucharist, that gift so excellent in itself and in its perpetuity, as the masterpiece of the wisdom, the power, and the generosity of God, according to the beautiful words of St. Augustine: "God, all-wise though He be, knows nothing better; all-powerful though He be, He can do nothing more excellent; infinitely rich though He be, He has nothing more precious to give, than the Eucharist." Our resolution shall be: First, often to thank Our Lord, by means of loving aspirations, for this magnificent institution; second, to make to Him, during the day, a fervent visit of thanksgiving. The words of St. Augustine shall serve as our spiritual nosegay.

MEDITATION FOR THE MORNING

Let us transport ourselves in spirit before the holy tabernacle; let us there adore Jesus Christ in union with the angels of the sanctuary, who form an invisible guard around Him day and night. Let us recollect ourselves, let us adore and let us bless, like them, the God of heaven, present in our midst.

FIRST POINT

✝ *The Eucharist is the Masterpiece of Divine Wisdom*

Supreme wisdom consists in proposing to itself the best ends and in attaining them by the best means. Now this is what we indeed find in the Eucharist. First, Jesus Christ desired to return to His Father, but without leaving us; these two designs seem to be incompatible with each other, but divine wisdom has accomplished them marvelously in the Eucharist. Second, it was the design of God the Father that the Church should live in the belief of His Son remaining among men, but here also there seemed to be an incompatibility: how to reconcile the presence of the object with the merit of faith! It is very true that before the death of the Savior it was possible to see Him and believe in Him, because His flesh, which was passible and subject to suffering, served as a veil for the divinity in which His disciples believed; but after His resurrection the splendor of His glorified flesh would have annihilated the merit of faith. What, then, did eternal wisdom do? It hid its glory beneath the Eucharistic veils, and by hiding it a double merit was provided for our faith: the merit of believing what we do not see, and the merit of not believing what we do see, since there are no bread and no wine in what solely appears to be such to us; whence results a continual exercise of our faith, as honorable to Jesus Christ as it is meritorious for us. Third, if the Savior had remained in the splendor of His glory, our eyes would not have been able to bear it, and we should not have dared to approach Him. What, then, did His wisdom accomplish? Through a merciful condescension it tempered the splendor by covering it with the Eucharistic veils. Fourth, He desired to teach us by His example the simplicity and modesty of the garments which cover our body; could He do so better than by veiling His own as He has done? Fifth, it was His plan to teach us, by means of the Eucharist, humility, a hidden life, universal detachment, the charity which practices devotedness; and in order to do so He lessens Himself within the limits of a particle. Sixth, He desired to attract us to receive Him frequently in communion; and in order to do so He quits His first form of flesh and blood, because we have a natural repugnance to eat human flesh and to drink human blood; He therefore substitutes for it the appearance of bread and wine, for which everyone has a liking, and He encloses Himself therein, whole and entire, even down to the most humble host, hiding so many great and divine things under mean appearances, in order to incorporate Himself wholly in us and to give Himself even to the sick; who could not receive Him under a larger form. Could there be more excellent ends and better means? Doubtless He might have veiled Himself beneath other appearances, but He preferred the appearance of bread, to make us understand that He is the "Bread of God come down from heaven, which gives life to the world", (John 6:33) that He divinely nourishes and satisfies all those who eat Him as they ought; that all Christians ought to form but one body and, as it were, but one bread, by the union of charity. To the species of bread he adds the species of wine, to make us understand, on the one hand, that the Eucharist is a complete repast, where, to the wheat of the elect, which is His body, is joined the wine which makes virgins; on the other side, that Mass is the sacrifice of Calvary continued, where the separation of His blood from His body is represented by the species of the wine separated from that of the bread; lastly, that the Eucharist produces in souls which receive it worthily a wholly divine ardor and strength, joy and transport O infinite wisdom! I recognize Thee and I adore Thee beneath the veils which cover Thee, and I joyfully repeat the words of Thy servant St. Augustine, "All wise as Thou art, Thou knowest of nothing more excellent to give us."

SECOND POINT

✝ *The Eucharist is the Masterpiece of Divine Power*

Here, indeed, Jesus Christ accumulates miracles which are infinite; the miracle of the change of the bread into the substance of His sacred body, and of the change of the wine into His precious blood; the miracle of His presence in His body and in His soul upon our altars, without His ceasing to be present in heaven; the miracle of the multiplication of His presence in as many places as there are hosts consecrated upon earth; the miracle of His presence whole and entire in each host, whole and entire in even each particle of each host, after the manner of spirits, who occupy no space; the miracle of the appearances of bread and wine preserved without any substance which sustains them, of whiteness without anybody which is white, of taste without anybody which has taste; the miracle of the production of all these wonderful effects by means of four or five words which the priest pronounces at the altar. O miracle of incomprehensible power, to which nothing is comparable excepting the ingratitude of men who respond so ill to such goodness, and the patience of God which suffers it! Of a truth, O my God! We have indeed good cause to repeat once more the words of St. Augustine, "All-powerful though Thou art, Thou couldst have done nothing more," and I understand why, before recounting the story of the Last Supper, in which Thou didst institute the Eucharist, St. John recalls to mind that God the Father has given all power into Thy hands (John 13:3).

THIRD POINT

✝ *The Eucharist is the Masterpiece of Divine Generosity*

Generosity is known by the sacrifices made for the person beloved, above all when we owe him nothing and expect nothing. Now, what has Jesus Christ done for us in the Eucharist? He gives us not only His graces, He gives Himself, to remain always with us, to unite us to Him and to transform us into Him, and at what a price? By reversing all natural laws by the most astonishing miracles, by abasing Himself, and lessening Himself through love for us; by devoting Himself to suffer irreverence, outrages, profanations, and sacrileges, to which He has been subjected since the day of the Last Supper. And what did He owe us that He gave Himself thus entirely to us? What did He expect from us? Less than nothing. He knew that most often He should receive from men nothing but indifference, coldness, abandonment, sometimes even the most dreadful outrages. O divine generosity, Thou hast accomplished Thy masterpiece! Infinitely rich though Thou art, Thou hadst among Thy treasures nothing more marvelous; and yet I love Thee so little, I honor Thee so ill, I am so cold, so tepid towards Thee. Ah, truly I am a shame to myself, and I cry to Thee: Mercy, pardon! I will set to work with all my heart to love Thee. *Resolutions and spiritual nosegay as above.*

Saturday in the Octave of Corpus Christi

SUMMARY OF TOMORROW'S MEDITATION

After having studied the Eucharist as a master piece of divine wisdom, power, and generosity, we will consider it tomorrow as a marvel in regard to a perfect life, and especially as the model of our duties towards God. We shall understand this by considering: First, the occupations of Jesus Christ in the Eucharist; second, the part which we ought to take in this divine life. Our resolutions shall be: First, to unite our homages to those which our divine Savior renders to God His Father in this great sacrament, and to endeavor to make them pass into our own hearts; second, often to utter acts of adoration, admiration, love, gratitude, supplication, and offerings of ourselves to God. Our spiritual nosegay shall be the words St. Paul spoke of Jesus Christ: "By Him, therefore, let us offer the sacrifice of praise always to God." (Heb. 13:15)

MEDITATION FOR THE MORNING

Let us adore Jesus Christ in the Most Holy Sacrament as the object of the complaisance of the heavenly Father. As once on the banks of the Jordan, so now He says: "This is My beloved Son in whom I am well pleased." (Matt. 3:17). Let us unite ourselves with the complaisance of the Father in His Son, and let us glorify the Divine Savior for it.

FIRST POINT

✝ ***The Occupations of Jesus Christ in the Eucharist***

Jesus, in His tabernacle, is neither dead nor idle; He is full of life and in continual action. He occupies Himself therein with the contemplation of God His Father; with taking delight in His infinite perfections, in praising, exalting, adoring, loving them, and confessing that in the presence of so much majesty no created being is worthy to subsist; and keeping this in view, He takes pleasure in lessening Himself within the limits of a particle, in order to glorify God by this profound abasement. He also occupies Himself at the same time with our dearest interests; He thanks God for us, He prays continually to Him for us, He asks pardon of Him for our faults, makes to Him for them reparation and honorable amends, and offers Himself in our place as a host of expiation. And who could fitly express the extent of this homage? He renders it at all times and in all places: at all times, because He never interrupts it during a single moment of the day or of the night; in all places, because for that He multiplies His presence on all the altars throughout the world, so that, O wonderful spectacle in the sight of heaven! At every moment there arrives from all points of both hemispheres, before the throne of God, the homage of this Divine Pontiff, and it goes straight to the heart of God, wounding it with love and ravishing His complaisance. Who could, above all, express the value of this homage? It is infinite, both because the hypostatic union with the divinity communicates to all the acts of Jesus an infinite merit, and because the Divine Savior, being incomparably more perfect and more enlightened in regard to the divine perfections than all the saints and angels, renders on that account more glory to God than the whole of heaven can render Him. It is there that God is more known, more praised, more honored, more loved than by all created beings, even if their homage were to be prolonged throughout eternity. Let us thereby judge of the excellence of the occupations of Jesus Christ in the Eucharist, let us rejoice at seeing God so magnificently honored, and let us unite ourselves to the homage which He renders to our sovereign Master and Lord.

SECOND POINT

✝ ***The Part we ought to Take in the Occupations of Jesus Christ in the Eucharist***

We ought: First, to offer them to God; second, to imitate them. First, we ought to offer them to God. Lord, we ought to say to Him, it is only in the interior of Jesus, Thy Divine Son, that Thou art known, honored, and glorified as Thou merits to be. My own occupations are mean, miserable, incapable

of honoring Thee worthily. I offer Thee, as a supplement to my indigence, the perfect homage which our Divine Head renders to Thee; I offer Thee His humble adoration, His praises so worthy of Thee, His abasement so profound, His thanksgivings so excellent, His prayers which are all powerful; I offer to Thee for myself, for the whole Church, for all creatures, and with my whole soul I praise the glory which His homage procures for Thee. Not knowing, of myself, how to speak to Thee worthily, I say to Thee all that my divine Jesus, the High-Priest of every creature, utters in the Blessed Sacrament. It is for me that He adores Thee, that He praises Thee, that He thanks Thee, that He asks of Thee mercy and grace; I say Amen to all the effusions of His heart; I offer them to Thee as mine, in virtue of my union with Him and the cession He has made me of His merits. Second, we ought to imitate the occupations of Jesus in the Blessed Sacrament. Every time that we pay a visit to the tabernacle, or that we pray or meditate in our oratory, let us represent to ourselves the occupations of Jesus in the Eucharist, and let us offer the same prayers, let us enter into the same sentiments, let us make the same acts of supreme esteem for God, of profound reverence, of perfect submission to Providence, of thanks, of expiation, of requests, of the abasement of our whole selves in presence of the Divine Majesty, of desire for His greater glory; of tender charity towards our neighbor, above all towards those from whom we suffer, or of whom we have cause to complain; of compassion for sinners, and of prayers for their conversion and ours; and let us endeavor, as much as we possibly can, to imitate the manner in which Jesus performs all these holy things. It is the most perfect manner of honoring God, as well as the surest means for obtaining graces. Do we employ these means? When we visit the Blessed Sacrament, do we offer by Him, in Him, and with Him our homage to the Most Holy Trinity? For want of giving up ourselves to these holy occupations, what time do we not lose in presence of the Blessed Sacrament, what fruitless visits do we not make to it!
Resolutions and spiritual nosegay as above

Second Sunday after Pentecost

SUMMARY OF TOMORROW'S MEDITATION

After having seen how the perfect life of Jesus Christ in the Eucharist teaches us our duty towards God, we shall see tomorrow how it teaches us our duty: First, towards our neighbor; second, towards ourselves. Our resolution shall be: First, to imitate, in our relations with our neighbor, the charity, the meekness, and the patience of Jesus in the Blessed Sacrament; second, to imitate as nearly as possible His spirit of mortification and humility. Our spiritual nosegay shall be the words of Our Savior: "I have given you an example, that as I have done to you, so do you also." (John 13:15)

MEDITATION FOR THE MORNING

Let us adore Jesus Christ, addressing to us in the Eucharist the same words which He addressed to His apostles during His mortal life: "I have given you example, that as I have done to you, so do you also." Oh, He is indeed the most finished model therein of a perfect life! Let us thank Him for the great example He has given us, and ask of Him, grace to imitate it.

FIRST POINT

✝ *The Eucharist Teaches us our Duty towards our Neighbor*

These duties may be reduced to three: to love, to bear with, to treat everyone with gentleness. Now, Jesus Christ in the Eucharist performs these three duties perfectly. First, what love He shows towards men! He is employed in a continual exercise of charity, day and night praying for us, day and night immolating Himself for us, and soliciting our salvation with ineffable ardor of zeal. Is it thus that we love our brethren? Do we love them with a practical love, which occupies itself with their happiness, which avoids all that might give them pain, which seeks, at the price of our own comfort, all that could give them pleasure? With a generous love, which devotes itself to others, and does not draw back in presence of any sacrifice whatever? Second, what patience Jesus exercises in the Blessed Sacrament! How He bears with coldness, with distractions, with negligence, with irreverence, even with profanations! It is thus that He teaches us to bear in others what displeases us their want of consideration and attention, their defects, their faults, their temper. Where there is no endurance, there is no charity. Second, what meekness Jesus shows in the Blessed Sacrament! During nineteen centuries He has borne with the abandonment of Christians who do not come to visit Him; with the blasphemies of the infidel who insults Him even in the sanctuary of His love; with the audacious sacrilege of thieves who have often taken Him out of the tabernacle, thrown Him into the dust, trodden Him under foot; and during all these nineteen hundred years He has never shown the slightest sign of displeasure. O calmness! O meekness! O benignity of my Savior! How Thou dost condemn our vivacity and our impatience, our hardness and our impetuosities, our temper, which cannot bear to suffer anything! Thou mightest launch thunders from out Thy tabernacle, and nothing comes from thence except grace, mercy, and meekness.

SECOND POINT

✝ ***The Eucharist Teaches us our Duties towards Ourselves***

We owe it to ourselves to mortify and humiliate ourselves: First, to mortify ourselves in our self-will, which, if it were to be given up to its caprices and its inconstancies, would prove to be our ruin; in our senses, which would otherwise be a door open to all temptations, a source of dissipation and of sensuality; lastly in our whole being, which, being thrown into disorder by original sin, tends always to avoid order; second, we owe it to ourselves to humble ourselves, by substituting for our self-love a sincere and profound humility, since it is written that pride is the root of all sin (Ecclus. 10:15). Now, what more beautiful model of mortification and of humility can we have than Jesus in the Blessed Sacrament? There self-will does not exist; we may do with Him what we will, we may shut Him in or we may expose Him, we may carry Him from one place to another; never does the hand which touches Him meet with the least resistance. Rather than make an act of self-will, He will allow Himself to fall into the dust, or will descend into a sacrilegious heart, side by side with the devil. In the Blessed Sacrament He makes no use of His senses; He has feet and does not walk, hands and He does not act, a tongue and He does not speak; it is a state of death in a living body. At the same time, what humility! He is really in the Blessed Sacrament the hidden God, (Is. 45:15) present, and nothing is seen of Him, glorious as is a risen body, magnificent as God Himself; and the Eucharistic veils cover everything! There is nothing which announces a man, still less a God; only the material appearance of bread is seen. What a lesson for self-love and vanity, which desire to attract notice, to obtain esteem, and which revolt against a hidden life, humiliation, and forgetfulness! *Resolutions and spiritual nosegay as above*

Monday in the Octave

SUMMARY OF TOMORROW'S MEDITATION

e will tomorrow consider the Eucharist: First, as the glory of the Christian; second, as his treasure. We will then make the resolution: First, to have more and more affection for the holy Eucharist, as being the dearest object of our love here below; second, to testify our love towards it by frequently visiting with great reverence, and by thinking frequently of it, even in the midst of our occupations. We will retain as our spiritual nosegay the words of the Apostle: "Let us go therefore with confidence to the throne of grace, that we may obtain mercy, and find grace in seasonable aid." (Heb. 4:16)

MEDITATION FOR THE MORNING

Let us adore the immense love of Jesus Christ in the institution of the Eucharist. Our divine Savior loved us during every moment of His existence, the first tear He shed after His birth was a tear of love, and His last sigh was a sigh of love. From Bethlehem to Calvary, every step was guided by love. Nonetheless, nowhere is His love better shown than in the institution of the Eucharist. Let us render to Him for it our homage of gratitude, of praise, and of love, and let us beg of Him to help us to meditate on this great mystery of His charity.

FIRST POINT

✝ *The Eucharist is the Glory of the Christian*

Moses, ravished with the honor which God had done His people in communicating Himself to them by frequent revelations, exclaimed: "Neither is there any other nation so great, that hath gods so nigh them, as our God is present to all our petitions." (Deut. 4:7) What then would he have said if he had seen what we see in the Eucharist? A God does us the honor to come and visit us and make Himself the companion of our pilgrimage! A God renews this descent and this visit every day, and in all the churches throughout the world! A God constitutes Himself to be captive and solitary in all the tabernacles, to remain day and night with us, and to make it easy for us at every moment to have access to His court and the honor of an audience! A God converts His churches into so many Paradises, because therein is the same God who is in heaven, surrounded by His angels, and that there we may associate ourselves with all the heavenly court, who form an invisible guard round about Him!

What glory for us! And yet this is only the least of the glories which we derive from the Eucharist; a much greater glory is that of nourishing ourselves with the flesh and blood of a God, and of incorporating Him and transforming ourselves in Him. O prodigy of greatness for a Christian! A Christian is more holy and more excellently consecrated than are churches and altars, than chalices and sacred vases. He is raised to a greatness which surpasses all human greatness, by as far as the heavens are above the earth. O Christian, who art so great! Respect thy dignity, and never lower thyself by vulgar actions and sentiments, still less by guilty actions and sentiments! O Temple of God! O living ciborium of the Eucharist! Do not profane thyself by what is impure or less perfect no matter what it may be!

SECOND POINT

✝ *The Eucharist is the Treasure of the Christian*

It is an infinite treasure of graces, from which we may always draw without ever diminishing it; where we shall always find wherewith to pay our debts towards divine justice, to provide for all our needs, for the needs of our relations and friends, for the needs of the whole universe; lastly, wherewith to enrich us for heaven and for eternity. O treasure which is above all treasures! According to the words of a council. Rich enough with such a possession, the Christian has nothing more to desire either in heaven or on earth (Ps. 72:25); he finds consolation there if he is afflicted, true glory if he desires it, knowledge if he is ignorant, strength if he is weak. It is a treasure which enables him to maintain, even with heaven, an ineffable and wholly divine intercourse; on the one side, he gives to the heavenly Father His adorable Son by the oblation of the holy sacrifice; on the other side, God gives him this same Son by communion, with all the graces which it may please him to ask, provided that they are in the order of Providence. It is a treasure which is not only exterior to ourselves, as are earthly treasures, but it is in us to the extent of being incorporated in us and becoming one with us. It is a treasure to be found everywhere where a priest exists with a little bread and a little wine; so that, for a Christian, there is neither exile nor privations; no exile, because, in his treasure, he finds paradise, which is the true country of the children of God; no privations, because the holy Eucharist stands in place of all things. It is a treasure which is imperishable, because, down to the end of time, there will be priests who will make this divine treasure descend from heaven; we shall enjoy it and be happy. Lastly, it is a treasure which is our life; the life of our body, in which it deposits the seed of immortality; the life of our mind, which it illumines and enlightens; the life of our heart, which it warms and in flames. Jesus Christ is our life (Coloss. 3:4), the Apostle says; it is no longer I who live, it is Jesus Christ who liveth in me (Gal. 2:20). Oh, what good reason had the Prophet to say: In Thee is the source of life (Ps. 35:10), the adorable source whence we may drink as much as we will and quench our thirst. It is, in a word, a treasure on which all our affections ought to be concentrated, since there where our treasure is our heart ought to be also; there where the body is, the eagles gather together. Is this the esteem in which we hold the holy Eucharist? *Resolutions and spiritual nosegay as above*

Tuesday in the Octave of Corpus Christi

SUMMARY OF TOMORROW'S MEDITATION

We will tomorrow consider the Eucharist: First, as the strength of the Christian; second, as his consolation and joy. We will then make the resolution: First, to have recourse to the Blessed Sacrament in our temptations, our troubles, and our discouragements; second, to cherish, as being the happiest and the best-employed instants of our life, the moments which we are able to spend in presence of the Blessed Sacrament. Our spiritual nosegay shall be the words of the Psalmist: "How lovely are Thy tabernacles, O Lord of hosts! My soul longeth and fainteth for the courts of the Lord." (Ps. 83:2)

MEDITATION FOR THE MORNING

Let us come back to the holy tabernacle; let us prostrate ourselves, filled with sentiments of reverence and love, before our God, who Himself burns with charity for us (Ps. 94:6). Praise, love, and benediction be to the Lamb who is immolated for us!

FIRST POINT

✝ *The Eucharist is the Strength of the Christian*

Experience proves this truth to us; it was the Eucharist which gave martyrs courage to brave torments and death; it is the Eucharist which gives the Christian virgin devotedness to enable her to succor all kinds of human woes in hospitals, on fields of battle, amidst pestilence and a thousand other perils; the soul which sees a God give Himself wholly to it feels that it is but just that it should give itself wholly to Him; it conceives not only a desire to do so, but also a firm resolution, a holy passion, which makes it find happiness in sacrifices, and renders it stronger than all obstacles. "He that eats this bread", says Jesus Christ "shall live forever." (John 6:59); he will derive from Me strength to gain eternal life (Ibid. 55). And whilst the Eucharist renders the Christian stronger by raising him above himself, sometimes as high as the most sublime virtues, it renders the enemy of our salvation weaker; for, as the councils and the Fathers of the Church say, it moderates the fire of the passions and calms the ardor of concupiscence. These are facts proved by experience: as long as we frequent the sacraments, we are sustained in the practice of good; as soon as we abandon them, we become relaxed and tepid, and we fall. The soul deprived of the nourishment which gives it strength and life falls away and dies.

SECOND POINT

✝ ***The Eucharist is the Consolation of the Christian***

How sad life would be without the Eucharist! Our churches would no longer have anything in them which would speak to the heart, nothing to which the heart could speak. The whole world would then be nothing but a place of exile, for it would not possess any memorial of our country, which is heaven. All the troubles of life would be left without a consoler, darkness would be devoid of light, doubters would seek in vain for counsel. But with the Eucharist, all is changed into joy and happiness. Our churches become a Paradise in which the soul can enjoy in advance the delights of heaven, and exclaim with the Psalmist: "Oh, how lovely are Thy tabernacles, Lord of hosts! My soul longs and faints for the courts of the Lord." (Ps. 83:2) It is there that we find a foretaste of our country. When we possess Thee, O my God, we have all things, and the contented heart has nothing more to desire (Ps. 72: 25). We read in the Old Testament that Anne, the mother of Samuel, found no consolation in anything except in going and letting her afflicted heart overflow before the ark of the Lord; how much more, then, when we are in trouble or in some pressing need, shall we find true consolation at the foot of our divine Ark, which is Jesus in the Blessed Sacrament! Never do we have recourse to Him there without bringing back with us solace for our heart. (Heb. 10:22) Men are only "troublesome comforters," Job said (Job 16:2). But Thou, O God of our tabernacles, Thou art the true Consoler; Thou dost raise up the heart which is cast down, Thou dost bring back serenity to the afflicted soul, and Thou makest repose and peace to follow troubles. Oh, how well did it become Thee to say: "Come to Me, all you that labor and are burdened, and I will refresh you!" (Matt. 11:28) The soul which recounts its sorrows to Thee in simplicity, as a friend speaks to a friend, or as a child to its father, always returns from Thee consoled; and those deprive themselves of the sweetest joys of their life who do not know how to come and pour out their afflictions before Thy tabernacles. *Resolutions and spiritual nosegay as above.*

Wednesday in the Octave of Corpus Christi

SUMMARY OF TOMORROW'S MEDITATION

After having considered what the Eucharist is in regard to us, we will meditate tomorrow on what we ought to be in regard to it. In the first rank of these obligations reverence must be placed. We shall then see: First, how profound ought to be our reverence for the Eucharist; second, what great blessings we shall obtain by means of this profound reverence. We will then make the resolution: First, always to maintain in church a profound reverence, a respectful demeanor, and restraint of the eyes; second, to observe strict silence, and not to speak to any one save God alone, except in case of necessity. Our spiritual nosegay shall be these words of Holy Writ: "How terrible is this place," (Gen. 28:17); "Reverence My sanctuary." (Lev. 26:2)

MEDITATION FOR THE MORNING

Let us adore in spirit Jesus Christ present in the tabernacles, let us abase ourselves with reverence in presence of His diminished greatness. Let us praise, let us bless the great God, who, through love for us, descends from so great a height to such profound humiliation. Whatever we may do, we shall never exalt Him sufficiently (Hymn Lauda Sion).

FIRST POINT

✝ *How Profound ought to be our Reverence for the Eucharist*

The more Jesus Christ abases His greatness in this sacrament, the more we ought to venerate Him, and the measure of His humiliations ought to be the measure of our homage. It is the rule which the heavenly Father has given to the world by His example: He beholds His divine Son humiliated in the cradle; at that moment He sends His angels to proclaim His glory to the neighboring inhabitants and to form a guard around the cradle of a Prince so great and so forsaken. He beholds Him on the banks of the Jordan mingling with sinners; immediately He opens heaven, and glorifies Him by means of the most splendid testimony. He sees Him upon Calvary, covered with opprobrium; immediately, in order to do Him honor, He raises the dead, makes the sun withdraw its light, rends the rocks, and shakes the earth. Now, if Our Lord ought to be honored in proportion to His abasement, shall we ever be able to conceive how great ought to be our reverence in presence of the holy Eucharist? For where did Jesus Christ ever abase Himself more profoundly? At least He had the form of an infant in the crib, and shepherds and kings came to adore Him; at least He preserved upon the cross some of the characteristics of a man, the masterpiece of the creation; but in the Eucharist, what do I see? Nothing which announces a man to me, still less anything which announces a God. O Eternal Wisdom, Thou didst hide Thyself beneath flesh, and behold, the flesh hides itself beneath the material appearance of bread! These weak species, which offer to my eyes nothing but the appearance of the commonest of aliments, veil the splendor of those same grandeurs of which a ray dazzled Moses upon Sinai and the disciples upon Tabor. The little particle fallen upon the sacred paten encloses the immense God, whom the vast extent of the heavens cannot contain, the King of heaven, the God of glory. O excess of humiliation which has seemed so great to the Eternal Father that, in compensation for it, He has not deemed it too much to have legions of angels around the tabernacles, who prostrate themselves there in continual adoration. I have seen them myself, says St. John Chrysostom, these adoring angels; they were there, like guards around their king, in an attitude of the most profound reverence, with their heads lowered, and their eyes cast down, like the four and twenty elders whom the beloved apostle saw before the throne of God (Apoc. 5:14). Let us hence conclude how great ought to be our reverence before the Eucharist, for where all heaven trembles and adores, it would ill become us to dare to indulge in a familiar attitude, to take our ease, to allow our spirit to be inattentive and our heart to be careless. And what are we then in presence of the Eternal Son of God, who has descended from the splendors of the saints? We are humble servants in the presence of the King of glory, said St. Thomas, drawing near to the tabernacles, overwhelmed with reverence. We are guilty sinners in presence of their Judge. Whence comes, St. Martin was asked, the trembling which has been remarked in you when you enter a church? How could I help trembling? Answered the miracle-worker of the Gauls; I am in the presence of my Judge! We are poor, miserable creatures in presence of the infinite majesty of their God, and what ought the creature to do when he is brought face to face with his Creator, if not to abase himself, to cast himself down in reverence, to confess that He is his Lord (1 Kings 3:15), that he himself is nothing but dust and ashes (Gen. 18:27), to repeat a thousand times the cry: Who art Thou, Lord, and who am I? Or rather to recall to himself the words of St. Teresa to her nuns: "My sisters, we ought to conduct ourselves in presence of the Holy Eucharist as all the blessed conduct themselves in heaven in presence of the Divine Essence." Do we think seriously of this when we are in the sacred edifice? Are we always overwhelmed with reverence and adoration?

SECOND POINT

✝ *What Great Blessings we Derive through Reverence towards the Eucharist*

The first blessing which we shall derive will be a notable increase in piety. Experience teaches us that when we have the courage to maintain, in presence of the tabernacle, a reverential attitude and a perfect recollection of the senses, we pray much better; on the one hand, because we cut off the cause of many distractions; and, on the other hand, grace, in recompense for the good will which we testify by so religious a deportment, infuses into the soul a superabundance of piety and fervor. If, on the contrary, there is but little reverence in the demeanor, exterior dissipation will induce interior dissipation. Never did behavior marked by too much freedom and want of restraint hide a reverential interior. The second blessing which reverence for the Eucharist produces is the edification of our neighbor. The good example given by a Christian who is perfectly recollected in presence of the tabernacle is a sermon to all who witness it; as on the other hand, an exterior which is wanting in recollection, a familiar manner characterized by no restraint, eyes which wander everywhere, a word said to a neighbor, tends to dissipate others, who dare not be more respectful than we are; it cools charity, lessens the religious sentiment, and often makes faith to totter. Have we not often inflicted blame on ourselves and on others by a demeanor wanting in reverence? *Resolutions and spiritual nosegay as above*

Thursday in the Octave

SUMMARY OF TOMORROW'S MEDITATION

e will meditate tomorrow on our second duty towards the Eucharist, which is to love it; and we will consider: First, how Jesus in the Eucharist merits all our love; second, how we ought to show our love to Him. We will then make the resolution: First, often, in the midst of our occupations, to offer aspirations of love towards Jesus in the Blessed Sacrament; second, to offer Him all our actions in a spirit of gratitude and of love. Our spiritual nosegay shall be the words of the Church: "Who would not love Him who has so loved us?"

MEDITATION FOR THE MORNING

Let us approach the holy tabernacle in spirit, animated by the feelings which Moses experienced when he approached the burning bush (Ex. 3:3); or with the desire of a man who, feeling cold, draws near to a great fire in order to warm himself. The holy Eucharist is a furnace of love; let us warm ourselves at its flame (4 Imit. 4:3).

FIRST POINT

✝ ***How Jesus Christ in the Blessed Sacrament Merits all our Love***

Jesus in the Blessed Sacrament merits the whole of our love by all kinds of titles. He merits it: First, as God, because the plenitude of the Divinity substantially inhabits this mystery, and is as worthy of being adored therein as it is in heaven itself where the angels and saints are consumed with an eternal love for it, which never grows cold or becomes relaxed. He merits the whole of our love, second, as God-Man, since, by means of this title, He unites to the ineffable amiability of God the Creator all the perfections and amiability which can belong to a creature. He merits all our love, third, on account of His Eucharistic being. O miracle of love! Not only does Jesus Christ abase Himself even more here than He did in the crib and on Calvary, since even His humanity disappears, but He multiplies Himself in thousands of places at one and the same time; He puts Himself within the reach of all and gives Himself to all who are willing to receive Him; He, moreover, shows Himself in certain respects more amiable than even in heaven. For in heaven He does not derogate in any degree from the dignity of His position: He is in His proper place, at the highest summit of glory; but in the tabernacle He descends to earth for love of us, and confines Himself within the smallest limits. In heaven He communicates Himself only to the saints, whose hearts are filled only with love for Him; here, He gives Himself even to sinners who do not love Him; He admits them to His audience, He gives them His flesh to eat, His blood to drink, all His sacred person to enjoy, if they desire to receive Him. In heaven He is surrounded by the praises of the whole heavenly court; here He is a butt to irreverence, coldness, profanations, and outrages. In heaven He is a King upon His throne; here He is a victim who immolates Himself for sinners, for His revolted subjects; a Mediator who supplicates, who asks for mercy, who interposes Himself between our crimes and divine justice. O God of the Eucharist! How amiable Thou art! How infinitely dost Thou merit our love! Oh, that we had millions of hearts to offer to Thee in gratitude! How ungrateful I am so often to have had so cold a heart towards Thee! Henceforth I will determine to love Thee, and to love Thee always more and more every succeeding day.

SECOND POINT

✝ ***How to Testify our Love to Jesus in the Most Holy Sacrament***

First, love desires to be recognized by love. We must, therefore, have a heart full of love for the holy Eucharist. And what could we love, my God, if we did not love Thee? Are we worthy to have a heart if we do not spend it wholly in loving Thee? If Thou wert to be found in but one place in the whole world, and if we could go but once to see Thee during our whole life, with what love should we not draw near to Thy sacred Person! But because we have Thee always near us, because at every hour of the day and night we can enjoy Thee, O shame! O ingratitude! We familiarize ourselves with Thee, we are no longer so touched by Thy love, and by dint of being loved we become ungrateful. It is indeed time to have done with such unworthy conduct, and, like St. Aloysius Gonzaga, St. Magdalene of Pazzi, St. Catherine of Siena, St. Francis of Assisi, St. Teresa, and so many other noble hearts, to be filled with nothing but love for the Eucharist. Second, the love of it ought to make us cherish and value all the moments which we are able to spend in adoration in our churches; above all, it ought to make us love Holy Communion and the thanksgiving which follows upon it, as being a delicious foretaste of heaven. Third, lastly, a memory full of love towards the holy Eucharist ought to follow us outside the church and accompany us everywhere. Our heart ought to remain ceaselessly in the holy ciborium with the sacred hosts, occupied in adoring, in loving, and in blessing the God whom love keeps hidden therein; constantly, in the midst of our occupations, we ought to keep Him company by fervent aspirations and the offering of all that we are. *Resolutions and spiritual nosegay as above*

SUMMARY OF TOMORROW'S MEDITATION

As the Eucharist is both a sacrifice and a sacrament, we will consider it separately from these two points of view. Considered as a sacrifice it is, above all things, a sacrifice of latria; that is to say, destined to honor the divine greatness and the supreme dominion of God over all creatures. In order to understand the honor which the holy sacrifice renders to God, we shall consider: First, that it is an homage of supreme esteem for the divine greatness; second, that this greatness is infinitely worthy of supreme esteem. We will then make the resolution: First, to assist at the Holy Sacrifice with profound reverence for the greatness of God, so perfectly honored by Jesus Christ; second, not to lose sight in the whole of our conduct, down to our most secret feelings, of the supreme esteem due to God above all things. Our spiritual nosegay shall be the words of Job: "Behold, God is great, exceeding our knowledge." (Job 36:26)

MEDITATION FOR THE MORNING

Let us adore the infinite greatness of God, so magnificently glorified in the Holy Sacrifice. Let us abase ourselves, in presence of its excellence, and let us pour forth our hearts in admiration of so great marvels, in love of so much beauty, and in praise of His infinite perfection.

FIRST POINT

✝ *How the Holy Sacrifice is an Homage of Supreme Esteem Offered to God*

By sacrifice considered in general is meant the destruction of a victim immolated in order to declare in the presence of heaven and of earth that all the excellence or the beauty of creatures is nothing, and ought to be counted as nothing, in comparison with the infinite perfection of God; that no created being is worthy to subsist in His presence; that divine greatness, which cannot ascend any higher, merits to be honored by an abasement which cannot be more profound, that is to say, destruction and nothingness; lastly, that God suffices perfectly to Himself in the infinite plenitude of His excellence. But if such is the signification of the supreme esteem offered to God by sacrifice in general, what is it in regard to the sacrifice of the altar? It surpasses all other sacrifices by as much as God surpasses His creature; for the value of homage increases in proportion to the dignity of him who renders it and the humble manner in which it is rendered. Now here, who can be greater than the Sacrificer who renders homage to God? He is God Himself. What can be more humble than the manner in which it is rendered? God Himself becomes the victim, and immolates Himself upon the altar as really as He did formerly upon Calvary. This is my body, the priest says over the bread; and in virtue of those words, there will be nothing there but the body. This is my blood, the priest says over the wine, and in accordance with the theological principle that the sacramental words produce what they signify and nothing more, there is nothing there but the blood, really separated from the body; and if it does not issue forth in great streams under the blow of the word as beneath the sacrificial knife, it is because it is retained in the veins of Jesus by the decree of the heavenly Father, which announces that Christ being risen from the dead shall die no more. Still the word has nonetheless virtue as regards the sacrifice; it is the sword which pierces the bosom of the victim, powerless though it be, by means of a miracle, to kill it, but always imprinting upon it the character of death and attesting to heaven as well as to earth the reality of the sacrifice. Could even God Himself conceive a higher idea of its excellence? O Supreme Lord, at whose feet a divine person dies mysteriously in recognition of Thy supreme domain over every creature, how incomprehensible is Thy greatness! O Being of beings, in presence of whom a God makes of Himself a victim, before whom the holy humanity of Jesus Christ, excellent though it be, owns itself to be unworthy to subsist, and hides itself under a particle of a host, how adorable Thou art! Yes, it is therein indeed that consists the most perfect homage which can be offered to God; it is the greatest possible glorification of the Divine Being; and one single Mass gives more glory to God than He could receive from all the homage of angels and saints put together throughout eternity.

SECOND POINT

✝ *The Divine Greatness is Eminently Worthy of the Supreme Esteem of which the Holy Sacrifice is the Expression*

Reason, in fact, shows to us God on a height which loses itself essentially in the infinite, on an elevation which homages that are in all respects divine, as is the Holy Sacrifice, can alone worthily honor. Whoever reflects attentively upon the greatness of God is profoundly astonished at the infinite perfections of the Divine Being; he discovers, in proportion as he meditates upon Him, always fresh perfections, beauties, and charms, compared with which all created objects are as nothing (3 Imit. 31:2). From supreme astonishment he passes into an ecstasy of spirit which clearly sees that, not only in this present life, but throughout eternity, the more he may sound these sacred abysses, the greater marvels will he discover; he enters into a ravishment of the heart which loves God because He is God, which loves God alone because God alone appears to him to be everything, which loves Him without reserve because His perfections have no limits, which, lastly, enjoys infinite pleasure on hearing this Supreme Being say of Himself: "I am who am" (Ex. 3:14), that is to say, I am the Being by essence, the very source of being; nothing exists except by Me. I am the Immutable Being, for to change would be to cease to be what one was in order to become what one had not been. I am the Eternal Being, for it cannot be said of Me, He has been, as though I existed no longer, nor, He will be, as though I had not yet been, but eternally ought it to be and it will always be said, He is. No one else has being except through Me, and then it is only a borrowed being. I am all by that alone, that I am." It is that which honors God in the sacrifice of the Mass, and, however great this homage may be, the Sovereign Being is infinitely worthy of it. May we always thoroughly understand this truth and always love God more and more for Himself, independently of the blessings we have received from Him; may we love Him above all things, because our greatest happiness is to love Him and our greatest misery would be not to love Him. *Resolutions and spiritual nosegay as above*

Saturday after the Octave of Corpus Christi

SUMMARY OF TOMORROW'S MEDITATION

We will continue tomorrow the meditation of this morning, and we shall see that the supreme esteem of God, of which the Holy Sacrifice is the expression, is in regard to the soul: First, a preservative against sin; second, a means for making progress in virtue. We will then make the resolution: First, to maintain habitually in our hearts an elevated sentiment of the greatness of God, and because of this consideration to perform all our actions in the best possible manner, in order to render them less unworthy of so great a God; second, not to neglect little things any more than great, because it is a great thing to please a Being so great, even in little things. Our spiritual nose gay shall be the words by which St. Michael confounded the rebel angels: "Who is like unto God?"

MEDITATION FOR THE MORNING

Let us adore the infinite greatness of God, before whom we are as nothing. Let us abase ourselves in His presence, confessing His incomparable excellence, which is incomparable above all things, saying to Him from the bottom of our hearts: O God, who art Thou, and who am I? Thou art greatness itself, and I am nothingness; Thou art infinite wisdom, and I am but sin. My weakness is confounded in the presence of Thy strength, my misery in presence of Thy mercy, and my heart dilates itself in admiration of Thy marvels.

FIRST POINT

The Supreme Esteem of God, of which the Holy Sacrifice is an Expression, is a Preservative against Sin. The soul which is deeply penetrated with an elevated idea of the greatness of God conceives an extreme horror of the least sin, because in all sin there is an implicit contempt, or at any rate but small esteem, for God, and nothing more than the sole thought of wanting in esteem for a Being so adorable thrills it with horror. The offers made it by the world cannot seduce it or its threats make it afraid, because, filled as it is with supreme esteem for God, it says to itself: Who is great like God, who is terrible like Him, and at the same time amiable like Him? Neither the assaults of the devil, nor the temptations of the flesh, nor the bugbear of human respect have any power over it, because it says to itself like Jonas did: "I fear the Lord, the God of heaven" (Jonas 1:9); like St. Peter: "We ought to obey God rather than man" (Acts 5:29); or like David: "What have I in heaven? And besides Thee what do I desire upon earth?" (Ps. 72:25) Full of these lofty thoughts, it feels only contempt for everything that the world esteems, and it is intolerable to it that for the love of such miserable things the world desires to make it offend God. Therefore to all its suggestions, and to those offered to it by the flesh or the devil, it replies by one single sentence: Who is like unto God? I esteem God alone, and all which is not God is as nothing to me. Armed with this thought, we do not sin; let us pray to God to make it sink deeply within us, and let us recall it to ourselves in all temptations, as well as when our courage is about to fail us.

SECOND POINT

✝ ***The Supreme Esteem of God, of which the Holy Sacrifice is an Expression, is a Means of Making Progress in Virtue***

The soul which is filled with a lofty sentiment of the divine greatness finds it easy to be humble, because, deeming that God alone is worthy to be esteemed and praised, it does not desire for itself either praise or esteem, things which essentially belong to God. It has the same facility in believing the truths of faith; it sees with joy that our great God is so superior to all our conceptions that our reason alone can say nothing of Him worthily, because He is ineffable, or comprehend anything exactly, because He is essentially incomprehensible to all others save Himself. Confidence in God seems to it to be very easy, because, plunged in the sacred abysses of the divine mercy, it feels that it can never confide in it too much. It is true, it says to itself, that I am full of misery; but Thou, O my God, art more full still of mercy. I am covered with sins; but Thou dost give me Thy blood, which effaces them. I am weak, but Thou art my strength; I have placed my confidence in Thee, and I shall not be confounded. It does not cost such a soul ought to be detached from all things, because, when it hears its great God say to it, as He did to Abraham: "I am thy protector and thy reward exceeding great" (Gen. 15:1); or to Moses: "I will show thee all good" (Ex. 33:19), it says to itself, I do not desire the insignificant gifts which the world offers to me. I only aspire to Thee, O my God! To Thee who art all good, the universal, eternal, infinite Good! Other good things are emanations from Thyself, but rivulets are not sufficient for me; I thirst for the source of life, which is in Thee (Ps. 35:10). I do not any longer wish for little drops of pleasure; I desire the torrents of delights of which Thy children drink in Thy bosom. I do not any longer wish for the content which touches only the surface of the soul; I aspire to the infinite joy which Thou dost taste in Thyself; I am impatient to plunge into it and drown myself therein. Inspired with these holy dispositions, it feels an insatiable desire to please its God as much as possible, even down to the smallest things, because it is an infinite honor in its eyes to do the least possible thing for the glory of so great a Master; and, whatever it does, it considers that it has never done enough. It imitates the saints of whom St. Thomas speaks, "Who do great things and look upon them as little" relatively to the greatness of God, for whom they labor; who do much and consider it but little; who labor a long time, and the length of time appears to them to be but as a moment." (Opusc. 61) *Resolutions and spiritual nosegay as above*

Third Sunday after Pentecost

THE GOSPEL ACCORDING TO ST. LUKE 15:1-10

"At that time the publicans and sinners drew near unto Jesus to hear Him: and the Pharisees and scribes murmured, saying: This man receives sinners and eats with them. And He spoke to them this parable, saying What man of you hath a hundred sheep, and if He shall lose one of them, doth he not leave the ninety nine in the desert, and go after that which was lost until he find it? And when he hath found it, lay it upon his shoulders, rejoicing; and, coming home, call together his friends and neighbors, saying to them: Rejoice with me, because I have found my sheep that was lost? I say to you, that even so there shall be joy in heaven upon one sinner that doth penance, more than upon ninety nine just who need not penance. Or what woman having ten groats, if she lose one groat, doth not light a candle, and sweep the house, and seek diligently until she find it? And when she hath found it, call together her friends and neighbors, saying: Rejoice with me, because I have found the groat which I had lost? So I say to you, there shall be joy before the angels of God upon one sinner doing penance."

SUMMARY OF TOMORROW'S MEDITATION

We will interrupt, tomorrow, our meditations on the Holy Sacrifice, in order to meditate upon the gospel of Sunday. We shall then see: First, on the one hand, how souls are lost; second, on the other hand, how Jesus Christ labors to save them. We will then make the resolution: First, carefully to avoid the very least faults as leading to greater ones, and to break off all ties which compromise our salvation; second, faithfully to obey the attractions of grace, which calls us to a more perfect life. Our spiritual nosegay shall be the words of our gospel: "There shall be joy in heaven upon one sinner that doth penance." (Luke 15:7)

MEDITATION FOR THE MORNING

Let us adore Jesus Christ presenting Himself to us, in the gospel of the day, under the double figure of a shepherd who runs after the sheep that has wandered away, in order to bring it back to the fold, and of a woman who, having lost a coin of great price, does everything she can to find it. Let us thank Him for these two figures, which show forth so well His mercy and the ardent desire he has for our salvation.

FIRST POINT

✝ *How Souls are Lost*

We shall find their history in the parable of the stray sheep of which our gospel speaks. First, the sheep runs after a plot of grass which pleases it, and it stops there where it grows; whilst it is grazing, the shepherd and the flock go in another direction; and behold it is lost. It is thus that the loss of a soul begins with a slight, almost insensible fault, one which is only half voluntary; it is the first step on the path which leads away from God. Second, the sheep sees that it has wandered away from the shepherd; it is not afraid either of having strayed from him or of the danger to which it exposes itself; it remains where it is. It is thus that after our faults, which we hardly look upon as such, we neglect to correct ourselves; we confess them without sorrow or without making a firm resolve not to fall into them again; we remain as we are. Second, the sheep, being without a guide, goes and throws itself into bushes and thorns, which embarrass it and from which it frees itself only rarely and with difficulty; it is the symbol of the attachments which keep the heart fast bound and lead it to the committal of more serious faults. Fourth, lastly, the sheep, struggling amongst the briars which tear its fleece, falls into a ditch, out of which it cannot rise. It is the figure of spiritual blindness, a deplorable state, a frightful darkness, in which the soul no longer sees what misery it is to lose the friendship of God, His graces, and His recompenses; to sacrifice Paradise, to expose itself to hell for the sake of a passing interest, a frivolous pleasure, a breath of honor, a vain satisfaction. If we wish to avoid so great a misfortune, let us avoid the smallest faults; let us correct them as soon as conscience shows them to us; and let us be always on our guard against attachments and the slight faults which lead to greater ones. Let us here seriously examine ourselves.

SECOND POINT

✝ *How Jesus Christ Labors to Save Souls*

Such is the love of Jesus Christ for souls which have quitted Him, that as soon as they return to Him He is always ready to pardon them, and is grieved at a want of confidence in His mercy. If they do not return, He pursues them with His exterior and interior graces until they do return. This is what He wishes to make us understand by the shepherd who leaves his ninety nine sheep to hasten into the wilderness after his wandering sheep. He does not cease from pursuing it until he has found it again. And when he has found it, O touching tenderness of the heart of Jesus towards poor sinners! Far from punishing it for its infidelities, He caresses it, takes it on His shoulders, He brings it back to the fold, and He makes a feast to celebrate its entrance into it; that is to say, that by the unction of His grace He attracts it, He brings it back, and He makes it enjoy so much sweetness on its return that it is rather carried than walks thither. Lastly, on its return to the fold, the delights of recovered innocence, the happiness of the friendship of God found once more, the joy of the hope of a blessed eternity, make of the day of reconciliation a festival day. The same truth is represented to us by the lost coin of our gospel. This coin, this precious stone, this inestimable jewel, are our souls, which St. Cyprian calls pretiosa monilia Christi, and which God destines to be the ornament of His Paradise. In order to save them, Jesus Christ has moved the world; He sends His priests to seek for them throughout the universe, and at the recovery of each one amongst them there is great joy in heaven. O inestimable value of souls! Happy are the priests employed in gaining them for Jesus Christ. Let us recall to mind all that Jesus Christ has done to save us. Let us thank Him for the past, and determine better to profit by His graces in the future. *Resolutions and spiritual nosegay as above.*

Third Monday after Pentecost

SUMMARY OF TOMORROW'S MEDITATION

The worship of latria which we render to God by the Holy Sacrifice, and to which we ought to associate ourselves, does not consist only in the supreme esteem of God, but also in a profound reverence for His greatness. We shall see tomorrow, First, how Christ in the Blessed Sacrament testifies His reverence towards His Father; second, how in our habitual conduct we ought to be reverential towards God. We will then make the resolution: First, always to speak to God in our prayers with profound reverence, accompanied with perfect modesty of demeanor; second, in all places to have great reverence for the presence of God, whose eyes are upon us day and night. Our spiritual nosegay shall be the words of the Psalmist: "I will worship towards Thy temple in Thy fear." (Ps. 5:8)

MEDITATION FOR THE MORNING

Let us adore God as being eminently worthy of the reverence of all creatures; and, in our powerlessness to reverence Him as He merits to be, let us offer Him all the reverence which Jesus Christ renders Him in heaven and upon our altars; "By Jesus Christ, as Jesus Christ and in union with Jesus Christ, glory and honor to Thee, God the Father."

FIRST POINT

✝ *Jesus in the Holy Sacrifice Teaches us, by His Example, Reverence for God.*

Isaias admired in the future Messias, by means of the prophetic light, the spirit of reverential fear of God (Is. 15:3); and, according to St. Paul, it is this profound reverence for the Divinity which gives to all His prayers their value and their efficacy (Heb. 5:7). He manifested it in the Garden of Olives by abasing Himself, in the presence of the majesty of His Father, to such a degree that He prostrated Himself with His face to the ground; He manifested it at the praetorium and on Calvary, by offering Himself there as our Victim to the greater glory of God, and He does not cease to manifest it in the highest heaven, where, as our Pontiff, He continually offers His adorable Victim, which is Himself. But it is, above all, in the Holy Sacrifice that this great and supreme reverence shows itself. There, in order to honor the infinite excellence of the Divine Being, Jesus, our High-Priest, falls down in adoration, and seems to desire to annihilate Himself by hiding Himself, with all His glory, under the symbols of death, under a little host or particle of a host; by depriving Himself of the use of all His senses, and by immolating Himself mysteriously, although in an unbloody manner: He, no longer the Son of man in a state of infirmity and resemblance to the flesh of sin, but the Eternal Son of God, reigning in His glory, the Divine Pontiff, holy, separate from sinners and raised above the heavens. Now, these extreme abasements, so in comprehensible in so great a Pontiff, in the very equal of God, eloquently tell us of the profound reverence with which He is penetrated towards the Divine Majesty, and with which He desires to inspire us. Let us pray to God to penetrate us with these lofty mysteries.

SECOND POINT

✝ *How, in our Habitual Conduct, we ought to be Reverential towards God*

Our duty as Christians is to associate ourselves with the perfect reverence and the profound abasement of Jesus Christ in the presence of God, our heavenly Father. Like Him, we ought to annihilate ourselves, through the feeling of our baseness in the presence of God, of our un worthiness compared with His sanctity. The Church in heaven gives us the example of it, for the angels praise Him, the dominations adore Him, the powers reverence Him with trembling, and the seraphim, covering themselves with their wings, dare not look upon so lofty a majesty (Preface of the Mass). The Church on earth does the same; for it is a constant fact that the more the saints excel in virtue, the more filled are they with reverence and with a kind of fear when they enter the house of God; the more, also, are they led to annihilate themselves in presence of the Divine Majesty, and to show their reverence for His presence in all places by a modest deportment, by a becoming language, by an irreproachable life; the more careful are they to look upon God always as God; that is to say, with perfect reverence, even if it be only in regard to the shortest prayer, or to a sign of the cross; the more reverence have they, lastly, for what belongs to God and to His worship, to the persons who are consecrated to Him, to the sacred vessels, to objects blessed by the Church, to ceremonies, to the Holy Scriptures, which St. Charles always read kneeling down and with head bare. Let us examine ourselves as to whether we have the profound reverence felt by the saints, the respect they manifested in the house of God and in prayer; their veneration for all that appertains to divine worship. *Resolutions and spiritual nosegay as above.*

Third Tuesday after Pentecost

SUMMARY OF TOMORROW'S MEDITATION

he worship of latria, which we render to God by the Holy Sacrifice, and with which we ought to associate ourselves, joins to the supreme esteem and profound reverence towards God perfect submission to His sovereign dominion. We shall see then: First, how Jesus in the Holy Sacrifice renders this submission to His Father; second, how we all ought to be in all things perfectly submissive to the sovereign dominion of God. We will then make the resolution: First, to keep ourselves always in a state of humble and loving submission to all the decrees of Providence; second, to immolate joyfully, even in things which cost us the most, our own will to the sovereign dominion and the good pleasure of God. Our spiritual nosegay shall be the words of the high priest Heli, when, on hearing of the death of his two sons, and the disaster which had befallen his people, he exclaimed: "It is the Lord; let Him do what is good in His sight." (1 Kings 3:18).

MEDITATION FOR THE MORNING

Let us adore the sovereign dominion of God over the whole universe, over the Church, and over the world, over all that belongs to us, over our will, over our body, and our soul. Let us be lost in adoration, in praise, and in love for this supreme dominion, and let us be inspired with profound submission to all that He wills, and all that He desires to do with us. "Lord, all things are in Thy power; Thou art Lord of all." (Esth. 13:9)

FIRST POINT

✝ *Jesus Christ in the Holy Sacrifice Teaches us, by His Example, Submission to God*

The whole life of Jesus Christ was a life of humble and loving submission to God His Father. "When He cometh into the world," St. Paul tells us, "He saith: Sacrifice and oblation Thou wouldst not, but a body Thou hast fitted to Me. Holocausts for sin did not please Thee. Then said I: Behold I come; in the head of the Book it is written of Me, that I should do Thy will, O God!" (Heb. 10:5-7) Until His last sigh He never departed for one moment, not even in the slightest of His actions or His words from this spirit of submission and dependence. "He that sent Me is with Me, and He hath not left Me alone, for I do always the things that please Him" (John 8:29), He said. "Father, all things are possible to Thee, remove this chalice from Me, but not what I will, but what Thou wilt." (Mark 14:36) "My meat is to do the will of Him that sent Me." (John 4:34) But this submission and this dependence were never so remarkable or so incomprehensible as they are in the Holy Sacrifice. He submits to descend therein from heaven to earth on all the altars throughout the world, each time that a priest summons Him; and at His arrival on the altar He immolates Himself mysteriously in order to recognize and confess that God, in His quality of supreme Lord of the universe, has a right of life and death over all created beings; and after having rendered this sublime homage, He remains in the tabernacle in a continual state of immolation, that He may continue to glorify the supreme dominion of God over every creature. He submits therein to all which it may please His Father to permit should be done to Him; to be carried wherever it is wished He should be taken, to be placed and lodged wherever it is desired He should be; He submits to be forsaken by men, to be left in the solitude and darkness of the tabernacle, to be exposed to the irreverence of bad Christians; He submits to allow Himself to be dropped, through inadvertence, or to be cast through malice on the ground, and to be trodden under foot; to be buried alive in a conscience soiled by sin, to submit to the evil deeds of thieves stealing away the consecrated vessels, or to fire, and other elements which may attack Him. Could there be a more complete submission to Providence, a more complete abandonment of our whole being to the sovereign dominion of God? How ill it would become me, after such an example, not to submit to all the decrees of Providence, to murmur or to complain! Let us consider in what we have failed, with respect to this duty, and let us determine to be more faithful to it.

SECOND POINT

✝ *We ought to Imitate Jesus Christ in His Perfect Submission to Providence*

Following the example set us by the adorable Victim immolated on the altar, we ought to abandon ourselves, together with all that we have and all that we are, to the good pleasure of God, to dispose of us and of all that belongs to us as He wills. There must be no exception in regard to this abandonment and this sacrifice. We ought to immolate to Him our bodies, to keep them in a state of perfect purity and modesty; our mind, that we may no longer have any thought enter into it except thoughts of God and according to God; our heart, in order no longer to love anyone but Him, and to love Him with all our strength; our whole being, in a word, the use of which ought to be not only devoted to nothing else except to serve Him, but to be offered in sacrifice to Him. O King of kings! Lord of lords! Sovereign Master of all creatures! we ought to say to Him, abased in Thy presence and filled with the sentiment of my dependence upon Thee, I joyfully recognize Thy supreme dominion; I am glad to be the servant of such a Master, content that Thou shouldst dispose of me as my Sovereign, as a thing belonging to Thee by a thousand titles, and which I should be happy to give Thee, even if it did not belong to Thee (2 Mach. 14:35; Wis. 16:13). O God so great! How horrible then is sin, which is a refusal of submission to Thy lofty majesty, and a species of insurrection against Thy supreme dominion! How just, on the contrary, is calm and resigned submission to all the decrees of Thy Providence, and how I desire to see all the hearts of the universe submitted to Thy great dominion! Also, O my God, I detest all sin, and whatever may be the way in which Thou shalt dispose of me and of all that belongs to me, I will always say: It is well, for the sole reason that it is Thy good pleasure (Matt. 11:26). *Resolutions and spiritual nosegay as above.*

Third Wednesday after Pentecost

SUMMARY OF TOMORROW'S MEDITATION

After having studied the Holy Sacrifice as a worship of latria, we will now consider it under another point of view, and we shall see: First, that it is an Eucharistic sacrifice, or of thanksgiving; second, that we ought to associate ourselves with this spirit of thanksgiving. We will then make the resolution: First, to occupy ourselves during Mass with thanking God for His love and His numberless blessings; second, to multiply during the day our thanksgivings for the goodness of God, saying to Him, by way of an ejaculatory prayer: Thanks, my God, thanks for all Thou dost continually for me, for the health Thou givest me, and the use of my limbs which Thou dost grant me, and the good thoughts with which Thou dost inspire me, etc. Our spiritual nosegay shall be the words of the Preface: "Let us give thanks to the Lord our God."

MEDITATION FOR THE MORNING

We will consider God as the universal Benefactor of heaven and earth. Let us render to Him, under this title, our thanksgivings and our praises. Let us esteem ourselves happy to have the Holy Sacrifice to offer to Him as Eucharistic, in supplement of our powerlessness to thank Him worthily, and let us say with St. Paul, "I give thanks to my God through Jesus Christ." (Rom.1:8)

FIRST POINT

✝ *Holy Mass is an Eucharistic Sacrifice, that is to say, a Thanksgiving*

Infinite gratitude is due to God, since from all eternity He has loved us with an infinite love, destining from then all the blessings He has lavished upon us since time began. And these blessings, what are they? First, the whole creation, since the whole of the universe was made for man; second, all that Providence has added, and continually adds, to the blessing of creation, whether in the spiritual order or the temporal order: and here the detail would be infinite; third, all the good which our neighbor does us, or desires to do us, since he is inspired thereto by the Spirit of God; fourth, the beneficent action of God in all these things; for it is an action of every moment, because the continual preservation of our being and that of others is equivalent to an ever new creation; it is a wholly gratuitous action, since God owes us nothing, since He had nothing to gain in giving us all these good things, and since, far from meriting His favors, we deserve His vengeance; it is an action of the most elevated order, since the blessings which it procures for us are of infinite value; it is His own Son given for our ransom; it is His Holy Spirit which He sends to us to shed His charity in our hearts, to make us Christians and Catholics; it is His blood with which He purifies us and nourishes us by the sacraments and the Sacrifice; it is His interior and exterior graces which preserve the soul from all the sins which it would commit without their succor, and which make it advance in virtue; lastly, it is His Paradise which He offers us and in a manner places at our disposition. Let us raise our thoughts higher still. We ought to count amongst our cause for gratitude: First, the glory that God procures to Himself by His works, by His Incarnation, by the praises which the three Divine Persons address to one another, since the glory of God ought to be dearer to us than our own glory, and because the Church makes us sing at the Holy Sacrifice: "We give Thee thanks for Thy great glory" (Gloria in Excelsis); second, the riches of grace which God has heaped upon the holy humanity of Jesus Christ, the Blessed Virgin Mother, all the angels, and all the saints, since by virtue of the communion of saints the graces which each one amongst them receives are as family possessions which call for the gratitude of all. But how shall we acquit such an immense debt as this? We have no other resource but the Holy Sacrifice, a resource which is unique, but also superabundant. For Jesus Christ, offering Himself at the altar as an Eucharistic Victim, renders to God as much as God has given and will ever give; He even gives Him more, because here the victim of thanksgiving is worth as much as God Himself. If, then, we receive all blessings by Jesus Christ, by Jesus Christ also we thank God worthily.

SECOND POINT

✝ ***We ought to Associate ourselves with the Spirit of Thanksgiving of Jesus Christ in the Holy Sacrifice***

Jesus Christ, in thanking God the Father, did not wish to dispense us from our debt; He desired, on the contrary, to invite us, by His example, to thank the Author of all good in associating us with His sublime thanksgiving; He desired to thank God by all His members united with Him, and thus to spread abroad, through the whole earth and in all heaven, the gratitude due to the Most Holy Trinity. Entering into His designs, heaven eternally thanks Him, and the Church on earth never ceases to sing: "Let us give thanks to the Lord our God." Let us penetrate ourselves with the same sentiments, and, from the bottom of a heart profoundly touched, let us several times during the day give thanks to God for all the good which He does to us; thanks for the good which He does to the whole of society: thanks for all which He does for the Church, which He enables to survive all her enemies, and to gain on one side what she loses on the other. Woe to him who does not understand this duty of gratitude! Ingratitude, says St. Bernard, dries up the sources of piety, the dew of mercy, the rivulets of grace, dissipates virtue, loses blessings, annihilates merits, ravages and destroys everything in the soul. Gratitude, on the contrary, for one blessing received, calls down new ones; and like the waves of the sea which return thither only to come back once more, so the blessings of God, which we cause to ascend to their adorable Source by means of thanksgiving, return to us with fresh abundance (St. Bern. Serm. ii. in Cant.). Lastly, gratitude animates us with fervor. "My God," St. Teresa, the patroness of generous and grateful souls, often said, "My God, to think we receive so much and give back so little!" Filled with this thought, she was ready to tear herself into pieces for the love of God; and she could not conceive it possible to lead in this world any other kind of life than that which is led in heaven, and which is an eternal canticle of thanksgiving. How far we are from having these sentiments! How little we thank God for His blessings, and how little sensible are we of them! Let us entertain better sentiments, and let our hearts overflow with thanksgiving. *Resolutions and spiritual nosegay as above.*

Third Thursday after Pentecost

SUMMARY OF TOMORROW'S MEDITATION

We will tomorrow consider that the Mass is not only a sacrifice of latria and Eucharistic, but also an expiatory sacrifice; and that through this title it is: First, a complete reparation for the offence which sin has committed against God; second, a superabundant satisfaction for the debts of the Church suffering and militant. We will then make the resolution, First, to renew in ourselves the spirit of penitence, and cheerfully to accept, with this object in view, all the trials of life; second, to be very keenly sensible of offences committed against God, to make reparation by acts of love and of honorable amend, and to do all that in us lies for the conversion of sinners. Our spiritual nosegay shall be the prayer of Joel: "Spare, Lord! spare Thy people!"(Joel 2:17)

MEDITATION FOR THE MORNING

Let us adore Jesus Christ as our Mediator and Pontiff, interposing between the anger of Heaven and guilty earth; turning away the thunder from above our heads and changing the lightning of divine anger into a rain of graces (Ps. 34:7). Let us thank Him for this charitable mediation to which the world owes its existence.

FIRST POINT

✝ *The Holy Sacrifice is a Complete Reparation of Offences Committed against God*

The Christian who, illuminated by faith, is able to appreciate how great an evil it is to offend God, is inconsolable for it. He sighs over it, he weeps over it, like the holy king David; his soul is overwhelmed by it, as was the soul of the holy prophet Jeremias; and when he considers how common this great evil is, when he looks at all the sins of the world collected together, he exclaims: "O heavenly Father! Father so worthy of all honor and all love, how afflicted I am to see that ungrateful men, instead of loving Thee, offend Thee! Oh, that I could offer to Thy offended honor a reparation equal to the offence." Then, out of the depth of his grief, his thoughts turn to the Holy Sacrifice; he there sees a God offering Himself in person as an expiatory host for all the sins of the world. "O God!" he resumes, filled with immense consolation, "behold what I was seeking for, behold a reparation for the sins of the whole world, not only equal, but superior to the offence. For, a God making satisfaction to Thee in person by means of His infinite abasement, honors Thee incomparably more than all the sins of devils and men put together can offend Thee. With all my heart I unite myself to this superabundant reparation; I unite myself to it by the horror and detestation I have for sin, by zeal for Thy glory and all the good works capable either of honoring Thee or of converting sinners and saving souls." Are these our dispositions?

SECOND POINT

✝ *The Holy Sacrifice is a Superabundant Satisfaction for the Debts of the Church Suffering and Militant*

Jesus Christ, in the Holy Sacrifice, is the great Penitent of the universal Church; and in offering Himself as an expiatory Victim, He shortens the sufferings of the suffering souls in purgatory; He solicits the gift of penitence for sinners, and He obtains the conversions which sometimes astonish the world. He cries aloud for mercy; He turns away the scourges with which God, in former days, visited the earth, and that is the reason of the patience of God in the midst of innumerable crimes and amidst all kinds of disorder. If His thunder does not burst forth, or if it stops after a few claps destined to serve as warnings to us, it is because in the same manner as Moses and Aaron once stood before the ancient Propitiatory, or rather in a much better manner than that of the leaders of the people of Israel, Jesus Christ, our High-Priest, pleads at the altar the cause of a guilty world, and appeases the anger of Heaven. Let us unite ourselves to the ardent zeal of Jesus Christ to solace the souls in purgatory and to make expiation for the sins of the world. God, in His admirable clemency, desires nothing so much as to see us resist His anger in union with Jesus Christ, to perform penance for sinners, to immolate ourselves for them as expiatory hosts, and to call down upon ourselves the thunder with which He is about to strike His people. He complains by His prophet of not having found enough of such souls to parry His blows. "I sought" He says in Ezekiel, "for a man who might set up a hedge and stand in the gap before Me in favor of the land, that I might not destroy it; and I found none." (Ezek. 22:30) You are not come back, He says by the same prophet, to place yourselves in front of My justice like a wall for the house of Israel. Now, if God thus complained under the Old Law, with how much more justice will He reproach us under the New Law, if we do not profit by the advantage of being able to offer Him, through our prayers, an expiatory host of infinite value? Have we, up to the present time, thoroughly understood this double duty of expiation for the souls in purgatory and for sinners upon earth? *Resolutions and spiritual nosegay as above.*

Third Friday after Pentecost

SUMMARY OF TOMORROW'S MEDITATION

We will tomorrow consider a fourth character appertaining to the Holy Mass, which is that of an impetratory sacrifice; that is to say, a sacrifice of prayer or of request, and we shall see that, in fact, the Mass is: First, the most excellent of prayers; second, that it is a prayer which is all-powerful over the heart of God. We will then make the resolution: First, better to perform our ordinary prayers; second, often to ask of God the spirit of prayer. Our spiritual nosegay shall be the words of our divine Master: "Amen, Amen, I say to you, if you ask the Father anything in My name He will give it you." (John 16:23)

MEDITATION FOR THE MORNING

Let us adore Jesus Christ on the holy altar, as the great suppliant of the universal Church. Let us ask Him to permit us to participate in the excellence of His prayer: "Lord, teach us to pray." (Luke 11:1)

FIRST POINT

✝ ***Holy Mass is the most Excellent of Prayers***

For, First, it is Jesus Christ Himself who prays at the altar; Himself who said to His Father, "Thou hearest Me always" (John 11:42); Himself, the equal of God, and God like His Father, who charges Himself with our prayers, supports them by His merits, and offers them consumed in the fire of His charity. Second, He presents them to His Father, begging of Him, in the most humble of states; He presents Himself as our Victim, making His wounds and His blood, which cries out louder than that of Abel, speak for us; He presents Himself as our High-Priest, with an immense desire to obtain all that He asks for, and He carries His desire into the depths of His Father's heart. Third, our prayer is united with His, but in the most favorable of conditions; for we give to the heavenly Father infinitely more than we ask of Him; we ask Him for His grace, and in return we give Him His own Son, by the oblation of the Holy Sacrifice, so that in the Mass Jesus Christ prays with us and in us, and we pray with Him and in Him. Could there be a prayer more excellent?

SECOND POINT

✝ *Holy Mass is a Prayer which is All-powerful over the Heart of God*

It is remarkable that it is the priest himself who decides upon the intention of the Sacrifice, who says to Jesus Christ what it is which he asks; and Jesus Christ, this willing proxy, presents to His Father all the requests with which He is charged, without ever finding them too numerous or too difficult. Now who is there that cannot see the supreme all-powerfulness of such a prayer? The most fervent prayers of the angels and saints put together do not approach it. They are never anything more than supplications of the servants of God; but the Mass is the supplication of the Son of God Himself, which is always heard and granted, says St. Paul, and even cannot be refused, because He is His well-beloved Son in whom He finds all His pleasure, His Son equal to God, and God like Him. We do not always see upon earth the effects of this divine Sacrifice. But when we enter into heaven, there where in the pure light of God are seen the secret springs by which everything is moved, and the relation between effects and their causes, we shall recognize a world of marvels obtained by the Holy Sacrifice both in the supernatural and the natural order. Whence we ought to see: First, what confidence we ought to have in the Holy Sacrifice and what happiness it ought to be to us to assist at it; it is the best of all moments for prayer, the most favorable moment for begging for all kinds of graces. Second, that the Church has good reason to put so often into the mouth of the priest during the action of the Sacrifice this invitation to prayer, Oremus; Let us pray, because at such a time we cannot ask too much and we can always obtain everything. If up to the present time our prayers have not always been granted, it has been because we have not made our supplications aright; we have made them without having a lively faith in these beautiful truths, without union with Jesus Christ, without recollection, perhaps even with a spirit full of distraction and a careless heart. Is it not true? *Resolutions and spiritual nosegay as above.*

SUMMARY OF TOMORROW'S MEDITATION

e will meditate tomorrow on the motives for the zeal we ought always to feel for hearing or saying Holy Mass; the first is, that of all religious exercises, it is the one which is most agreeable to the Most Holy Trinity; the second is, that it is the one which is the most profitable for us and for the Church. We will then make the resolution: First, never to fail, in as far as is possible, either to say or to hear it every day; second, to bring with us to it a lively faith and deep piety. Our spiritual nosegay shall be the beautiful words of the Imitation: "When the priest celebrates he honors God, he gives joy to the angels, he edifies the Church, he succors the living and the dead, and he procures for himself all kinds of graces." (4 Imit. 5:3)

MEDITATION FOR THE MORNING

Let us adore Our Lord, the supreme High-Priest, consummating upon the altar, by the ministry of the priest, as well as upon the cross in His own person, the sacrifice which glorifies God and which saves the world. Let us thank Him for admitting all of us to participate in the merits of this solemn act. "Come to Me" (Matt. 11:28), He cries aloud to us; let us promise Him to respond to this amiable invitation with eagerness and love.

FIRST POINT

✝ *Holy Mass is, of all Religious Acts, the one which is the most Agreeable to the Most Holy Trinity*

It is to the Most Holy Trinity alone that the Holy Sacrifice can be offered and what better acts could be offered to Him than the one which procures for Him infinite glory, which renders infinite thanksgiving for all His benefits, and which satisfies His justice by an infinite reparation? Now the sacrifice of the Mass unites these three great advantages, as we have shown in our preceding meditations; whence we ought to conclude that we can do nothing which is more agreeable to God than to assist at the Holy Sacrifice when we do not offer it, and to come and welcome His Son at the moment when He descends, from amidst the splendors of the saints, upon the altar, to offer Him our praises and our love, to unite our prayers with His, the sacrifice of ourselves with the sacrifice which He makes therein of His own person ; and through Him to adore, to love, and to bless the Most Holy Trinity, to whom He offers

Himself. A great monarch who should send his son to visit his provinces would be offended by the negligence of those among his subjects who did not come and welcome his beloved son; and he would, on the contrary, be flattered by the eagerness with which his other subjects would come and welcome him and make the air resound with their exclamations of love and devotion. It is the same with the Holy Sacrifice; in the same degree in which the Most Holy Trinity beholds with displeasure the indifference which leaves almost alone in the church the celebrant with his humble server, it beholds with delight a numerous assemblage of the faithful collected together before the altar, praying and adoring with the priest. Mary and John, at the foot of the cross, assisting at the death of the Savior on Calvary, were the objects of the complaisance of the Most Holy Trinity; they were the type of Christians assisting at the sacrifice of the Mass, since it is the same sacrifice on the altar that it was on Calvary. Let us hence learn to assist as often as possible at Holy Mass, and let us have a horror of those who do not assist at it when they might.

SECOND POINT

✝ *The Holy Sacrifice is, of all Religious Acts, the one which is the most Profitable to us and to the Church*

First, it is evident that no prayer, not even that of the whole of the angels, is to be compared in value to that of Jesus Christ immolating Himself upon the altar, and making all His wounds, as though they were so many supplicating voices, to pray for us. To neglect by our absence through insufficient motives, so powerful a prayer, is to be our own enemy; it is to sin against our dearest interests. Second, to offer the Holy Sacrifice, or only to unite with the priest who offers it, assisting at it in the spirit and intention with which he offers it, is, as we have already seen, to procure joy for the Church triumphant, solace for the Church suffering, the most efficacious aid for the Church militant. Could there possibly be anything more profitable for the universal Church? For the sake of the love we bear to our brethren in heaven, ought we not to esteem ourselves happy to be able to help them to glorify and to thank the Lord? For the sake of the sufferings of the souls in purgatory, ought it not to be a joy to us to solace them by the Divine Sacrifice? Third, if we are alive to the woes of the Church militant, to the troubles of all kinds to which all the children of Adam are subjected, what happiness for us to come to their aid by this same sacrifice. Oh, how these thoughts ought to make us assiduous in assisting at Holy Mass, as far as is possible to us. Have we this zeal in hearing and in piously assisting at it? *Resolutions and spiritual nosegay as above.*

Fourth Sunday after Pentecost

THE GOSPEL ACCORDING TO ST. LUKE 5:1-11

"At that time, when the multitudes pressed upon Jesus to hear the word of God, He stood by the Lake of Genesareth. And He saw two ships standing by the lake; but the fishermen were gone out of them and were washing their nets; and going into one of the ships that was Simon's: He desired him to draw back a little from the land, and sitting, He taught the multitudes out of the ship. Now, when He had ceased to speak, He said to Simon: Launch out into the deep, and let down your nets for a draught. And Simon, answering, said to Him: Master, we have labored all the night, and have taken nothing, but at Thy word I will let down the net. And when they had done this, they enclosed a very great multitude of fishes; and their net broke; and they beckoned to their partners that were in the other ship, that they should come and help them; and they came and filled both the ships, so that they were almost sinking. Which when Simon Peter saw he fell down at Jesus' knees, saying: Depart from me, for I am a sinful man, O Lord. For he was wholly astonished, and all that were with him, at the draught of fishes which they had taken: and so were also James and John, the sons of Zebedee, who were Simon's partners. And Jesus saith to Simon: Fear not, from hence forth thou shalt catch men. And having brought their ships to land, leaving all things, they followed Him."

SUMMARY OF TOMORROW'S MEDITATION

e will meditate tomorrow upon the gospel of the day, and we shall learn from it: First, the causes of the little progress we make in virtue; second, the means for making progress in the future. We will then make the resolution: First, to maintain in ourselves a firm determination to advance in virtue; second, in all things to set before ourselves Jesus Christ as the model of this progress, and to do everything in union with Him. Our spiritual nosegay shall be the words of the Apostle: Let us increase always in Jesus Christ, who is the adorable Head of which we are the members. (Eph. 4:15)

MEDITATION FOR THE MORNING

Let us adore Jesus Christ instructing us in the gospel of the day upon the causes of our insignificant progress in virtue, and on the means whereby to make real progress in the future. Let us thank Him for the great goodness with which He instructs us; and let us ask of Him grace to understand and to practice what He teaches.

FIRST POINT

✝ *The Causes of our Little Progress in Virtue*

Our gospel shows us three causes. First: The apostles had labored all night and had taken nothing (Luke 5:5). There is nothing astonishing in that; what could they take when they could not see anything? It is the unhappiness of those who labor without faith: some of them mechanically, and without any definite intention, like the animals; others from purely natural principles, like the honest pagan; others from principles of interest and self-love, like the men of the world; such as these obtain nothing from what they do, and spite of a great deal of labor they never advance. Those alone make progress who, living a life of faith, are guided in all that they do by an upright and pure intention to please God, keeping constantly the eyes of their heart fixed upon the divine good pleasure. As the eye of their intention is simple, the whole body of their action shines with a splendor of sanctity which is worthy of heaven (Matt. 6:22). Second, the apostles had labored without Jesus; He had not been with them during the night: this was the second cause which rendered their fishing useless. If it be not the spirit of Jesus which animates us, His example which directs us, His love which inspires us, we lose time and do not advance. As the shoot draws its life from the vine, and is dried up and dies if it be separated from it, so Christian action has no life and no merit except by its union with Jesus (John 15:4). In order to labor usefully, we must therefore do everything, say everything, and think everything through the spirit of Jesus, and in union with Him (Canon of the Mass). Third, the apostles had labored under the inspiration of their own will; Jesus Christ had not yet told them where they ought to cast their nets; therefore they had caught nothing. But when once He had given them His orders, and they were able to say: We have cast in the net where Thou hadst commanded (Luke 5:5), they worked wonders. In the same way, all that we do without consulting Our Lord, according to our own pleasure and our own fancy, is time lost, even as, on the contrary, all that is done under the inspiration of His grace, through obedience to the spirit of Christ, makes us advance in the practice of solid virtue. Let us recognize by these signs the reason of our little progress, and let us correct ourselves.

SECOND POINT

✝ *Means whereby to make Progress in Virtue*

First means: To have a determined will always to tend to more lofty perfection. O Christian soul, do not remain stationary near to the earth and its vain enjoyments; advance constantly towards the sea of holy love; advance every day, every hour, every moment; gain the open sea, and run in the path of the commandments and of counsel; tend always to higher perfection (Luke 5:4). To desire always to love more and more, to desire to be always more recollected, more humble, more fervent; to desire always to perform the present action better than the one which preceded it; to desire always to advance, because not to advance is to go back; this is the first means for making progress. Second means: Never to allow ourselves to be discouraged by failure. The apostles had labored all night without taking anything; but as soon as Jesus spoke, they cast in their nets and redoubled their efforts (Luke 5:5). In the same way, after our faults we ought not to allow ourselves to be cast down, but derive from those very faults a motive for doing better, in order to repair past evil by present good; we must be animated by a double measure of love, that we may repair the unhappy moments in which we have not loved; such is the second means of making progress. The third is to keep ourselves in a state of humility after we have received graces. St. Peter, on seeing the miraculous draught of fishes which he had just made, falls on his knees before Jesus Christ, recognizing himself to be unworthy of the favor he had just received, and exclaiming that he was nothing but a sinner (Luke 5:8). Following his example, we ought to refer to divine goodness the little good which is in us, or which is done by us, without esteeming ourselves any the more for it, without taking pleasure in it, and without congratulating ourselves upon it as though it were as product of our own nature. We ought, in the midst of the greatest graces, to look upon ourselves in the presence of God as being sinners unworthy of standing before Him, more unworthy still of His favors, and make an exact share between God and ourselves: all that is good belongs to God, evil only belongs to me. Alas Lord, I confess, to my confusion, that I have but little practiced these three means; but henceforth I will apply myself to them with my whole heart; I will every day endeavor to do better; I will every day encourage myself to do so, and I will constantly maintain the humility incumbent on me because of my wretchedness. *Resolutions and spiritual nosegay as above.*

SUMMARY OF TOMORROW'S MEDITATION

e will meditate tomorrow upon the occupations of the soul during Holy Mass, and we shall see how suitable it is to occupy ourselves: First, with the passion and the death of Jesus Christ; second, with the ends of the Sacrifice; third, with the love which God the Father and Jesus Christ His Son testify to us in this mystery. We will then make the resolution: First, no longer to assist at Holy Mass from habit or routine, without some fixed and precise object to prevent the soul from being distracted; second, to occupy ourselves with one of the three considerations we have just indicated. Our spiritual nosegay shall be the words of the Council of Trent: "Therein is immolated in an unbloody manner the same Jesus Christ who on the altar of the cross immolated Himself in a bloody manner."

MEDITATION FOR THE MORNING

Let us honor the most holy Virgin upon Calvary as being the most finished model of the spirit which ought to animate us during the Holy Sacrifice. Occupied wholly with what was passing before her eyes, with the glory of God and the salvation of the world, for which she offers the adorable Victim, with the love of God who delivers up to death His innocent Son, and with the love of the Son who delivers up Himself, she offers herself and immolates herself in spirit in order to make of herself with her dear Son but one sole and same victim. Let us admire her sublime occupations and adore the Holy Spirit, who produces them.

FIRST POINT

✝ *How Suitable it is to Occupy ourselves during Holy Mass with the Passion and Death of Our Savior*

What, in fact, can be more suitable than to think of what passes before our eyes? Now, at the altar, everything speaks to us of the passion and the death of the Savior: the cross surmounts the tabernacle and is seen upon all the sacred vestments; the stole represents the chains by which Jesus was attached to the pillar; the girdle the scourges which lacerated His flesh, the maniple the cords with which He was bound; the passing to and fro of the priest from one side to another of the altar recalls to mind the different tribunals at which He was made to appear. The Mass itself is a lively and real reproduction of the sacrifice of Calvary; it is the same Victim and the same Priest. It is true that in it Jesus Christ borrows the person of a man to render His invisible priesthood visible; but in reality it is always Jesus Christ who consecrates, Jesus Christ who immolates Himself, Jesus Christ who prays. Is not all this to show us that during Holy Mass we ought to meditate upon His passion and death, inspired by the same pious sentiments with which we should have been animated had we assisted, together with Mary and St. John, at His agony upon Calvary; that consequently, we ought to sacrifice ourselves, body and soul, to the great living God, in order to form, with Jesus Christ, but one sole victim?

SECOND POINT

✝ *How Suitable it is to Occupy ourselves during Mass with the Ends of the Sacrifice*

These ends, as we have already shown, are, first, to render to God the worship of latria by a supreme esteem for His greatness, respect for His lofty majesty, and submission to His supreme dominion over us; second, to thank Him for His numberless benefits; third, to make reparation for the offence of sin, and to inspire ourselves with a lively desire to destroy its reign upon earth; fourth, to ask God for all the succor and all the graces of which the whole world stands in need, and which we ourselves also need. Now what can be more suitable than to occupy ourselves with all these holy things? Not to do so would be, first, to miss the object of the Sacrifice, because these are its ends; second, it would be to deprive our soul of the most excellent resources of piety, since we can think of nothing which is better, nothing which is more glorious to God, nothing which is more useful to ourselves; it would be, third, to render the prayers of the liturgy unintelligible to us, because these ends are, as it were, the key which opens the meaning of them.

THIRD POINT

✝ *How Suitable it is, during Mass, to Occupy ourselves with the Love which God the Father and Jesus Christ His Son Testify to us in this Mystery*

God the Father, at the moment of the Sacrifice, opens His bosom to give us His Son, in order that He may be our victim, our pontiff, our mediator, our food, our consolation, our all; and God the Son, accepting this mission, gives Himself to us without reserve, offers and immolates Himself for us, remains with us as the companion and consoler of our exile, the supplement of our religion and of all our duties towards His Father, the model of all virtue and of all holiness, the life of our life, the strength of our weakness; in a word, He spends Himself wholly for us. Now where God is so prodigal of His love, what can be more suitable than for us to occupy ourselves with this love, than to exert ourselves to render to so good a Father, to so generous a Son, love for love, and to imitate the blessed spirits, overwhelmed by an eternal ecstasy of love in presence of the eternal love of God? (St. Chrysostom, de Sacerd., lib. 3, cap. 2) Do we occupy ourselves during Holy Mass with some of these thoughts, according as grace attracts us? *Resolutions and spiritual nosegay as above.*

Fourth Tuesday after Pentecost

SUMMARY OF TOMORROW'S MEDITATION

We will meditate tomorrow upon the lively faith, the profound humility, and the ardent love which we ought to bring to the Holy Sacrifice. We will then make the resolution to bring to the Holy Sacrifice these three virtues, and our spiritual nosegay shall be the words which formerly the deacon pronounced in the assembly of the faithful: "Holy things are for those who art holy."

MEDITATION FOR THE MORNING

Let us adore the infinite goodness of Jesus Christ descending upon the altar at the summons of the priest, and immolating Himself there for us. Let us beg of Him to make us thoroughly understand the dispositions with which we ought to welcome His arrival amongst us.

FIRST POINT

✝ *The Lively Faith we ought to Bring to the Holy Sacrifice*

As in this ineffable mystery the senses tell us nothing of what is really contained in it; as the eyes, the taste, the hand, far from instructing us, hide the truth of things from us, we cannot appreciate the mystery of the altar except in proportion to the faith we bring to it. With a languishing faith, the august action of the Sacrifice does not touch us any more than does the most indifferent of actions; the Holy Table is nothing but a common table, the bread of heaven is but as common bread, and the Eucharistic wine but as ordinary wine. The beautiful prayers of the liturgy say nothing to the soul; we allow the most burning words to slip over a cold and icy tongue, without associating our hearts with our lips, and we return from the Holy Sacrifice just the same as when we went to it, without repenting of our faults and without resolving to lead a better life. With a lively faith, on the contrary, we behold in the sacrifice of the Mass the very sacrifice of Calvary; we see there the sacrifice in heaven, where the Lamb is, as it were, immolated before the throne, in the midst of angels and saints, who sing His glory and render to God, through Him, infinite praise. We associate ourselves with all the princes of the heavenly court, to sing with them the canticle of eternity. We adore, we thank, we pray with our whole soul for ourselves, for those belonging to us, for the Church, for the whole world; and the angels, like heavenly messengers, go from thence to open the prisons of purgatory and to shed over the whole world the graces obtained by the offering of the divine Host (St. Chrysostom, Horn, 28, ad Antiocli). Oh, what good reason then has the Church to call the Eucharist the mystery of the faith (Inter verb. Cone. Cal.), and how fervently ought we to repeat the prayer of the apostles: "Lord, increase our faith" (Luke 17:5). Do we understand the need we have of it?

SECOND POINT

✝ *The Profound Humility which must be Brought to the Holy Sacrifice*

The whole liturgy of the Mass breathes nothing but humility; that is to say, the annihilation of the soul, confounded in presence of the greatness of God and overwhelmed by the sentiment of its misery. Hardly has the priest reached the altar before the holy liturgy makes him pause, in order that he may think of the majesty of God, before Whom he is about to present himself. It makes him implore the assistance of grace to perform an action so holy, and it bows him down under the weight of his indignity. It makes him implore the assistance of all heaven and ask for grace and pardon, and it is not till after the Lord has shown him mercy that he dares ascend the steps of the altar of God; arrived at the summit of the holy mountain, he resumes his accents of humility: "Thou who takest away the sins of the world, have pity on us. Purify my heart and my lips." He continues these expressions of humility at the offertory: "I offer Thee this sacrifice for my sins, my offences, my innumerable negligences. Receive me in the state of confusion to which my sins reduce me. Do not let my soul be lost with the wicked; have pity on me." After the consecration he repeats the same words of humility, calling himself a sinner, and exclaiming: "Forgive us our sins, deliver us from evils, past, present, and future. Thou who takest away the sins of the world, have mercy upon us. Lord, I am not worthy to receive Thee." What continual accents of humility uttered by the priest and the faithful, who ought to associate themselves with him!

THIRD POINT

✝ ***The Fervent Love which ought to be Brought to the Holy Sacrifice***

O Jesus, when should we love Thee, if it be not at the solemn moment in which, coming down from the heights of heaven, Thou dost descend upon the altar through love of us; at that moment when, surrounded by the angels, Thou dost transport Thy court into the midst of us, and makest a paradise of our churches; at that moment in which Thou dost offer Thyself in sacrifice for us, adoring, thanking in our stead, expiating our sins, asking pardon for us, and presenting all our needs to the Most Holy Trinity; at that moment, lastly, in which Thou dost give up Thyself wholly to an exercise of love for us, always ready to give Thyself wholly to us if we desire to receive Thee by communion? Ah, that is the moment above all for loving Thee, the moment when the heart ought to be melted with love of Thee, when to love Thee we need all the love of heaven. Even then it would not be enough; in our poverty we must at least offer all that we have, all that we are, in order to live only by His love, and to desire nothing more, either in this world or in the next, except to love Him always more and more. Is this the ardent love with which we assist at the Holy Sacrifice? Have not the angels of the sanctuary often seen us, and with astonishment, cold, icy, distracted? What a subject of confusion for us! *Resolutions and spiritual nosegay as above.*

Fourth Wednesday after Pentecost

SUMMARY OF TOMORROW'S MEDITATIONS

We will meditate tomorrow: First, upon sacramental Communion; second, upon spiritual Communion. We will then make the resolution: First, to renew in ourselves love for Holy Communion; second to communicate spiritually every day, and even several times during the day. Our spiritual nosegay shall be the words of the Psalmist: "Thou hast prepared a table before me" where I may obtain strength "against them that afflict me." (Ps. 13:5)

MEDITATION FOR THE MORNING

Let us adore the infinite goodness of Our Lord identifying Himself with us by Holy Communion, and making of our heart an earthly paradise, wherein He delights to dwell (Prov. 8:31). Can we ever be sufficiently grateful for such great love?

FIRST POINT

✝ *Sacramental Communion*

Holy Communion exercises its beneficent action on our souls and our bodies. Through it we unite ourselves so intimately with Jesus Christ that He dwells in us and we dwell in Him (John 6:57), and are so entirely transformed into Him that we become, in a manner, but one flesh and one blood with Him (Cyr., Cat. My si. 4); that we are as so many Jesus Christs; not that Jesus Christ changes Himself into us, but that we are changed into Him. In fact, the more worthily we approach Holy Communion, the better we become; and in the same degree that we separate ourselves from it, the farther we go away from virtue. When we communicate with faith, we feel that it would not be right that the tongue on which has been laid the body of a God should be profaned by indulging in frivolous or uncharitable conversations; that the body which has been the living ciborium of the sacred Host should be soiled by the slightest indecency; that the heart which has been the sanctuary of the Divinity should open itself to anything that is not holy and pure. Hence it is that Holy Communion corrects vices, moderates passions, deadens the furnace of concupiscence, and cures our spiritual languors. Afflicted, it consoles us; discouraged, it revives us; cast down, it raises us; cold, it warms us. The woman who suffered from a bloody flux felt certain that she should be healed if she could only touch the robe of the Savior; what is it then to receive His body, His blood, His soul, His divinity? It would be impossible to express what blessings Holy Communion, properly received, brings to us. It is the wheat of the elect; it is the vine which makes virgins, and gives to the soul a love for purity and innocence. The presence of Jesus Christ in us strengthens our will in regard to charity and all the other virtues. "He that eateth Me" says Jesus Christ, "the same also shall live by Me," (John 6:58) that is to say, he will no longer lead an earthly and animal life, but the life of Jesus Christ, a life of humility, of purity, of obedience, of meekness, and patience, and he will be able to say: "I live, now not I, but Christ liveth in me" (Gal. 2:20). To these effects of Holy Communion upon our souls we must associate its beneficent action upon our bodies. First, it sanctifies them by consecrating them to be as it were the ciborium of the body of Jesus Christ, and by teaching us to keep them in perfect purity, as though they were so many sacred vessels. Second, it cools the ardor of concupiscence. If you do not so often feel, says St. Bernard, fits of anger, of envy, of sensuality, and other vices, render thanks to the body of Jesus Christ (Serm. 19, in Cant.). Lastly, it lays in our souls the germ of a glorious resurrection. "He that eateth

My flesh and drinketh My blood," Jesus Christ says, "Hath everlasting life, and I will raise him up in the last day."(John 6:55) Let us thank Jesus Christ for so many graces attached to a good communion.

SECOND POINT

✝ *Spiritual Communion*

Spiritual Communion consists in the ardent desires of a heart full of love and which hungers and thirsts after Jesus Christ (Ps. 62:2). O God! It says to Him, how I desire to receive Thee within me, to bear Thee in my bosom, to unite myself with Thee heart to heart, and henceforth to be only one with Thee! Jealous of enjoying so great happiness, I will endeavor to lead a better life, that I may communicate oftener. This Communion through desire, otherwise called spiritual, is infinitely useful to the soul. It gives it a taste for divine things, it animates it to lead. A perfect life, it strengthens it in practicing virtue, and even sometimes produces more fruit than does sacramental Communion made with less love. It has also this advantage, that it may be made every day, at every moment during the day and night, and in all places, whether profane or sacred. Do we make this Communion, at any rate at each Mass at which we assist and at each visit to the Blessed Sacrament? *Resolutions and spiritual nosegay as above.*

Fourth Thursday after Pentecost

SUMMARY OF TOMORROW'S MEDITATION

We will consider tomorrow: First, the importance of preparing ourselves well for Holy Communion; second, the manner in which we ought to prepare ourselves. We will then make the resolution: First, to prepare for our communions better in future than we have done until now; second, to encourage ourselves every day to lead a more holy life that we may communicate better. We will retain as our spiritual nosegay the words of the prophet Amos: "Be prepared to meet thy God." (Amos 4:12)

MEDITATION FOR THE MORNING

Let us adore Our Lord in the Most Holy Sacrament, warning us, by His prophets, to prepare ourselves for His coming. What goodness in this divine Jesus, to desire not only to come to us, but to warn us of the obligation we are under to prepare ourselves rightly to receive Him! May our heart be dilated with praise and thanks giving for conduct so full of love!

FIRST POINT

✝ ***The Importance of Preparing ourselves well for Communion***

We owe it, first, to Our Lord. He who was about to receive into his house a great monarch would carefully prepare the apartments which the sovereign was intended to inhabit; he would cleanse them with solicitude, and would decorate them in the best possible manner; what preparation then ought we not to make in order to receive a god within us? (1 Paral. 29:1) We owe it, second, to ourselves; for communion without preparation would only lead to our ruin; and the measure of the graces which he who communicates receives is more or less great, in proportion to the dispositions he brings to it. We cannot read without trembling the story in the gospel of the wicked man who, on account of having presented himself at the wedding-feast without the nuptial robe, was cast, with his hands and feet bound, into the exterior darkness; it is the type of him who would dare to present himself at the Holy Table without being worthy of it. O my God, keep this misfortune far away from me. Do not ever permit me to present myself at Holy Communion without having prepared myself with all the care so holy an action requires.

SECOND POINT

✝ ***The Manner of Preparing ourselves for Holy Communion.***

First of all we must cleanse our souls of everything that might wound the holy eyes of God. Now, there are two things which wound them: First, sin; not only mortal sin, which God has in horror, but also venial sin, which is to the soul, in the presence of God, what spots and ulcers are on the face; second, attachment to creatures, because attachments divide the heart, and are on that account displeasing to the heavenly Spouse, who desires to have the whole heart. In the second place, on the days which precede Holy Communion, we must be wholly occupied with this great thought: I am preparing myself to communicate, and consequently we must perform all our actions in a holy manner, in a spirit of preparation, and multiply holy aspirations toward Jesus Christ, often asking ourselves, Who is He who is about to come to me? It is the Lord. Who am I, that I am going to receive Him? O Lord, I am not worthy. What is He going to do with me? He desires to make of me a saint. What is it that procures for me so great a happiness? It is His pure love; it is, on His side, gratuitous goodness. I do not in the least deserve it. Lastly, during the day we must often have a great desire to receive Our Lord, and if we do not feel it, we must at any rate have a lively wish to experience it, and offer in place of it the dispositions of the Blessed Virgin and of all the saints. Thirdly, on the eve of Holy Communion we must be more recollected, more separated from the world, less occupied with worldly affairs; we should leave less liberty to the senses, above all to the eyes, like the saint of whom St. Jerome says: His eyes desired in so lively a manner to behold Jesus Christ that they did not deign to look at anything else (St. Jerome, de Nepot.). At night we must go to sleep with the thought of the communion to be made the next day, return to it during the night when we awake, and at our rising in the morning; until the moment when we approach the Holy Table we must persevere in prayer and in holy desires. Is it thus that we act? *Resolutions and spiritual nosegay as above.*

Fourth Friday after Pentecost

SUMMARY OF TOMORROW'S MEDITATION

e will meditate tomorrow upon the three principal dispositions which we ought to bring to Holy Communion; that is to say: First, humility full of respect; second, a love full of confidence; third, and a great desire to unite ourselves to Our Lord. We will then make the resolution, first, to form within ourselves these holy dispositions before and during Holy Communion; second, to preserve and perfect them every day in our soul. Our spiritual nosegay shall be the words of St. Thomas: "Oh, how wonderful a thing it is! The supreme Master gives Himself as food to His poor and humble creature."

MEDITATION FOR THE MORNING

Let us adore the immense goodness of the Son of God giving Himself to us in Holy Communion. His infinite love is communicated to us. Therein without reserve; His body, His blood, His soul, His graces, His divinity, He gives all, O God, prodigal of Thyself, could there be a heart ungrateful enough not to be melted with love for so much love?

FIRST POINT

✝ *The Humility full of Reverence with which we ought to Communicate*

This feeling ought to spring up within us from the meditation of a double thought, Who art Thou, O Lord, and who am I? Thou, so great, the Sovereign of the universe, the God of eternity, and I such a little, miserable creature; I, a worm of the earth, Thou, so holy, before whom the heavens are not pure, and I so evil, who have soiled my past life by so many sins, who still sin every day, and should sin still more if Thy grace did not prevent me. Ah, Lord,

I am seized with reverence and confusion in Thy presence: with reverence, whilst considering Thy lofty majesty, Thy infinite holiness; with confusion, whilst considering myself; and it only remains for me to say with St. Elizabeth: "Whence is this to me, that the mother of my Lord should come to me?" (Luke 1:43); with the centurion of the gospel: "Lord, I am not worthy that Thou shouldst enter under my roof" (Matt. 8:8); with the prodigal son: "Father, I have sinned against heaven and before Thee; I am not now worthy to be called Thy son" (Luke 15:18,19); with the publican who stood at the door of the temple, not daring to lift up his eyes, and striking his breast: "God, be merciful to me a sinner" (Luke 18:13); lastly, with the Psalmist : "What is man, that Thou art mindful of him?" (Ps. 8:5) Alas, Lord, when I think that in Thy presence the pillars of heaven tremble, and that the highest seraphim dare not look upon Thy lofty majesty, ought I not to be confounded and overwhelmed with a feeling of reverence and of humility?

SECOND POINT

✝ *The Love full of Confidence with which we ought to Communicate*

Love, says St. Bernard, cannot rest satisfied unless it is reciprocated (Serm. 83, de Cant.). Now the Eucharist is the great sacrament of love. It is therein that the love of Our Lord displays all its riches and expends itself wholly for men. It is therein that He gives Himself to us without reserve, without limit; body, blood, soul, divinity, He gives all. We must therefore in return give to Him an undivided love, a love which gives itself wholly up to Him, a love which delivers itself up with an absolute abandonment to all which He desires of us; a love which cares for nothing else than Him, which takes pleasure only in Him, so as to be able to say with St. Bonaventura: "The Lord Jesus is my only love; may nothing please me, may nothing have any charm or attraction for me, save Him alone! He is everything for me; may I then be everything for Him, and may my heart become one with Him." (Stim am., pp. 1,6) Lastly, He deserves we should have a love filled with confidence in His goodness. For to have no confidence in a friend is tantamount to offending him; not to place all our confidence in a benefactor is to wound him. Now, is there a friend, is there a benefactor comparable to Jesus in the Blessed Sacrament, in which He gives Himself wholly and entirely to us by Holy Communion?

THIRD POINT

✝ *The Holy Desires with which we ought to Communicate*

This heavenly bread ought to be eaten with great hunger (St. Augustine); it produces its fruits in the soul in proportion to the desire with which it is received (Luke 1:53). We ought then to desire Holy Communion with our whole soul. We ought to desire it as being the greatest happiness of our life, as the infant desires its mother's breast, as the thirsty stag sighs after the fountains of water, as David desired water from the cistern of Bethlehem (St. Ambrose, Apol. David). We ought to desire it as the man who is ill desires to be cured, as the woman with the bloody flux, who said: "If I shall touch only His garment, I shall be healed;" (Matt. 9:21) As the sick to whom it sufficed to approach the Savior to recover health, because "Virtue went out from Him and healed all" (Luke 6:19). Let us here examine ourselves. Do we bring to Holy Communion these three dispositions on which we have been meditating: humility love, and holy desires? *Resolutions and spiritual nosegay as above.*

Fourth Saturday after Pentecost

SUMMARY OF TOMORROW'S MEDITATION

We will meditate tomorrow: First, on the importance of the act of thanksgiving after Communion; second, on the manner of making it. We'll then make a resolution: First, to be very faithful in performing our thanksgiving rightly; second, often to remember during the day, the communion we made in the morning, the good sentiments which we then experienced and the resolution we made to live in a more holy manner. Our spiritual nosegay shall be the words of the Psalmist: "What shall I render to the Lord for all the things that He rendered to me," (Ps. 115:3) in the one sole benefit of Holy Communion?

MEDITATION FOR THE MORNING

Let us adore Our Lord teaching us by His example in the cenacle to make an act of thanksgiving after Holy Communion (Matt. 26:27,30). Ah, what sentiments, full of tenderness and love, flowed then from His heart toward His Father! Let us unite ourselves with His fervent thanksgiving.

FIRST POINT

✝ ***The Importance of the Act of Thanksgiving after Communion***

Reverence, gratitude, our own interests, makes it a duty incumbent on us. First: Reverence. When Our Savior honors us so far as to come to us, is it not just that all the powers of our soul should assemble together, as it were, around Him, to keep Him company, to render to Him their homage, to hold intercourse with Him, to speak to Him, and to listen to Him? Would it not be strange irreverence to leave Him alone in the bottom of our hearts, to pay no attention to Him, and to occupy ourselves with other things? Is it thus that we receive a great personage or a friend who comes to visit us? Second: gratitude. We ought to thank God the Father, who gives us no longer the manna which He gave to the Israelites in the desert, but His own Son (1 John 3:1). We ought to thank God the Son, who gives Himself wholly to us, who gives Himself continually, without ever exhausting Himself. Oh, here indeed have we good reason to say: "Thanks be to God for His unspeakable gift" (2 Cor. 9:15). If we did but comprehend what gratitude this gift of God deserves (John 4:10), our hearts would melt with love. Third: our own interests. For it is in the moments which follow upon Communion that the soul can best enjoy Jesus Christ, be filled with His spirit, and be penetrated with His love; it is then that Jesus Christ is best disposed to enlighten, inflame, and touch the soul and that the Sacrament produces its principal effect, provided that it does not meet with any obstacle. To neglect the act of thanksgiving would be to place an obstacle in the way of grace; it would be to imitate the poor man who will not wait for the alms which the rich man is about to make him. Let us here examine ourselves. Have we always given at least a quarter of an hour to our act of thanksgiving? During this quarter of an hour, have we not allowed our mind to wander through not having done ourselves a little violence, through not having maintained an attitude of recollection, or through our not having been willing to subject ourselves to the acts suitable to this exercise? Have we not deferred, or abridged, or interrupted our thanksgiving through the merest pretext? Alas, whence comes it that we have derived so little fruit from so many communions? The ill performance of our thanksgiving has been the most ordinary cause.

SECOND POINT

✝ ***The Manner of Making our Thanksgiving***

The first means is to listen to what Jesus Christ says to the heart at so precious a moment, and to follow the attractions of grace. The second is to produce acts, first: of adoration, admiration, and love; of adoration, which consists in annihilating ourselves in presence of the infinite greatness of Our Lord, offering Him the adoration of the angels and saints in supplement of ours, and remaining in a state of abasement at His feet; of the admiration which fills us with profound astonishment that so great a God should descend so low; of love, with the effusions and transports and ecstasies of heart which make us attach ourselves to Jesus alone, desire nothing else but Him in the world, and count all things beside Him as nothing. Second: to produce acts of the thanksgiving we owe to Him for so great a benefit and which we beg of Him to offer to God in our stead. Third: to make the requests which we ought to address to Him, telling Him in all simplicity and confidence what are our needs and our miseries, like a child that speaks to its father. It is then the moment to ask everything and to obtain everything (Ps. 68:14). Fourth: to offer the whole of ourselves to Him, consecrating to Him all that we are and all that we have, to be disposed of in accordance with His good pleasure (Cant. 2:16). Lastly, we must make the good resolutions which ought to be the fruits of our Communion. Is it thus that we perform our acts of thanksgiving? *Resolutions and spiritual nosegay above.*

Fifth Sunday after Pentecost

THE GOSPEL ACCORDING TO ST. MATTHEW 5:20-24

"At that time, Jesus said to His disciples: Unless your justice abound more than that of the scribes and Pharisees, you shall not enter into the kingdom of heaven. You have heard that it was said to them of old: Thou shalt not kill, and whosoever shall kill, shall be in danger of the judgment. But I say to you, that whosoever is angry with his brother, shall be in danger of the judgment; and whosoever shall say to his brother, Raca, shall be in danger of the council; and whosoever shall say, Thou fool, shall be in danger of hellfire. Therefore, if thou offer thy gift at the altar, and there thou remember that thy brother hath anything against thee, leave there thy offering before the altar, and go first to be reconciled to thy brother; and then coming, thou shalt offer thy gift."

SUMMARY OF THE MORROW'S MEDITATION

We will meditate tomorrow upon the first sentence of this gospel: "Unless your justice abound more than that of the scribes and Pharisees, you shall not enter into the kingdom of heaven," and we shall learn thence that true and solid virtue is, first: interior, second: humble, third: gentle and affable. We will then make the resolution: First: to give to our virtue these three characteristics; and, to apply ourselves especially tomorrow to be meek and humble towards everyone. We will retain as our spiritual nosegay the words of our gospel: "Unless your justice abound more than that of the scribes and Pharisees, you shall not enter into the kingdom of heaven!"

MEDITATION FOR THE MORNING

Let us adore with love and trembling Our Lord addressing to us, for the good of our souls, these serious and solemn words: "Unless your justice abound more than that of the scribes and Pharisees, you shall not enter into the kingdom of heaven." These Pharisees fasted twice a week, they made long and frequent prayers, they were exact in paying the taxes, and preached almost continually. He who would do as much in the present day would pass for a saint in the opinion of the world; and yet in order to be one in the eyes of God, Jesus Christ declares to us that we must do much more. Let us thank Him for this lesson, and let us beg of Him to enable us rightly to comprehend the characteristics of true and solid virtue.

FIRST POINT

✝ *True Virtue is Interior*

The Pharisees gave their principal cares to the exterior. Exact down to a scruple in observing the slightest ceremonies of the law and the traditions of their fathers, they affected to appear everywhere with a well regulated exterior; and in the bottom of their hearts they violated this same law by objects and intentions wherein an eye to the creature had more share than an eye toward God; they were, says Jesus Christ, like to whited sepulchers which appear beautiful to the eyes and within are full of corruption. Oh, how many Christians are there still at the present day who are true whited sepulchers, great observers of insignificant practices, and within full of hatred, jealous, susceptible, filled with defects which they try to hide from man! Such is not true and solid virtue. It does not suffice to appear righteous in the eyes of the world, which only sees the exterior; we must be so in the eyes of God, who sees into the bottom of the heart (1 Kings 16:7). We may perform all kinds of good works, of great acts of edification, but if the intention be not pure and holy, if human aims and secret motives of self-interest, if the desire to make ourselves esteemed, if vanity and pride inspire us, our virtue is false, because it is only exterior; it is an alloy which will not be received by God; it is a disguise which will only render us more worthy of condemnation. Let us here examine our conscience.

SECOND POINT

✝ *True Virtue is Humble*

The Pharisees sought only to be esteemed by men; they prayed in the midst of the public places, that every one might see them; they had trumpets blown before them when they gave alms; in a word, the only object they had in their works was to obtain reputation and esteem (Matt. 23:1). Oh, how many Christians resemble them! Jealous of deference and preeminence, they desire to be esteemed and honored and deferred to in everything (Ibid. 6,7). True virtue is very different. It is humble, and has no thought of itself. It is not for us to esteem ourselves, nor to wish to be esteemed; it is for God to judge and recompense us. To Him alone be all honor and glory (1 Tim. 1:17). However little we do, provided it be from a desire to please Him, we shall be recompensed for it; and however great may be the things we do, if we perform them with the object of being praised by men, we shall receive no recompense. It is true that we ought to edify our brethren by good example; but, if the good work appear in public, the intention whereby we propose to ourselves to please God ought always to remain in the secret of our heart. Have we these sentiments of a truly humble soul, which in all things has regard only to God, without any thought of self or any creature whatever?

THIRD POINT

✝ *True Virtue is Gentle and Affable*

The Pharisees, full of esteem for themselves, felt only contempt for others. "I am not as the rest of men" (Luke 18:11), the Pharisee said when he was praying in the temple; and they dared to blame Jesus Christ because He ate and conversed with sinners. It is not thus that true virtue acts. It does not feel contempt for any one, and never addresses any hard or disagreeable speeches to any one whatever; as it places itself beneath the whole world in its own esteem, it behaves to all with consideration and respect, with kindness and charity; no words except such as are marked by gentleness and kindness ever issue from its lips (Cant. 4:11). Let us examine whether this is a characteristic of our virtue, and whether we do not sometimes give way to ill-tempered speeches, calculated to wound and grieve our neighbor? *Resolutions and spiritual nosegay as above.*

SUMMARY OF TOMORROW'S MEDITATIONS

e will meditate tomorrow upon frequent communion, and we shall see: First, that frequent and fervent communion is a source of great good; second, that frequent and tepid communion is a great evil. We will then make the resolution: First, to live in so holy a manner that we shall be able to communicate often; second, to watch over ourselves after our communions, that we may profit by them. We will retain as our spiritual nosegay the words of St. Augustine: "Live in such a way that you may be able to communicate every day."

MEDITATION FOR THE MORNING

Let us adore the Eternal Father, who, having adopted us as His children, gives us daily, on the altar, His dear Son to be the food of our souls. Let us adore the Son, who, in the ardor of His love, desires nothing but to unite Himself to us in communion. Let us adore the Holy Spirit, who, having no other desires than those of the Father and the Son, invites us often to partake of this divine nourishment. What goodness on the part of the three Divine Persons and how we ought to thank them for these tender invitations!

FIRST POINT

✝ *Frequent and Fervent Communion is a Source of great Good*

Holy Communion is a divine repast which God makes us take, that supernatural life may be maintained within us. Now, as our bodies cannot subsist upon one sole repast, but require several reiterated repasts, in the same way the life of our souls can only be preserved by frequent communion, and it is to each one of us that is addressed the words of the angel to the Prophet Elias: "Arise, eat, for thou hast yet a great way to go." (3 Kings 19:7) The bread which he must often eat in order to have strength to walk along the road which leads from earth to heaven is the Eucharistic bread, the bread which makes men strong. Sorrowful experience shows us indeed that when we only rarely communicate we neglect prayer and pious exercises; we watch but very little over ourselves; we allow ourselves to be carried away by worldliness, the love of pleasure, of our own ease, and of earthly possessions, and by pride; whilst those who communicate often and fervently prepare themselves for it by means of a better life during the days which precede it, and they sanctify in a better manner the days which follow it. The grace of the sacrament sustains them, fortifies them, and enables them to make progress in virtue. Therefore all pious souls ardently desire often to sit at the Holy Table; they rejoice at the approach of the days when they communicate, and are ravished when several follow immediately one after the other. Their heart is filled then with holy gladness, like that of Zacheus, when Our Lord said to him: "This day I must abide in thy house." (Luke 19:5) It is with them as it is with the heavenly spirits who feed continually upon God without ever being satisfied; the more they communicate, the more they still desire to communicate. Have we, like these holy saints, a great desire often to communicate? Do we not feel a kind of indifference, and almost a dislike for the Bread of angels? Do we not absent ourselves from it, under the pretext that such frequent communions would take too much time, would oblige us to lead a more holy life, inconvenience us, and constrain us to do violence to ourselves? Have we not even sometimes insinuated, when speaking to others, that to communicate so often is to be wanting in reverence to Jesus Christ?

SECOND POINT

✝ *Frequent and Tepid Communion is a great Evil*

First: to ally together frequent communion and tepidity, which derives no fruit from it, which leaves the soul always in the same state, without any reformation of its defects, without any progress in virtue, is to accumulate upon our heads the abuse of graces, the responsibility of which is sufficient to make us tremble. Second; when we have the misfortune of familiarizing ourselves with communion, so as to make of it a routine which says nothing to the heart, religion has no longer anything in it which can stir the soul; there is in it the coldness of marble, the insensibility of stone; and is not that a great misfortune? Third; to communicate often without mortifying ourselves, without renouncing the idle satisfaction which tepid souls take in creatures, is to paralyze the whole effect of communion, as would be the case with a man who, after having partaken of excellent food, were to eat other things that would be injurious. We cannot nourish ourselves carefully at one and the same time with Our Lord and the world. Fourth; lastly, not to take to heart the work of our sanctification is to render ourselves unworthy of often eating the bread of the children of God, according to the words of the Apostle: "If any man will not work, neither let him eat." (2 Thess. 3:10) What then is to be concluded from this? That we must absent ourselves from Holy Communion because we are tepid? No; but that we must issue from out of our tepidity and communicate often. *Resolutions and spiritual nosegay as above.*

SUMMARY OF TOMORROW'S MEDITATIONS

e will meditate tomorrow upon visiting the Blessed Sacrament, and we shall see: First; that to visit it is a duty incumbent on us; second, that our dearest interests invite us to do so. Our resolution shall be: First; to be faithful in making a visit every day to the Blessed Sacrament; second; never to pass before a church without entering into it for a few moments, in so far as it is possible for us to do so. Our spiritual nosegay shall be the words of Our Lord: "Behold I am with you all days even to the consummation of the world" (Matt. 28:20).

MEDITATION FOR THE MORNING

Let us adore Jesus Christ residing upon our altars like a king in his palace, always accessible to His subjects, in order to give audience to them and to overwhelm them with His more than royal gifts. Oh, how worthy He is, in this state, of all our praise and all our benedictions! "To Him that sitteth upon the throne, and to the Lamb, benediction and honor, glory and power forever and ever." (Apoc. 5:13)

FIRST POINT

✝ *It is our Duty often to Visit the Blessed Sacrament*

If there were in the world a place where Jesus showed Himself under a sensible form as He formerly did in the midst of Judea, where He conversed familiarly with anyone who went to visit Him, one should doubtless consider it a duty and a happiness to go and converse with Him, if the distance to be traversed were not too great. What would it be for us, then, if He Himself were to make the first advances, and if He were to come and establish Himself near us, almost at our very door, saying to us: Come to Me! It is a great pleasure to Me to hold intercourse with you, and to dispense to you My treasures. How eager should we be to meet Him and how worthy of condemnation should we consider him to be who did not do so! O men of little faith that we are! Have we not then in the Eucharist the same Jesus Christ whom the Magi adored, whom Judea saw passing by and doing good to all and healing every one (Acts 10:38); He of whom the heavenly Father said: "Let all the angels of God adore Him." (Heb. 1:6) The true Solomon is not satisfied to have in Jerusalem, that is to say in heaven, a throne more magnificent than any throne ever was; He willed to have also in the midst of us, and within our reach, a more simple throne, where

He could receive us at any moment (Cant. 3:9). From it He cries, "Come to Me;" (Matt. 11:28) "I am with you all days even to the consummation of the world." (Matt. 28:20) "My delight is to be with the children of men." (Prov. 8:31) Every day I reach forth My arms to you (Is. 65:2). Come to Me, My heart and My hands abound in graces wherewith to enrich you (Ps. 33:12). And behold, O hardness of the human heart! These tender invitations do not touch us. The Queen of Saba came from the extremities of the earth to visit Solomon, and we have in our tabernacles much more than a Solomon (Matt. 12:42). Men of the world attach great value to being received by a prince or a monarch; and yet we, to whom Jesus, our divine King, offers so frequent an audience and as prolonged a one as we desire to have, visit Him so little! A friend takes pleasure in being with his friend, whilst we have so little pleasure in conversing with Jesus! He seems to be the only one amongst our friends whose society has no charm for us (Tertullian). Let us be afraid lest, having shown so little eagerness to appear before the throne of His mercy that we may find grace there, we may be hereafter taken before His divine justice to receive our condemnation (Hymn Dies Ire), and lest He should say of us: I have been abandoned in My tabernacles and you have not visited Me (Matt 25:43).

SECOND POINT

✝ *It is in our Interest to Visit the Blessed Sacrament*

Tabernacles are the thrones of grace where Jesus Christ dispenses His favors, and bestows them on all who visit Him. Let us go to Him and tell Him our needs with simplicity and confidence, and we shall be solaced. One sole visit to the Blessed Sacrament often gives back calm and peace to the troubled soul; it had come to Him sorrowful and languishing, and it returns full of consolation and of joy; it had come tepid, feeble, and full of distractions, and it returns warmed, encouraged, and recollected. It would be impossible to express how many graces the soul receives in these holy visits. It is there that Jesus Christ accomplishes in a very special manner His promise, "Ask, and you shall receive" (John 16:34). There we obtain the illumination which enlightens, the divine unction which touches, the grace which sanctifies, to such a degree that we may almost be sure of the salvation of a soul that is faithful in making its visit every day to the Blessed Sacrament (Ps. 33:6). There, lastly, we obtain, besides graces for ourselves, graces for our neighbor, for our parish, for the Church, for the whole world, because the treasures of Jesus Christ in the Blessed Sacrament are inexhaustible. How then is it, that having within our reach the source of so many blessings, we go so seldom to draw from it, and that when Jesus Christ asks for nothing better than to give us His graces we show so little zeal in going to receive them? Let us here examine our conscience. Have we a fixed time for visiting the Blessed Sacrament? Are we faithful to it? Do we not sometimes look upon the moments as less well employed which we pass at the foot of the altar? Do we not prefer to them the visits of friends, or certain worldly visits as useless as they are dangerous? Lastly, is it to the tabernacle we have recourse in our temptation and our discouragement, in order to seek consolation and strength? *Resolutions and spiritual nosegay as above.*

Fifth Wednesday after Pentecost

SUMMARY OF TOMORROW'S MEDITATION

We will meditate tomorrow on the manner of visiting the Blessed Sacrament, and we shall see that we must bring to it: First: exterior devotion; second; interior devotion. We will then make the resolution to bring this double devotion to our visits, and our spiritual nosegay shall be the words of the Psalmist: "How lovely are Thy tabernacles, O Lord of Hosts!" (Ps. 83:2)

MEDITATION FOR THE MORNING

Let us adore Our Lord Jesus Christ always present in His tabernacle, there to receive our adorations and to give us audience every moment during the day and the night that we come to visit Him. Oh, how much so great love merits all our thanks and all our homage! "Come, let us adore and fall down and weep before the Lord." (Ps. 94:6)

FIRST POINT

✝ *On Exterior Devotion in our Visits to the Blessed Sacrament*

This exterior devotion seems only a secondary thing, and yet it is fundamental. If the exterior is not religious, the demeanor recollected, the eyes kept under restraint, the whole deportment modest, the visit will, of necessity, be fruitless and bad. If we permit ourselves to look at what is in the church, at what is going on, at those who come and go, we shall think of all these things, of all these persons, and God will be forgotten. If, lastly, we permit ourselves to indulge in a shameless exterior, negligent, free and familiar, marked by an unconcerned air, a word said to our neighbor, the whole of our interior will soon become as careless as our exterior, and we shall have no energy for prayer, we shall not think either of the lofty majesty in whose presence we stand, nor of the legions of adoring angels which surround us, nor of the immense needs which we have to expose for ourselves and for the whole Church; and far from this visit being a profit to us, it will be converted into a double sin, a sin against Jesus Christ, to whom we have been wanting in reverence, and a sin against our neighbor, whom we shall have scandalized.

SECOND POINT

✝ ***On Interior Devotion in our Visits to the Blessed Sacrament***

First; in going to make a visit we must prepare ourselves by recollection and a holy joy at the thought that we are going to spend a few moments in Paradise, in the company of Our Lord and of His angels. Arrived in presence of the Sacrament, we must do three things: render our homage, present our requests, and study the Eucharistic life of Jesus Christ in order to imitate it. First; render our homage; and in order to do so, we must speak to Our Lord in all simplicity; tell Him just what our heart inspires us to do, whether they are joys or sorrows, and if we do not know what to say to Him, to express to Him, with simplicity, our powerlessness to keep ourselves very humble in His presence, feeling ourselves but too much honored to be suffered to appear before Him; to offer to Him the most pure and fervent homage of the legions of angels who surround His tabernacle, and to protest to Him that we love Him and desire to love Him always more and more; that we adore Him as our Lord and our God, that we thank Him for His presence in our midst, for innumerable communions and numberless sacrifices, and for all the graces of which the Eucharist is the source. If, in the midst of these effusions of our heart, it pleases Our Lord to give us some good thoughts, some pious sentiments, we must listen to Him in silence, receive with great reverence and affectionate gratitude whatever He may deign to say to us, and endeavor to make it take root in us through meditation; then we must offer to Our Lord all that we have, and all that we are, and unite ourselves with all the homage He renders to His Father, like all the angels of heaven by the eternal Amen of Paradise. Second; we pass from thence to the presentation of our requests, and like a poor man at the feet of one who is rich, we pray for our own needs, for the needs of persons in whom we are interested, and the needs of the whole Church, for the conversion of sinners, for the sanctification of the just, and we present these requests accompanied with a great desire that God should everywhere be sanctified, that His reign should extend over all hearts, and that everywhere His holy will should be respected. Third; thence we pass on to the study of the Eucharistic life of Our Savior, of His perfect religion towards God, His Father, His charity, meekness, and patience towards His neighbor, His humility and His mortification in regard to Himself: we then draw from these considerations strong resolutions to conform our life to the many beautiful examples He sets before us; and we fix upon some acts of this new life which ought to be the fruit of our visit. Lastly, when our visit is over, we leave our heart in the holy ciborium with the divine Host, that it may there continue its adorations, its love, and its good resolutions. Then we watch over our interior and over all our senses, so that distractions do not make us lose what we have gathered together of graces, of fervor, and of holy resolutions during our visit. Is it thus that we make our visits to the Blessed Sacrament? *Resolutions and spiritual nosegay as above.*

Fifth Thursday after Pentecost

SUMMARY OF TOMORROW'S MEDITATION

After having meditated upon what God has done for us since His incarnation in the womb of Mary down to His daily presence in our tabernacles, we will meditate now upon what we ought to do for Him, that is to say, upon the Christian life it is incumbent on us to lead for His sake. We will begin by meditating successively upon its general principles. The first principle is, that to advance in the Christian life or in the perfect life we must desire ardently and constantly to do so. We will endeavor to make this principle sink deeply into us, by considering: First, that it is supremely just ardently and constantly to desire to lead a perfect life; second, that this great desire is the best means for becoming perfect. We will then make the resolution: First, every morning when we awake to say to God, and often to repeat during the day, the following aspiration, accompanied by a great desire that it should be granted to us: "My God, give me grace to lead today a really Christian life." Second, to watch over ourselves during the day, in order to avoid everything that may be contrary to the perfection of a Christian life. Our spiritual nosegay shall be the words of the Psalmist: "My soul hath coveted to long for Thy justifications." (Ps. 118:20)

MEDITATION FOR THE MORNING

Let us adore Our Lord Jesus Christ teaching us that the first thing to desire and to seek after the Christian life, which is nothing else but the reign of God within us (Matt. 6:33), and that those are blessed who are devoured by this desire to such an extent that they hunger and thirst after it (Matt. 5:6). Let us thank Him for so precious a lesson, and ask of Him the understanding and the love of it.

FIRST POINT

✝ *We ought to Desire Ardently and Constantly for Perfection in the Christian Life*

The Christian life is the sole good desirable in this world, for it is the only one which is necessary, since without it there is no heaven, but only hell eternal; it is the only solid good, because without it all is vanity, uselessness, and trifles. Vanity of vanity (Eccles. 1:2) Solomon, who had enjoyed all the good things of this life, exclaims. "All is vanity," adds the author of the Imitation, "except to love God and serve Him alone" (1 Imit. 1:3). What, in fact, do all other goods result in? What is the use, at the hour of death, of having been rich, great, wise, a man of ability, an illustrious man enjoying great renown? (Matt. 16:26) All that is of no value in the eyes of God, of no value for eternity. All that, consequently, does not merit the least of our desires. But the true Christian life, that is what infinitely merits to be ardently desired and sought after every day and at each moment of our life, because it is that which saves, which consoles us in this world, which rejoices us in eternity, and puts the soul in possession of God, who of Himself alone is all good, as God said to Moses (Ex. 33:19). All the goods of this world, says St. Paul, seem to me to be vile and but as dust, compared with the possession of Jesus Christ in my heart, through the practice of the Christian life (Philipp. 3:8). "As the heart panteth after the fountains of waters," exclaims David, "so my soul panteth after Thee, O God"(Ps. 41:2). Is it thus that we aspire after the perfect life, that is to say, after the true Christian life? Is all that forms us to it, all that leads us hither, dear and precious above all things? Do we prefer our spiritual exercises to everything beside? Do we look upon the moments of our life which we consecrate to them as the best employed of all our moments? Do we not imitate those tepid Christians who regret, as though it were lost time, the moments which they give to the care of their salvation, who willingly abridge their spiritual exercises; who, given up entirely to outward things, and to a perpetual dissipation, scarcely ever live within themselves with God and their soul; who, lastly, make but small account of grace, desire it little, and are not afraid of losing it?

SECOND POINT

✝ *The best Means for being Perfect is to have a great Desire to become so*

When we have not a great desire for anything, we do not take any great pains to obtain it. The least dislike makes us stop; the smallest difficulty repels us. It is the story of the idler with his sterile desires which are the cause of his death (Prov. 21:25), with his weak intentions of which hell is full; who says sometimes, I should like; never I will, I am resolved. (Prov. 13:4; Ps. 66:11) But, on the contrary, when we desire anything ardently, this great desire, this strong will increases a hundredfold the strength and the energy of the soul in striving to attain to it. With what does not an ardent desire for riches, honor, and glory inspire a man of the world? Neither labors, nor watchings, nor perils of death, cost him anything if he may but acquire his object. Oh, if we desired as ardently, if we willed as resolutely. To raise ourselves to the true Christian life, in the same proportion as the man of the world desires and pursues the false goods of the world, how quickly should we become perfect! We should precipitate ourselves along the path of perfection, like a spark in a place filled with reeds, says the Holy Spirit (Wis. 3:7); and we should need to be moderated rather than encouraged. It would then be that heaven would come powerfully to our aid, and would second our enthusiasm. When God sees at His feet a soul which ardently desires to love Him, which hungers and thirsts to love Him more and more, He pours down upon it torrents of graces (Apoc. 21:6). Wisdom, it is written, allows herself to be seen by those who love her; she allows herself to be found by those who seek her; she prevents them that desire her (Wis. 6:13,14). God fills with good things those who thirst after a better life (Luke 1:53), and Daniel owed the visit of the archangel Gabriel solely to the ardor of his desires (Dan. 9:23). Hence it was that St. Thomas, being questioned by his sister as to how she could save herself, "By willing it", he answered. It is enough really to will it; that is to say, to will it with our whole heart, with all the vehemence of our desires. Have we this firmness of will, this decided resolve to become a saint, and do we burn with the desire to become better every day? *Resolutions and spiritual nosegay as above.*

Fifth Friday after Pentecost

SUMMARY OF TOMORROW'S MEDITATION

e will continue to meditate tomorrow upon the desire to lead a perfect life, and we shall see: First, that this desire is a sign of predestination; second, that it increases in the soul in proportion as we advance in virtue. We will then make the resolution: First, ceaselessly to aspire towards a higher degree of perfection; second, often to recall to ourselves how the saints loved and served God, and to be ashamed that we are so far from them, and to excite ourselves to love and serve God as they did. Our spiritual nosegay shall be the words of the Psalmist: "The just in his heart hath disposed to ascend." (Ps. 83:6)

MEDITATION FOR THE MORNING

Let as adore Our Lord Jesus Christ proclaiming those to be blessed who hunger and thirst after perfection, that is to say, who have a great desire for it, and promising to them that they shall have the complete satisfaction of their desire in heaven (Matt. 5:6). Let us thank Him for this lesson and this promise.

FIRST POINT

✝ *An Ardent Desire for the Perfect Life is a Sign of Predestination*

It is enough to make us tremble to hear the Holy Spirit saying to us by the mouth of the Sage: "Man knoweth not whether he be worthy of love or hatred" (Eccles. 9:1). But to calm the fear which such words inspire, there is a disposition of the heart which ought to reassure us; it is an ardent desire to lead a perfect life, or the desire to please God and to love Him always more and more. As long as we feel that we have this disposition of the heart, we have nothing to fear, for it is love bearing its most certain characteristic. Now, Jesus Christ has said: "He that loveth Me shall be loved of My Father," (John 14:21), consequently he shall be saved. Therein consists, says St. Bernard, the most evident proof that God lives in us, because He alone can produce such a desire, and make Himself desired in making Himself enjoyed (Serm. 2, de St. Andrea). Therein, lastly, according to the witness of the Holy Ghost, consists the true seal of the just. "The path of the just" says the Book of Proverbs, "as a shining light, goeth forwards and increaseth even to perfect day" (Prov. 4:18). The more they advance, the more they tend to advance still further, and they never say: It is enough. They are always hungering and thirsting after greater righteousness, they are always tending to become better, according to what is written of them that "they shall go from virtue to virtue" (Ps. 83:8), and are very different from the base souls which do not perceive even their falls, who often do not esteem that to be sin which really is sin, and regard as an imperfection what is sometimes even a serious fault. Let us examine our conscience; do we there recognize the characteristic of predestination on which we have been meditating?

SECOND POINT

✝ *The Desire for the Perfect Life Increases in the Soul in Proportion as it Advances in Virtue*

There is a great difference between the enjoyments of the world and the enjoyments of religion. We ardently desire the first before we possess them, because we are ignorant of their nothingness and of their incapability of rendering us happy; and after having obtained them at the cost of great trouble and anxiety, we are almost immediately afterwards disgusted with them, because experience makes us feel the vacuity of them. The contrary takes place with regard to the enjoyments of religion; before tasting them we have no desire for them, because we do not suspect the charm of them; but as soon as we have tasted them, that we have felt their excellence and sweetness, we ardently desire them, because we feel the value of them ever more and more. Virtue is so beautiful, it is so suited to the heart of man, that the more we practice it, the more zeal we are inspired with towards the exercise of all the acts of it. "Whosoever drinketh of this water" says Jesus Christ, "shall thirst again" (John 4:13), that is to say, he will always be desiring to advance more and more in the practice of virtue. The world and its false joys will be insipid to him, he will feel a disgust for them, according to those other words of Our Lord: "He that shall drink of the water that I will give him shall not thirst forever" (Ibid.). All his desires will tend towards the pure joys of virtue, and he will at once be satisfied and hungry; for the characteristic of spiritual goods is that they both satisfy and excite hunger, that they quench and excite thirst. We are satisfied because we find in God all good; we are hungry, because in tasting it we find it so delicious that we desire it ever more and more. The ravished heart sings the praises of God and of virtue, but it is a song which is ever new, because fresh beauties are continually revealing themselves to our love and admiration. Let us judge by the measure of our desires, to what degree of virtue we have attained.*Resolutions and spiritual nosegay as above.*

Fifth Saturday after Pentecost

SUMMARY OF TOMORROW'S MEDITATION

We will meditate tomorrow upon two other principles of the Christian life. The first is, that to whatever degree of virtue we may have attained, we ought always to look upon ourselves as being very far from what we ought to be; the second is, that to cease to make progress in virtue is to go back. We will then make the resolution: First, to encourage ourselves to give to all our actions all the perfection of which we are capable; second, to examine, after every action, into the defects with which it has been mingled, and to repair them by performing in a better manner the following action. Our spiritual nosegay shall be the words of the Apocalypse: "He that is just, let him be justified still, and he that is holy, let him be sanctified still." (Apoc. 22:11)

MEDITATION FOR THE MORNING

Let us adore Jesus Christ in the period of His adolescence, increasing in wisdom and in grace; that is to say, giving exteriorly more and more dazzling signs of His interior wisdom and grace (Luke 2:52), in order to teach us that we ought always to increase in virtue always to go forward without ever making a pause. Let us thank Him for so useful a lesson, and let us endeavor to put it into practice.

FIRST POINT

✝ *Whatever may be the Degree of Virtue to which we have Attained, we should always Look upon Ourselves as being very Far from being what we ought to Become*

I, do not believe, St. Paul said, that I have attained perfection. Forgetting the good I have been able to do, and advancing towards that which it still remains for me to do, I strive to reach the goal (Philipp. 3:13,14). This should be our model. We ought never to think that we have done enough for our salvation. We must forget the good we have done, and have no more remembrance of it than as though we had never done it, because the recollection of it would produce in us pride and negligence. The good which it remains for us to do we must always keep before our eyes, in order always to labor at it. The debtor, as long as he has not paid his whole debt, is not rendered tranquil by the thought that he has paid a portion of it. He thinks constantly on what it remains for him to pay, and he neglects no means of doing so. The traveler does not halt on his journey under the pretext that he has performed part of it; he continues his road until he has reached his destination. The athlete, who knows that the prize of the race is only to be gained on reaching the goal, always presses forward until he has attained it. The man engaged in business never fails to make use of opportunities for making profits under the pretext that he has already gained large sums. We ought also to reason thus in regard to our salvation, and the more charity there is in our heart, the better we shall understand that we have neither loved nor served our great God sufficiently; the more miseries to be cured we shall discover in ourselves, the more defects to be corrected, the more we shall see, in the interior paths, immense distances to be traversed; in the examples set us by Jesus Christ and the saints, models from which we are far distant; in our accounts with God, fearful debts to pay for innumerable graces received and for slight penance performed. Is it thus that we reason?

SECOND POINT

✝ ***To Cease to Advance in Virtue is to go Back***

Such is the maxim of all the masters or doctors of the spiritual life. He who does not advance goes back (St. Bernard, Serm. 2, in Purif.) where there is no progress there is relapse (Ibid.); to cease to desire to be better is to cease to desire to be good (Ibid.); not to rise in virtue is to descend. A man placed in the midst of a rapid river, if he ceases for one single moment to act and to endeavor to make head against the current, will soon be carried away by the waves. Our evil nature is the river which ceaselessly tends to drag us down towards what is evil; consequently there is no salvation except on condition of incessant efforts to advance in a contrary sense. We cannot say: I will remain just what I am, neither better nor worse. It is impossible; man never remains in the same state (Job 14:2; either he makes an effort to become better, and then each effort is an act of virtue which tends to perfect him, or he languishes without doing anything to advance, and this languor is of itself a falling away (St. Bernard, Ep. 254). It is a guilty abuse of grace. "The earth," says St. Paul, "that drinketh in the rain which cometh often upon it, but bringeth forth thorns and briars, is reprobate, and very near unto a curse." (Heb. 6:7,8). The earth St. Paul speaks of is evidently our soul, upon which the graces of God do not cease to rain down; and not to profit by them is evidently to attract anathemas towards ourselves. It is therefore very true that not to advance is to go back; that not to rise is to descend; there is no middle course. Now, is it not a great misfortune to turn back after having journeyed onward for a long time? If Our Lord declared him to be unfit for the kingdom of heaven who only looked back (Luke 9:62), how will it be with us who turn back? Let us here examine our conscience. Do we not go back in the path of virtue instead of advancing? Let us endeavor to comprehend how dangerous it is for our salvation. *Resolutions and spiritual nosegay as above.*

SAINTS

WHOSE FEASTS, BEING ON FIXED DAYS, DO NOT FOLLOW THE VARIABLE COURSE OF THE LITURGY

APRIL 25TH

ST. MARK

SUMMARY OF TOMORROW'S MEDITATION

e will meditate tomorrow upon St. Mark; and we shall admire in him: First, the amiable character of his virtue; second, his apostolic zeal. We will then make the resolution: First, to endeavor, like St. Mark, to make our virtue amiable to all, in everything; second, to try and bring back to God the souls which have wandered away from Him and to make those better which are already good. Our spiritual nosegay shall be the words of St. Paul: "I also in all things please all men, not seeking that which is profitable to myself, but to many: that they may be saved." (1 Cor. 10:33)

MEDITATION FOR THE MORNING

Let us adore the goodness of God in raising up St. Mark not only to be one of the most beautiful patterns in His Church of Christian piety and of apostolic zeal, but also for having given to us, through him, one of the four gospels. Let us thank Him for this double benefit, and let us bless His Providence towards His Holy Church.

FIRST POINT

✝ The Virtue of St. Mark was Amiable in its Character

We see, in fact, that he gained the hearts of all who were brought into contact with him. St. Peter loved him as his son and even gave him the name of son (1 Pet. 5:13). He instructed him himself, took him as his companion on his travels, brought him with him to Rome, and at the request of the Christians the pious disciple wrote his gospel as a compendium of the preachings of his master. St. Peter approved of the gospel and gave it to the churches to be read as a faithful exposition of the life of Jesus Christ. St. Paul loved St. Mark no less than did St. Peter; he styled him a very useful cooperator in the work of the holy ministry, and begged Timothy to bring him with him as being a friend and a precious help (2 Tim. 4:11). The people were touched, as well as the apostles, by the amiability which characterized the virtue of St. Mark; and this innocent prestige was the secret of his great success in his preaching of the gospel. The fact is that at all times and all places virtue which is amiable in its features honors religion, gains hearts towards it, makes it to be loved and respected. We easily believe that the religion which forms such perfect virtue, so gracious in all its relations, so amiable in all its procedures, comes to us from heaven, and from a God who is all love and goodness. St. Mark, by conforming his conduct to it, only realized, it is true, in his person, the idea of true virtue such as St. Paul exhibits it to the faithful of Philippi, when he presents it to them as an admirable composition of all there is most pure, of all that is just, of all that is holy, of all that is amiable (Philipp. 4:8). Is this characteristic of our virtue? Do we never allow anyone to suffer anything from us, and are we amiable towards all, above all towards those whom we dislike?

SECOND POINT

✝ St. Mark had a Lively Apostolic Zeal

St. Mark, a Jew by origin, was no sooner converted after the resurrection of the Savior, than he no longer breathed anything but zeal and devotedness to make Jesus Christ known and loved. After having taken part in the labors and sufferings of St. Peter and St. Paul, he left Rome, at St. Peter's order, to go and evangelize Egypt and the neighboring provinces, which was one of the countries the most attached to idolatry, the most infected by vice and superstition. Having arrived in the fallow land where the Gospel had not been preached, he sets to work, goes from town to town, from province to province, touches hearts, inflames them with the desire of perfection, with the love of eternal riches. He forms disciples and leaves them everywhere where he has been to keep up the good he has begun, whilst he himself goes to evangelize other nations. In a little time the whole country is Christianized. At Alexandria the number of the faithful becomes so great that the holy apostle, Eusebius informs us, is obliged to establish different churches or parishes there, with priests to serve them, and in these parishes the Christians lived like religious, having only one heart and one soul, and practicing the most sublime virtues. In the remainder of Egypt were formed those fervent Christian bodies which later on peopled the deserts of the Thebais, and astonished the world by their eminent virtues. So much success irritated the rage of the pagans, some of whom attempted the life of the apostle, and crowned his labors by martyrdom. Such was the zeal of St. Mark; and ours, what is it? Are we sensitive in respect to the evils suffered by religion and to the loss of souls? Do we do what we can to hinder God from being offended and to incline hearts to love Him? *Resolutions and spiritual nosegay as above.*

April 30th

THE MONTH OF MARY

SUMMARY OF TOMORROW'S MEDITATION

In order to prepare ourselves for the month of Mary, which is about to begin, we will meditate tomorrow, first, on the motives for celebrating in a holy manner this blessed month; Second, on the manner in which to celebrate it. We will then make the resolution: First, to be faithful every day during the month in performing this holy exercise; second, often to recall to remembrance that every day during this month ought to have a special characteristic of holiness; our prayers ought to be more fervent, our charity better practiced, all our actions more perfect; third, to labor during this month more specially to correct our besetting sin. Our spiritual nosegay shall be the words of the Church, "We fly to thy protection, O holy Mother of God."

MEDITATION FOR THE MORNING

Let us adore the Holy Ghost inspiring the Church with the devotion of the month of Mary. He first inspired certain pious souls with it, then religious communities, then a few parishes, and lastly it was spread throughout the whole Church. On all sides, at the present day, there is a universal outburst of devotion towards the Mother of God, an always increasing zeal for the exercises of this holy month. Let us bless the Spirit of God for this constant growth, which opens to all the faithful sources of grace and salvation.

FIRST POINT

✝ Motives for Celebrating in a holy Manner the Month of Mary

First motive, love for the Blessed Virgin. What, in fact, is Mary's love towards us? First, she is our mother; now who is there that would not delight to meet together as a family to honor a mother? Who is there who would not hasten to these charming meetings in which are celebrated the greatness, the virtues, the kindness of this beloved mother; where, in her honor, the most beautiful canticles rejoice our souls, the most beautiful flowers display their richest colors and exhale their sweetest perfumes? Should we be children of Mary, if such exercises were not full of delight for us? Second, Mary is our queen; now should we be Christians if we did not come to these delightful meetings to which we are invited by this great queen and gracious sovereign; if we did not have it at heart to surround her throne, to offer her our homage, to lay at her feet the tribute of our devotion, and to animate each other to be in a greater and ever greater degree her subjects and faithful servants? Third, Mary is our great benefactress, all the graces which we have received since our birth have passed through her hands, and we are indebted for them to her. It being so, do we not owe her a public testimony of our gratitude, and should we have a heart if we did not hasten to come every day during the month to offer her our thanks? Already three times a day we honor her at the sound of the Angelus; one day in the week, Saturday, is consecrated to her; almost every month a feast is celebrated in her honor; why then should we not, every year, consecrate a month to her glory, and, above all, the month of May, which does not possess any feast of Mary, which is the most beautiful month of the whole year, in which all nature, which is renewed, invites us to a renewal of faith and of fervor, in which all the flowers bloom under the symbol of which the Church presents to us the Blessed Virgin: the rose with its rich colors (Ecclus. 24:18), the lily (Cant. 2:2). The violet, which hides beneath the grass and embalms the air with its sweet odor?

The second motive is our own interest. First, we cannot but gain much by meditating every day during this month on the mysteries and the virtues of Mary; by looking at ourselves in this beautiful mirror of purity, of innocence, and of holiness, in which we may see by comparison in what we are wanting and where virtue appears in such beautiful guise that its charms make us love it and incline us to practice it. Second, Jesus and Mary will aid us in this work of interior reformation: Jesus, that He may reward our zeal in honoring His mother, and Mary by taking account of what we do for her. Therefore the month of Mary is like a second season of Lent, and every year numbers during its course many sinners converted, many tepid souls warmed, many parishes renewed. Third, the succor thus afforded us is all the more seasonable because experience shows us the dangers of this season, which precisely on account of its charm tempts us to lead an effeminate, sensual life, given up to the love of pleasure. Fourth, it is the time for placing ourselves entirely under Mary s protection. It is when all hearts are united together to honor her that we may ask more, and hope for more graces for society, which is so sick.

The third motive is the desire of the Church. The Church, in order to attract us to the feet of Mary during this month, grants us three hundred days of indulgence every day, and a plenary indulgence to whoever shall have followed the exercises regularly during the whole month. She ornaments the altar of Mary with the richest decorations, the most splendid lights, the most lovely flowers, makes the most beautiful canticles to be sung, integrated with pious instructions. Is all this not sufficient to show us that her most ardent desire is that we should celebrate this holy month in a pious manner?

SECOND POINT

✝ How to Sanctify the Month of Mary

First, we must assist every day at the exercise of this holy month; this reunion glorifies Mary and edifies ourselves. The example set us by others, the canticles, the lights, give a greater impulse to devotion; the instructions inflame. If we cannot attend these reunions, we can at least read in private the meditation for every day, before a little altar surmounted with a statue of Mary, ornamented with flowers and lights. Second, we must look upon each day of the month as a feast of the Blessed Virgin; salute Mary in the morning at the first moment of our awaking; consecrate to her the whole day, and often, during its course, renew this consecration; we must rise promptly and at a fixed hour; offer to her, as a present from a child to its mother, each one of our actions, in proportion as we perform them; we must add to them a little prayer and a small sacrifice, but it must be a prayer of the heart, and an interior sacrifice, such as that of the will, of the temper, of self-love, and an exterior sacrifice, such as that of an impulse of curiosity or of useless words. Lastly, we must live in such a manner that the love of Mary may embalm the whole day, occupy and rejoice our heart. Third, we must be converted; we have all of us need to be. Mary will accept our devotion only on this condition; and if we only have a little good will, she will obtain this grace for us. Fourth, we must imitate the Blessed Virgin in all things; it is the homage of which she is the most jealous; consequently we must apply ourselves to praying to God as she does, with her recollection and her piety; to conduct ourselves towards our neighbor as she does, with her charity, her gentleness, her devotedness; to be humble and modest as she is; to employ our time well, and to perform all our actions in the best possible manner. *Resolutions and spiritual nosegay as above.*

May 1st

FEAST OF ST. PHILIP AND ST. JAMES

SUMMARY OF TOMORROW'S MEDITATION

We will meditate tomorrow, first, upon the virtues of St. Philip; second, on those of St. James. We will then make the resolution: First, to imitate the detachment of these two apostles, who left all to follow Jesus Christ; second, to endeavor to be, like them, men of work and of prayer, always usefully occupied, and always by our prayers calling down the blessing of God upon our labors. Our spiritual nosegay shall be the words of the Gospel, "Leaving all things, they followed Him." (Luke 5:11)

MEDITATION FOR THE MORNING

Let us adore Our Lord Jesus Christ choosing for the apostolate St. Philip and St. James, and making of them two suns, with which to illuminate the universe (Ecclus. 17:16). Let us thank Him for the beautiful present made to His Church, and let us congratulate these two apostles on having been the objects of the choice of the Savior, for it is not they who chose Him, but He Himself who chose them (John 15:16) Honor, praise, and glory be to Jesus Christ!

FIRST POINT

✝ The Virtues of St. Philip

I observe in him, first, promptitude in obeying grace: he no sooner knew Christ than he left everything which attached him to this world, and gave himself unreservedly to his Divine Master in order to follow Him. I observe, second, his zeal in making Jesus Christ to be known by others; he preaches to everyone, and gains, amongst others, Nathaniel, a precious conquest which the Savior deemed to be worthy of eulogium. I observe, third, his intimacy with Jesus Christ; it is to him that the people address themselves in order to be presented to the Savior, and it is he also whom the Savior consults upon the means of feeding the great multitude who had followed Him to the desert. I observe, fourth, the supreme love which draws from his heart these beautiful words "Lord, show us the Father, and it is enough for us" (John 14:8). Alas! How few there are, even amongst Christians, who, like St. Philip, desire nothing but God alone, and are able to say with perfect truth like him, I desire only God; provided that I love Him in this life, and that I see Him in the next, that suffices me; I am content. I observe, fifth, the generosity of His love, which joyfully accepts the portion which falls to him after the resurrection, that is to say, to go and preach the Gospel under the icy skies of Scythia. He goes there without hesitation, and evangelizes these countries with a zeal which wins for him the glory of martyrdom. Let us compare our conduct and our sentiments With the conduct and sentiments of the holy apostle. What a contrast, and what matter for making generous resolutions!

SECOND POINT

✝ The Virtues of St. James

St. James had this special characteristic, that he so greatly resembled in his face the Son of God that Judas, fearing lest the Jews might take him for Jesus Christ, gave them as a signal the cruel kiss by which he betrayed Him. There was a better resemblance still between him and the

Savior: the resemblance of holiness and of innocence. During his whole life he kept the flower of his virginity. He was so mortified that he never ate flesh, lived upon vegetables only, and never drank wine. He possessed the spirit of prayer in so great a degree that he was almost always in the temple, he alone having the right to enter within the sanctuary, where he prayed so constantly, with his face on the ground, that on his forehead and on his knees, according to what historians relate of him, the skin became as hard as that of a camel. Therefore the people held him in such veneration that they gathered around him to touch the hem of his garment, and that they gave him the surname of the Just, in consideration of his great zeal for the salvation of souls through the preaching of the Gospel and of his charity towards the poor. He crowned all these virtues by martyrdom, being thrown from the summit of the temple by his enemies, and stoned whilst, like St. Stephen, he was praying for men. My God! How far are we from possessing the holiness of this apostle! What have we in common with this innocence of life, this perfect mortification, this spirit of prayer, this zeal for souls, this charity which pardons everything, which renders good for evil, which prays for its enemies; this perfect love which accepts martyrdom joyfully, and offers up to God the sacrifice of its life? *Resolutions and spiritual nosegay as above.*

May 3RD

INVENTION OF THE TRUE CROSS

SUMMARY OF TOMORROW'S MEDITATION

We will consider tomorrow: First, that the true cross of Christ is found everywhere; second, we shall see how we ought to carry it. We will then make the resolution: First, not to look at the trials of life in the same manner as do philosophers and pagans, as though they were purely natural events, but to see in them the hand of God, who ordains them and who permits them from motives of love towards us; second, to bless God for the evils we suffer, as well as for the good He sends us, often repeating the words of the holy man Job: "The Lord gave and the Lord hath taken away: blessed be the name of the Lord." (Job 1:21)

MEDITATION FOR THE MORNING

Let us adore Jesus Christ ascending Calvary, laden with His cross, and inviting us to take up ours courageously also, and to bear it whilst following Him (Matt. 16:24). Let us thank Him for the example He gives us and the invitation He addresses to us.

FIRST POINT

✝ The True Cross of Christ is to be Found Everywhere

We attach great value to relics of the holy cross, which was found buried in the ground on Calvary by the Empress St. Helena, and we look upon it as a happiness to possess one. But there is a cross which is better than these particles, most venerable though they are by their having been stained with the blood of a God: it is everything we meet with in this life which annoys us and is opposed to us. The pagan or the philosopher sees in these things only effects springing from natural causes; but the Christian, who is enlightened by faith, sees in them the hand of God, who disposes, ordains, or permits everything for our greater good, to render us like to His Divine Son, whose whole life was nothing but a cross and a martyrdom; to form us to the solid virtues of patience, of resignation, and of humility; lastly, to make us acquire more honor and glory in eternity. Now all trials, looked at in this light, are the true crosses which Jesus Christ recommends to us, holy crosses, precious crosses which are found everywhere. Sometimes we find them in our bodies: they are sufferings and infirmities, sicknesses, cold, heat, the mortification of our comforts, of our tastes, of our sensualities, the uneasy or restrained use of our limbs or our senses; sometimes we find them in our hearts: they are the death of someone who is near and dear to us, a reverse of fortune which obliges us to descend from the rank we occupy; they are the association with difficult and disagreeable characters; they are the thousand desires we cannot satisfy, the thousand unpleasant circumstances we meet with. Here we find them outside ourselves: they are a humiliation which is inflicted on us, a want of consideration, the preference of another to ourselves, a calumny or a raillery of which we are the object; they are persecutions coming to us from persons who do not bear good will towards us, who do not understand us, who hate us and seek to do us evil. There again we find them within us: they are temptations against purity, against hope, against even God Himself, aridities, darknesses, distractions, and dislikes in regard to our practices of piety; scruples and doubts which fatigue us, sometimes even pure imagination; we fancy things which do not exist in reality and we turn them into cruel trials. "In a word," says the author of the Imitation, "the cross is everywhere, you cannot escape from it; above you and below you, outside you and inside you, you will everywhere find the cross." (2 Imit. 12:4) Happy he who receives it and bears it as he ought, "looking on Jesus, the author and finisher of faith, who having joy set before Him endured the cross" (Heb. 12:2), contempt, ignominy. Do not let us complain, do not let us be discouraged, having set before us Him who suffered so great contradiction from sinners. Have we as yet resisted unto blood, fighting against sin? Is it thus that we regard all the trials of life? Do we receive them with submission and love, as coming from the hands of God?

SECOND POINT

✝ How we must bear the Cross

We must bear it with respect, love, and joy. First, with respect. Nothing is more venerable than the cross. St. Paul placed his glory in it (Gal. 6:14).

St. John of the cross saw in it his Paradise upon earth. "What do you desire to have," Jesus Christ once asked him, "as a reward for all your great labors?" "Lord Jesus," he answered, "to suffer and be despised for Thy sake." And in point of fact, a soul which is crucified and weighed down under suffering is the image of Jesus Christ, the object of the complaisance of the heavenly Father, it is beautiful in the eyes of God and of His angels, worthy of the respect of heaven and of earth. It bears the seal of Paradise, the seal of the elect, and this is why, in the eyes of the saints, a good cross is worth more than all riches, a good affront worth more than all honors. Second, we must bear the cross lovingly. It is the consequence of what we have been meditating upon. Love follows upon esteem; we love things in proportion to the respect in which we hold them. Therefore we see that Jesus Christ passionately loved the cross; He was born upon it; He lived upon it; He died upon it, therefore the cross is most lovable; for, whatever men may say, the judgment of God is worth more than that of the world. Look again at St. Andrew, that illustrious lover of the cross; as soon as he saw it in the distance he cried out with transport: "O good cross, cross which I have so much loved, so much desired, sought after so greatly, I salute thee!" Third, we must bear the cross joyfully. To suffer patiently and without murmurs is the act of beginners; but in proportion as we study the cross we find in it our joy and our delight, we bless God for it, and we render to Him a thousand thanksgivings. We go farther still; we esteem ourselves to be unworthy of so great an honor, and we are plunged into profound astonishment that Heaven should have considered us to be worthy of so great glory. "The apostles went from the presence of the council rejoicing that they were accounted worthy to suffer reproach for the name of Jesus," it is written in the book of the Acts (5:41). Oh, how far are we from possessing the great sentiments of the saints: the respect, the love, the joy with which they welcomed the cross! *Resolutions and spiritual nosegay as above.*

FEAST OF THE SACRED HEART

FIRST MEDITATION

SUMMARY OF TOMORROW'S MEDITATION

e will meditate tomorrow upon the foundation of the devotion to the Heart of Jesus, by considering it: First, in His holy soul, burning with love for us; second, in His heart of flesh, a symbol of the love with which He burns. We will then make the resolution: First, to renew in our souls devotion to the Heart of Jesus, to honor it better than we have done until now, and to endeavor to increase every day in love towards Him; second, to keep a picture of the Sacred Heart before our eyes during our work and in our prayer book, in order that we may exercise ourselves constantly in the practice of loving it. Our spiritual nosegay shall be the well-known prayer: "O Heart of Jesus, burning with love for us, kindle our hearts with love for thee!"

MEDITATION FOR THE MORNING

Let us adore Jesus Christ burning with incomprehensible love for us, and presenting to us His material heart as the symbol and victim of this love, to inflame the coldness of ours, and to urge us to render Him love for love, heart for heart. O adorable Heart of my Savior! At all times Thou oughtest to have been loved, but in these our days we ought to love Thee far more. The Spirit of God inspired the souls of all with this devotion, the people respond to it, crowd into Thy sanctuary, and cry towards Thee with their whole soul. Would it be possible for me, amidst such heartfelt demonstrations, so general an attraction, not to burn with love for Thee!

FIRST POINT

✝ The Devotion to the Heart of Jesus, Considered in the Love with which it Burns for us

In ordinary language, the soul, in regard to its being loving, is designated under the name of heart; and in regard to its being intelligent, it is spoken of under the name of mind. Now, what do we not owe to the love of Jesus for us? We owe Him two principal duties: love and reparation. First; love.

Alas! Where shall I find a heart burning enough, where shall I find flames sufficiently ardent, worthily to love such a Heart? Who will inspire my soul, in order to recognize so much love, with all the fervor of the seraphim, ill the fire of heaven? And even that would be nothing in comparison with the sacred flames with which the Heart of Jesus is inflamed for me. Thy Heart, O my God! Is an unfathomable abyss of charity and tenderness; it is a furnace of love, wherein we are more loved than all the angels of heaven can conceive it possible to be. At every moment of the day and night Thou dost consume Thyself for us poor sinners; Thou dost offer and immolate Thyself for each one of us. Who would not love a heart which loves us so much! Oh, woe to him who does not love so much love! (1 Cor. 16:22) Woe to them who cannot say with the Apostle: "The charity of Christ presses us!" (2 Cor. 5:14) Second, after the duty of love comes the duty of reparation, and it is that which is the special characteristic of the devotion towards the Sacred Heart. This devotion has been provided by Providence for these ages of decadence, of coldness, of carelessness in regard to religion, of incredulity, of profanations, of crimes, and of disorders, as a reparation which is indeed due to the love of Jesus, who is not loved, who is outraged and blasphemed even in the sacrament of His love, whose very existence is denied. It is a duty for every Christian soul to enter into this great design of God, to love the Heart of Jesus for those who do not love Him; to offer to Him, prostrate in His presence, the most fervent homage in reparation for so many outrages. O Incarnate Love! Holy of Holies! I see Thee torn out of the tabernacle, cast into the mire, trodden under foot. Pardon, O Love which art not loved, and which, nevertheless, art so amiable and so loving! Pardon, reparation, honorable amends! I offer myself to Thee as a victim of expiation; henceforth I desire to live only to love Thee, to make reparation for my sorrowful past, and to expiate all the crimes of the world. Alas! We have so little loved so much love! We have done so little to repair all the wrongs of all countries and of all ages inflicted upon the Heart of Jesus! Let us begin, then, at once; it is indeed time we should do so.

SECOND POINT

✝ The Devotion to the Heart of Jesus, Considered in His Heart of Flesh, the Symbol of the Love of His holy Soul

If all nations look upon the heart as being the most noble part of the whole human body, and consequently agree in rendering to it, in the person of kings, of heroes, or of persons dear to us, a very special honor which is not given to the other portions of the body, why should we not also render to the Heart of Jesus a special worship, a worship distinct from that which we offer to the whole of

His body? If a Divine Person is adorable in all His parts, why should we not render divine honors to a heart which is the heart of a God, which is a real part of a Divine Person? If, for the same reason, the Church renders a special worship to the sacred wounds of the Savior and to His adorable blood, and honors them by a special feast, how much more ought we to honor the Heart of Jesus? For the heart is, in all languages and amongst all peoples, the symbol of love. The Heart of Jesus in particular is the source of the precious blood which redeemed us upon the cross, which purifies us in the sacraments, and quenches our thirst at the altar. The heart is the principle of the life of Jesus, of that life which is so precious to us; it is therein that is maintained, and that thence is conveyed to all the senses, vital warmth, strength, and motion. This Heart is the organ which felt in the most vivid manner all the affections of His holy soul: sorrow oppressed it, fear compressed it, and all our sins weighed upon it with infinite weights; love warmed it and dilated it; from the first moment of its creation all its beatings have been beatings of love for us, and throughout all eternity we shall be able to read therein, impressed upon it in characters of fire, the love wherewith it loves us. Is it not just to render to such a Heart a very special worship, distinct from the general homage which is given to the body of the Savior? Let us renew in ourselves devotion to this adorable Heart; let us look at it lovingly; let us delight to kiss it. *Resolutions and spiritual nosegay as above.*

FEAST OF THE SACRED HEART

SECOND MEDITATION

SUMMARY OF TOMORROW'S MEDITATION

We will meditate tomorrow upon the excellence of this devotion, and we shall be convinced of it by considering that, of all devotions, it is: First, the one which is most conformable to the spirit of Christianity; second, the most sanctifying; third, the most consoling. We will then make the resolution: First, often to study the Heart of Jesus and its ineffable perfections, and to multiply as much as possible our acts of adoration for His greatness, of love for His charity, of gratitude for His benefits, of confidence in His goodness, of zeal for His glory; second, to honor

His Divine Heart on the first Friday in every month by special prayers, every day at nine o'clock and at three o'clock by the aspiration which will serve as our spiritual nosegay: "O Heart of Jesus, burning with love for us, make us to burn with love for Thee!"

MEDITATION FOR THE MORNING

Let us adore the Spirit of God inspiring the Church to establish amongst her children the devotion to the Sacred Heart as the resource for the world in the decadence of the present age. In the midst of the evils which afflict her, this holy Church seems to take in her hands the Heart of her divine Spouse, and presenting it to the faithful, burning with love, palpitating with tenderness: See, she says to them, how God has loved you (John 3:16). Can you do aught but love Him who has loved you so much? Let us respond to the desire of the Church, and let our hearts be filled with praise and love of the Sacred Heart of Jesus.

FIRST POINT

✝ The Devotion to the Sacred Heart is the one which is most Conformable to the Spirit of Christianity

The spirit of Christianity is love, the sacred fire which Jesus came from heaven to bring down to earth (Luke 12:49). To love is the whole of the Gospel; it is the whole of religion (Rom. 8:10). Now, in the devotion to the Sacred Heart all is love; it is the love itself of Jesus Christ, and we honor Him by loving Him. There exists, as it were, a holy emulation between Jesus Christ who loves and the soul which desires not to allow itself to be surpassed in love; which longs that this Sacred Heart should be everywhere loved, everywhere honored; which is afflicted at seeing it so misunderstood; and which, on its side, endeavors to compensate such treatment by means of a constantly renewed love. All the feasts of the year, the cross, the altar, all the sacraments, all the mysteries, everything in religion, preaches love to us; and this love, which presents itself to us under all kinds of forms, whence does it come to us, if not from the Heart of Jesus? What is it, if it be not the Heart of Jesus itself, burning with love for each one of us, and inviting us to love Him? (Prov. 23:26) It is a palpable proof that no devotion is more in conformity with the spirit of Christianity.

SECOND POINT

✝ The Devotion to the Sacred Heart is the most Sanctifying of Devotions

This adorable Heart, in fact, offers to us at once the motive, the example, and the grace of holiness, First, the motive; what could be more suited to make us keep ourselves from sin than the sight of the Sacred Heart saddened by sin to such an extent that He would have died of it, if a miracle had not enabled Him to survive His grief (Matt. 26:38), what more calculated to inspire us with zeal for our sanctification than the study of this Heart, which calls us to it through so many attractions, through so much love, by so many sacrifices? Second, the holiness preached to us by the Heart of Jesus He also teaches us by His example. A type of all the virtues, He is the perfect model of recollection, of prayer, of union with God, of zeal, and of sacrifices for God. A pattern of charity, of devotedness, of endurance of His neighbor, He is at the same time a pattern of humility, of patience, of silence, of forgetfulness of self, of a life given up entirely to God and to souls, and He urges us to take Himself as our model (Matt. 11:29). Third, we find, in this devotion, the grace of holiness; for, said Blessed Margaret Mary, nothing is better calculated to raise the soul in a very short time to the loftiest degree of holiness. This sole means suffices to re-establish fervor in the most relaxed communities, and to enable those who live according to their rule to attain to the height of perfection. Those who labor for the salvation of souls, she adds, will find in this devotion the gift of touching the hardest hearts, and will obtain for their ministry the most marvelous success. It is because the Divine Heart is the fountain of all graces; they issue from thence, like the waters of the ocean, to fertilize the field of the Church. It is the throne whereon mercy is seated, and where invocations to it are never made in vain (Heb. 4:16). It is the strong tower against which all temptations are powerless (Ps. 60:4). It is the place of reconciliation between God and the world (2 Cor. 5:19). It is the source of all benedictions (Eph. 1:3). Oh, how ill-advised have I been until now! I desired to have virtue, and I have not been to seek it at its source; I desired to have the fire of charity, and I did not go to kindle myself with it at its hearth!

THIRD POINT

✝ The Devotion to the Sacred Heart is the most Consoling of Devotions

The Heart of Jesus, St. Bonaventura says, is the dwelling I have chosen for myself; it is there that my heart is in repose (Ps. 131:14); it is there that I will speak to the Heart of my Jesus, and that I shall obtain all that I desire.

What consolation, indeed, to think that we are infinitely loved by this Divine Heart; that at every moment it is ready to listen to our requests; that at every moment it prays for us and calls us to it that it may enrich us in our poverty, console us in our troubles, cure us in our infirmities, and defend us in our temptations (Matt. 11:28). Let us listen to its appeal. Afflicted, we shall find in it consolation; sinners, we shall find in it righteousness; tepid, we shall find in it fervor; weak, we shall find in it strength; just, we shall find in it perfection; dying, we shall find there confidence and happiness; for it is sweet to die, after having been constantly devoted to the Heart of Him who is to judge us.
Resolutions and spiritual nosegay as above.

FEAST OF THE SACRED HEART

THIRD MEDITATION

SUMMARY OF TOMORROW'S MEDITATION

After having meditated upon the foundation and the excellence of the devotion to the Sacred Heart, we will meditate tomorrow on its practice, and we shall see that it consists in three things: First, in exterior worship; second, in interior worship; third, in imitation. We will then make the resolution: First, to study the Heart of Jesus in our meditations, our communions, our visits to the Blessed Sacrament, and to excite ourselves by means of this study to adore it, to love it, to live constantly in a state of union with it; second, to endeavor to imitate it in all its virtues, but especially in its gentleness and humility. Our spiritual nosegay shall be the very words of the Savior Himself: "Learn of Me, because I am meek and humble of heart!" (Matt. 11:29).

MEDITATION FOR THE MORNING

May our hearts be dilated and open to love. Today again let us meditate upon love; let us adore and love the Heart of Jesus (Brev. Paris); let us resolve to love it always. O Sacred Heart, may I forget my right hand, may I forget myself, if ever I forget Thy love and Thy benefits, if I ever cease to love Thee, to place in Thee my confidence, and to take Thee as my model. (Brev. Rom.)

FIRST POINT

✝ On the Interior Devotion Due to the Heart of Jesus

All the powers of our soul ought to be employed in its service, like subjects in the service of their Master; that is to say, our understanding ought to study it; our will, to offer it homage; our memory to render it everywhere and always present. First, our understanding ought to study it; for to know its excellence and its amiability, its dignity and its greatness, its virtues and its holiness, the treasures of grace contained in it, the sufferings which it has endured for us: this is the condition apart from which there is no salvation; this is the secret of eternal life (John 17:3); this is the supereminent holiness compared with which all the rest is as nothing; the bottomless and shoreless ocean of holiness, where in we always find more and more to admire and imitate in proportion as we study it more and more. How have we fulfilled this first duty? We have learnt many things during the course of our life; have we learnt to know the Heart of Jesus? Have we through prayer, meditation, and reading sought to know it well? When we have once known the Divine Heart, our will feels itself urged to offer its homage to it. There is no possibility of restraining its transports and its praises; we adore so much greatness, we adore so much charity; we give thanks for so many benefits; we burn with zeal to make such graciousness loved; we feel the outrages inflicted upon it; we desire to immolate ourselves for its glory; and whatever we do, we think that it is not, after all, enough. Such is the homage which the will owes to the Divine Heart. On its side, memory ought to render it always and everywhere present; present in our prayers and meditations, in order to offer to the heavenly Father His infinitely holy prayers as a supplement to ours; present in our communions, in order to admire the ineffable union of the richest with the poorest of hearts, of the holiest with the most miserable of hearts; present in our visits to the Most Blessed Sacrament, in order to unite us with it and to fill ourselves with its virtues; present before, during, and after every action, that we may begin, continue, and terminate them all in its sentiments and its dispositions; present at every hour that strikes, that our heart may dilate itself wholly in it; present in our troubles in order to console us, in our joys to moderate them, in our anxieties to calm us, in our hastiness to make us pause in our languor to reanimate us, in our discouragement to raise us, in our coldness to warm us.

SECOND POINT

✝ On the Exterior Worship Due to the Heart of Jesus

In order that the interior worship on which we have been meditating should be maintained and developed in us, it is infinitely useful that an exterior worship should prevent the forgetfulness of it and recall it to our soul by sensible acts, such as: First, the annual celebration of the feast of the Sacred Heart, accompanied by special devotions; second, the consecration of the first Friday in each month in honor of the Divine Heart; third, the rendezvous given every day at nine o'clock in the morning and at three o'clock in the afternoon to the Sacred Heart, in order to say to it, in common with all the souls devoted to it: "O Divine Heart, I love Thee, I adore Thee, I invoke Thee, with all our associates for all the moments of my life, and above all for the hour of my death." Fourth, the presence of a picture of the Sacred Heart upon our table, or in our book, with the characteristics under which it is represented, the cross, the wound whence the blood flows, the thorns, the flames, all of which have a language full of love which sinks into the soul and does it good. Fifth, different prayers to the Sacred Heart, above all the frequent use of ejaculatory prayers, such as this: "Heart of Jesus, burning with love for us, make our hearts burn with love for Thee."

THIRD POINT

✝ On the Imitation of the Heart of Jesus

Jesus Christ teaches us it Himself: "Learn of Me, because I am meek and humble of heart."(Matt, 11:29) We ought then to imitate it, first, in its meekness: the meekness of heart which regulates all our relations with one another, prevents all contests and all disputes, impetuosities of our character, resentment, and antipathies; which triumphs over evil by good, indifference by affection, hardness by tenderness, and introduces into social and family relations the kindness and cordiality which are the charm of life. We ought to imitate it, second, in its humility; the humility which consists not only in recognizing that we are nothing but nothingness and wretchedness, ignorance and depravation, all of which is but too evident, but also in thinking, speaking, and acting in a manner which is in harmony with this knowledge; that is to say, in not esteeming ourselves, but on the contrary despising ourselves profoundly; never saying anything to our own advantage, never seeking to attract notice, but to see, without any feeling of vexation, the matter for contempt which is in us, and to accept this contempt as being most legitimate; to be content to see others honored, and ourselves left in obscurity; others praised and ourselves forgotten or held in small esteem. If this practice seems difficult to us, let us study the Heart of Jesus, thirsting for contempt and suffering (Ps. 68:21); impatient to be plunged into a bath of ignominy (Luke 12:50), and we shall be ashamed of our self-love and of our pretensions. *Resolutions and spiritual nosegay as above.*

June 11th

FEAST OF ST. BARNABAS

SUMMARY OF TOMORROW'S MEDITATION

e will meditate tomorrow upon this apostle; and we shall see: First, what was his meekness; second, his prudence; third, his simplicity. We will then make the resolution: First, to behave towards our neighbor in all things with perfect gentleness, keeping the mastery over our disposition, repressing our vivacity and our bad temper; second, to unite prudence and simplicity together, in our conduct and the whole of our conversation. Our spiritual nosegay shall be the beautiful eulogium which the Holy Spirit pronounced upon St. Barnabas: "He was a good man full of the Holy Ghost and of faith." (Acts 11:24)

MEDITATION FOR THE MORNING

Let us adore Jesus Christ sending His apostles to preach the Gospel throughout the world, and recommending them to associate with their ministry three principal virtues; that is to say, meekness, prudence, and simplicity. "I send you as sheep in the midst of wolves. Be ye therefore wise as serpents and simple as doves." (Matt. 10:16). Let us admire the manner in which St. Barnabas excelled in these three virtues, and let us ask for a participation in them ourselves.

FIRST POINT

✝ Meekness of St. Barnabas

The Holy Spirit tells us Himself that Barnabas was a good man; that is to say, of so gentle a disposition and such engaging manners that he gained the hearts of those whom he evangelized. By means of gentleness and tenderness he strengthened the disciples of Antioch in the service of God, and obtained the large number of conversions of which the Acts of the Apostles speak (Acts 11:24). Through the same spirit of meekness he took with him as his companion in his travels John Mark, whose company was refused by St. Paul, because he had quit them in Pamphylia without any consideration for the need in which they might be of him. Through this he preserved the disciple in question from discouragement, and utilized his ministry for the good of religion and of souls; and the rupture with St. Paul which was the consequence of St. Barnabas meekness, after having been made without bitterness, was turned by the disposition of Providence into a means for making the Church spread. Happy those whose hearts are meek, they shall possess the earth (Matt. 5:4), says the Gospel; that is to say, they shall gain all hearts, they shall lead them to virtue, and they shall make peace, charity, and happiness reign all around them. They shall be loved by God and by men: by God, who directs the heart of the meek in all their ways (Ps. 24:9), by men, who permit anything to be done provided that they are treated with meekness. Let us examine what degree we have reached in regard to this beautiful virtue of meekness, which is the flower of charity, the aroma of true piety, the chain which links hearts together, and the charm attendant upon our relations with one another. In order to attain to it, we must watch carefully over ourselves, over our disposition, our will, our interests, our tongue. We must reflect before speaking or acting, and ask ourselves whether we should be pleased if others were to speak of us in the way we are tempted to speak of them, or if we were to be treated in such or such a manner.

SECOND POINT

✝ Prudence of St. Barnabas

St. Barnabas had the prudence of the serpent of which the Gospel speaks. In the same way as the serpent exposes the rest of its body in order to preserve its head, St. Barnabas gave up all his goods that he might save his soul and purchase the Gospel. He sold land which he had and laid the price of it at the feet of the apostles. Chosen to accompany St. Paul when he was taking the alms of the Christians of Antioch to the faithful of Judea in a time of famine, he acquitted his mission with perfect tact. Designated for the apostolate, he would not, though he was an enlightened man and a doctor of the infant Church, begin his functions until after the Holy Ghost had ordained him (Acts 13:2). The whole of his ministry was distinguished in the same manner by a heavenly prudence; therefore what good did he do, and what conversions were the fruit of his apostolate! Let us here examine ourselves, and let us see that prudence, which alone renders apostolic zeal fruitful, is not less necessary to the faithful in their conduct and their language. Indiscretion in actions and words troubles charity, engenders hatred and discord, and casts everything into disorder. Let us see whether we are not wanting in regard to this point.

THIRD POINT

✝ Simplicity of St. Barnabas

St. Barnabas possessed the simplicity of the dove in the same degree as the prudence of the serpent; this eminently holy man, as he was styled by the Holy Ghost, sought God only in all things, simply and without any subterfuge. The recital he gave, together with St. Paul, before the council at Jerusalem, of the marvels worked through their ministry, reveals in him an apostle who thought only of the good of religion, the glory of God, and the salvation of souls. In addition to the simplicity of the dove, he had also its sighs. Who can conceive how deeply he groaned over the resistance made by the Jews to the Gospel, or what it cost his heart to say to them with Paul: "To you it behooved us first to speak the word of God, but because you reject it and judge yourselves unworthy of eternal life, behold we turn to the Gentiles." (Acts 13:46). Have we this simplicity, this uprightness of intention which has God alone for its object in all things? *Resolutions and spiritual nosegay as above.*

June 21st

FEAST OF ST. ALOYSIUS GONZAGA

SUMMARY OF TOMORROW'S MEDITATION

e will meditate tomorrow upon St. Aloysius Gonzaga, and we will consider three principal features of his life: First, his innocence; second, his mortification; third, his charity. We will then make the resolution: First, to become saints, cost us what it may, and in order to do so, we will often ask ourselves in what manner St. Aloysius would perform such and such an action, would offer such and such a prayer, that we may animate ourselves to imitate his example. Second, to avoid, with the greatest care, even the smallest faults and to be faithful to the smallest graces. Third, to aspire ceaselessly to the mortifying of ourselves more and more, and to love God always more and more. Our spiritual nosegay shall be the words taken from the Book of Wisdom upon the death of the just carried away in the flower of his age: "In a short space he fulfilled a long time." (Wis. 4:13)

MEDITATION FOR THE MORNING

Let us adore God, who is admirable in His saints; let us especially bless Him for having made of St. Aloysius so pure and ravishing a model of virtue, that his memory is dear to the whole Church, and also for having raised him in heaven to so high a degree of glory, that St. Magdalene of Pazzi, who was permitted to contemplate him there, spoke of it with exclamations of surprise: "Oh how great," she said, "is the glory of Aloysius, the son of Ignatius!" Let us at one and the same time congratulate this amiable saint on the beautiful portion bestowed on him by grace and endeavor to imitate him, for, as he said, "The best way of honoring the saints is to imitate their virtues."

FIRST POINT

✝ The Innocence of St. Aloysius

Innocence is, as it were, the special characteristic of our saint and the first thought that the memory of him awakes in us. The slightest shadow of the smallest sin frightened him, and a few free speeches, of which he did not understand the meaning, which escaped from him in his childhood, occasioned his pure soul so great grief, that he fell into such a fainting state that he was not able to finish his confession on that day. All his life he was so ashamed of it, that he never recurred to it excepting with tears, groaning over what he called the time of his licentiousness. He aimed in everything at what was the most perfect, weighed all his words in the balance of the sanctuary, watched over all the movements of his heart, in order to root out of it all that remained in it of nature, mastered his disposition to such an extent that he was able to keep in restraint the slightest of the vivacities belonging to his temperament, and was so firmly attached to the performance of even the least of his duties and the whole of his exercises of piety, that even fits of burning fever with which he was attacked did not seem a sufficient reason for omitting any of them. Every week he confessed his imperfections with so lively a contrition that on several occasions it was thought that he was on the point of expiring. With still greater reason, he took every precaution against falling into sin. His noble birth called him to the court, but his faithful guardianship over his senses, his continual vigilance over himself, all was employed in defending his virtue. Not being reassured by this experience, he left the world and entered into the Society of Jesus. Once more, not feeling reassured in this new position, he observed in the whole of his person a restraint which might have caused him to be taken for an angel: a modesty in his eyes, a discretion in his words, an exactitude in keeping his rule, which allowed him at the hour of his death to say that he could not remember to have violated it in even the smallest article. Lastly, he was the admiration of all, even of the most advanced, who remained persuaded at his death that he had taken into the presence of God the holy robe of his baptismal innocence, shining with whiteness. Let us here examine ourselves; let us compare our selves with him; let us humble and correct ourselves.

SECOND POINT

✝ Mortification of St. Aloysius

Everything in St. Aloysius was mortified: his senses, his imagination, his disposition, his self-love. He kept his senses in restraint to the extent of interdicting them the most innocent kind of satisfaction, never even raising his eyes to look at his mother before he left the world, nor in churches to look at the decorations of the altars, and in addition macerating his body by rude instruments of penance. He had so entirely obtained the mastery over his imagination that he was able to say: "Not a single thought, not a single idea ever enters into my mind except such as I allow to do so." He had so entirely conquered his disposition, that nothing could trouble the tranquility of his soul, interfere with its gentleness, disturb the lineaments of his face, so that those who had never known him believed him to have been born without passions. He had so completely annihilated his self-love by keeping continually in a state of entire contempt of himself, that he looked upon himself as being the refuse of the world. He was astonished at having been admitted into the Society of Jesus, and "I cannot conceive" he said, "what they will do with such a miserable creature as I am." The good opinion of men caused him extreme grief, as though it were an outrage against truth, and their contempt gave him a delight that showed itself upon his face. Every opportunity which presented itself to him of being humiliated seemed to him to be a piece of good fortune, and he canvassed for shame and confusion in the same manner as others canvass for honor and glory. It was thus that our saint had mortified everything within him; he was, according to the words of a great saint, an unknown martyr; he even avoided the attaching himself to the most precious of graces, that God alone might have the whole of his heart. What a lesson for us! Let us recall to ourselves the words of the Imitation: "We advance towards perfection only in the degree that we do ourselves violence." (1 Imit. 25:2) And also the words of St. Aloysius: "We do not love God unless we have an ardent and continual desire to suffer for His love."

THIRD POINT

✝ The Charity of St. Aloysius

St. Aloysius, before he had reached the age of eight years, had, according to the testimony of St. Charles and of St. Robert Bellarmine, already made great progress in the path of perfect charity. From that time forward, his charity was always on the increase; and as the more we love God the more desirous are we to hold intercourse with Him, he was soon seen to spend as much as five consecutive hours in prayer, and also a portion of his nights. Even in the midst of his studies he preserved in the bottom of his soul a sense of the presence of God, and remained lovingly united with Him. The sole thought of the divine goodness filled him with transports; the sight of the crucifix kept him sometimes motionless during whole hours, wrapped up in the contemplation of the wounds and the sufferings of Jesus. Tabernacles ravished his heart even more. In presence of this memorial of divine love, he watered the pavement with his tears and seemed as though he were chained to Jesus Christ by love, until the moment when he was obliged to ask Our Lord to permit him to leave His presence when obedience summoned him elsewhere. Then he withdrew bodily, but his heart remained there without his being able to take it away, spite of the orders laid upon him by his superiors and his own efforts to obey them. The Holy Sacrifice was above all, the moment in which his burning charity shone forth; and it would be impossible to tell either the abundance of his tears at the consecration, or his transports at the Communion, or the holy outbursts of his heart at the act of thanksgiving. Let us humble ourselves at being so far distant from so much love, and let us confess the cause of it: that we do not beg God fervently enough to give us His love, that we do not utter frequently enough acts of love, that we do not meditate sufficiently on the motives for loving, that we do not sufficiently keep up the fire of holy love in our hearts, by the spirit of recollection, when it is kindled by grace. *Resolutions and spiritual nosegay as above.*

June 24th

FEAST OF ST. JOHN THE BAPTIST

SUMMARY OF TOMORROW'S MEDITATION

e will meditate tomorrow upon the zeal which St. John Baptist exercised: First, in sanctifying himself; second, in sanctifying others. We will then make the resolution: First, not to love the world, and to prefer to it family life and the charms of our home. Second, to endeavor, like St. John, every day to make progress in the virtues, especially in humility and mortification. Third, to influence every one surrounding us for good, by our example and our counsels. Our spiritual nosegay shall be the eulogium Our Lord pronounced upon St. John: "He was a burning and a shining light." (John 5:35)

MEDITATION FOR THE MORNING

Let us adore God announcing to Zacharias, by the ministry of the holy angel Gabriel, the birth of John Baptist, and, six months later, sanctifying him in the womb of his mother, at the voice of the Blessed Virgin. All rejoiced at his birth (Luke 1:11), and asked each other, "What will this wonderful child be at some future day?" (Luke 1:66.) Let us thank Our Lord for having, thirty years afterwards, resolved this question, by proclaiming St. John Baptist the greatest among the children of men, a prophet, and more than a prophet, a new Elias, a burning and shining light. Let us at the same time glorify St. John Baptist as being him of whom the prophets said: "Behold, I send My angel before Thy face, who shall prepare the way before Thee. A voice of one crying in the desert. Prepare ye the way of the Lord." (Mark 1:2,3) Let us honor him as the angel of the great council, the friend of the Spouse, the patriarch of the hermits, the sacred link between the old and new alliance, the intrepid preacher of truth, the martyr of chastity, which he defended at the peril of his life, and let us ask for grace to imitate his virtues.

FIRST POINT

✝ The Zeal of St. John for his own Sanctification

John Baptist, understanding the holiness to which God called him, retired into the desert to occupy himself solely with this great affair; to forget there the world and all that passes in it, and to give to his sanctification all his thoughts and all his moments. And what does he do in this retreat, far from men, and alone with God? "The child grew" says the Gospel, "and was strengthened in spirit" (Luke 1:80). He grew in the knowledge of God, of His perfections and His infinite amiability, His law and His oracles; he grew in the knowledge of himself, which is the basis of all virtue, which teaches man to count himself as nothing and to look upon God as all; he grew in the knowledge of the world, by the serious reflection which makes a man remark and observe, by meditation and the habit of thought. In growing thus, he was strengthened, on the one side, in the spirit of faith, of charity, of zeal, of all the virtues of which he was to give to the world lessons and examples; on the other side, in resistance to all the passions of which the heart is the source, to all the vices of which it contains the germs, to seductions and the dangers of the world. God does not call us all, as He did St. John, to a life of retreat, but He calls us all to be saints; to use the world as not using it that is to say, not to make use of its spirit or its maxims; to separate ourselves from it, in so far as our position will permit, not to frequent it or mingle in its dangerous pleasures and in its corrupting feasts; to live alone with God in the secret of domestic life, in the practice of our religious duties. To the life of retreat St. John added the practice of the most sublime virtues. How mortified he was! He took his rest upon the bare ground, and for his raiment had only the skin of a camel, that is to say, a coarse hair shirt; he fed upon locusts and a little wild honey, and he had nothing to drink except the water of the torrents, which made the Savior be told that he seemed neither to eat nor drink (Luke 7:33). It is thus that he preaches to all that we cannot be saved unless we die to ourselves, each according to his condition, his temperament, and the duties of his state. What humility he showed! The Jews, impressed by the splendor of His holiness, sent an embassy to him to ask if he were not the Messias; and, without being swelled with pride at the high opinion entertained of him, utterly rejecting the praises addressed to him, he replies that he is nothing more than a sound which beats upon the air; that he is not worthy to untie the strings of the shoes of Him who he is taken to be, of Him who will increase and grow, whilst as to himself, he never can make himself small enough (John 3:30). And what charity was his! He is, said

Jesus Christ, a burning and a shining light. Lastly, how entire was his conformity to the will of God! Everyone hastened after Jesus Christ to see the miracles which He worked, and to hear the words which came from His mouth. St. John deprived himself of this enjoyment, which seemed to be so holy a one; the will of God had placed him in the desert; he would not leave it till he had received a command to. What admirable holiness, and how far are we from posscssing it!

SECOND POINT

✝ The Zeal of St. John for the Sanctification of Others

Every day St. John preaches energetically on the borders of the Jordan, whither his great virtue attracts the Jews. He reproves sin, he baptizes sinners, he converts soldiers, and instructs them in their duties with wisdom and marvelous discretion. He does not stop there; he goes in search of Herod until he finds him amongst his guards, reproaches him for his sin of incest, and urges him to put an end to so horrible a scandal (Mark 6:18); and, at the same time, and in a most admirable manner, he tempers his strong and generous zeal with so much prudence and gentleness, that he does a great deal of good, even to this wicked prince (Ibid. 20). So much zeal did indeed deserve the glory of martyrdom. Heaven bestowed upon him the grace of it, and he died a martyr of chastity. Alas! If we had as much zeal for the salvation of our brethren, what good we should do them by our example, our counsels, our gentle insinuations, and all the other means which we are able to use when we love. *Resolutions and spiritual nosegay as above.*

June 29th

FEAST OF ST. PETER

SUMMARY OF TOMORROW'S MEDITATION

e will meditate tomorrow upon the prince of the apostles, and we propose to gather from his feast: First, an increase of faith. Second, an increase of love. We will then make the resolution: First, to apply ourselves to the leading of a life of faith that is to say, to judge, to think, to speak, and to act in a spirit of faith. Second, every day to excite ourselves to love God with a humble, fervent, and generous love. Our spiritual nosegay shall be the words of St. Peter: "Lord, Thou knowest all things: Thou knowest that I love Thee." (John 21:17)

MEDITATION FOR THE MORNING

Let us adore Our Lord Jesus Christ raising Simon Peter above all the apostles, above St. Paul himself, through that primacy of honor and of jurisdiction which constitutes him throughout all ages as the Bishop of the whole universe, the center of the Catholic faith, shepherd of the whole flock, the infallible doctor and the father of the great Christian family. Let us thank Our Lord for the honor He bestowed upon the apostle, and let us venerate a dignity so lofty in his person and in that of all his successors, in whom he lives, speaks, and governs.

FIRST POINT

✝ We ought to Gather from the Feast of St. Peter an Increase of Faith

What feast, in point of fact, is more suitable for increasing faith than the celebration of a saint who is at the same time the pattern of faith and the guardian of the faith? Now, St. Peter is such a one. First, he is the pattern of faith. His faith is wholly supernatural, it comes direct from heaven. "Who do you say that I am?" asked Christ of His apostles. "Lord," exclaims St. Peter, "Thou art the Christ, the Son of the living God." "Blessed art thou, Simon Bar

Jonah" replied Jesus Christ, "because flesh and blood hath not revealed it to thee, but My Father who is in heaven." (Matt. 16:15-17). His faith is generous; he renounces all to follow Jesus Christ (Matt. 19:27). His faith is lively: at the word of his Master, he casts himself into the water (Ibid. 28). His faith is proof against scandal: several of the disciples would not believe Jesus Christ announcing for the first time the institution of the Eucharist. As for me, said St. Peter, I believe in Thy love and I remain faithful to Thee. "To whom shall we go? Thou hast the words of eternal life." (John 6:69) Let so beautiful a faith teach us to esteem God above all things, to renounce ourselves, to renounce all earthly goods, to renounce everything, in a word, so that we may attach ourselves to Jesus Christ alone, without allowing ourselves either to be seduced by scandals or to be arrested by human respect. Let us examine our conscience, and see whether, instead of living the life and thinking the thoughts of faith, we do not act and speak like the world, according to its false principles and its anti-evangelistic maxims. Second, St. Peter, the pattern of faith, is also its guardian, for it was to him that Jesus Christ said: "Thou art Peter, and upon this rock I will build My Church. I will give to thee the keys of the kingdom of heaven, and whatsoever thou shalt bind on earth shall be bound also in heaven, and whatsoever thou shalt loose on earth shall be loosed in heaven." (Matt. 16:18,19) "I have prayed for thee, that thy faith fail not, and thou being once converted, confirm thy brethren." (Luke 22:32). Solemn words which established St. Peter to be forever the foundation, the depositary, the infallible doctor and the guardian of the faith, for the foundation of an immortal Church ought to endure as long as the Church itself, and the people having more need to be confirmed in the faith in proportion as they are removed from the origin of religion and its advance in the ages, Peter ought always to live in his successors, speak to them, as said the Fathers of Chalcedon, and remain in this manner the everlasting centre of Catholic unity. He who attaches himself to St. Peter does not deceive himself; he who separates from him is already dead. It is a holy doctrine, precious above all in our age of confusion and of blindness, since, without discussing what philosophy and the passions say, it guarantees us that by attaching ourselves to the Chair of Peter, believing and doing what Peter tells us, we are sure to be in the right. Where Peter is, there is the Church, and where the Church is, there is eternal life. It is that which ought to make us love the Roman Church so much, and engrave in our hearts the words of Fenelon: "Every Catholic is Roman;" and those of Bossuet: "O holy Roman Church, we will forever cling to thy unity in the bottom of our hearts. Other churches may lose the faith and perish; but thou, O Church of Rome, thou wilt always preserve in purity the sacred deposit of the truth, always thou wilt feed the sheep and lambs, without distinction and without exception, on holy doctrine."

SECOND POINT

✝ We ought to Gather from the Feast of St. Peter an Increase of Love for Jesus Christ

St. Peter teaches us, by his example, to love Jesus Christ with a humble, fervent, and generous love. First, with humble love. "Simon, son of John, lovest thou Me more than these?" said Jesus Christ to him words which show us that Jesus Christ will not confide the guidance of souls except to hearts which love Him with a quite special love. And what does St. Peter reply? He does not say, I love Thee more than these, but simply, "I love Thee." He dare not compare himself to any one, still less to prefer himself to any one whatsoever. Asked two other times, he still mistrusts himself. "Lord," he says, "Thou knowest." (John 21:15-17) His lofty position and the brilliant success of his apostolate cannot in any degree influence or change this humble love. Until his death he does not cease to consider himself a sinner; far from forgetting the sin he committed in denying his Master, he weeps every day over his fault, and his cheeks are worn by his tears of penitence. As fervent as he was humble, he preaches Jesus Christ to all Israel, to the whole of the nations of the Gentiles, and between Jerusalem and Rome; he preaches it in the midst of a thousand labors, a thousand persecutions, a thousand sufferings; he propagates the Gospel everywhere; he founds, confirms, and governs the churches. Lastly, his love is equally generous; for, after having been imprisoned and scourged, he returns joyful and triumphant at having been deemed worthy to suffer for his good Master. After long labors he is condemned to the punishment of the cross by the most cruel of tyrants; he accepts gladly such an opportunity of giving to Jesus Christ the greatest proof of love, the testimony of his blood, and only asks one favor from his executioner, which is, that he should be nailed to the cross with his head towards the ground, feeling that a death entirely similar to that of his God would be too great an honor for him. Let us judge thereby whether we love God, and above all whether we love Him with a humble, fervent, generous love; if we love Him upon Calvary as well as upon Tabor, when we have to suffer as well as when we can enjoy. *Resolutions and spiritual nosegay as above.*

June 30th

COMMEMORATION OF ST. PAUL

SUMMARY OF TOMORROW'S MEDITATION

e will consider tomorrow how the great heart of St. Paul was: First, wholly given to Jesus Christ; second, wholly to his neighbor for the sake of Jesus Christ. We will then make the resolution: First, not to serve God in only half a manner, by a guilty mixture of self-love, of our own comfort, and of our tastes, with the love of God. Second, to endeavor not to inflict pain on any one, and to contribute to the happiness of all by whom we are surrounded. Our spiritual nosegay shall be: "For me to live in Christ." (Philipp. 1:21)

MEDITATION FOR THE MORNING

Let us adore Jesus Christ raising St. Paul from this world to the third heaven, and there instructing him with His own mouth; delegating him to the nations of the Gentiles to announce to them the riches of the Gospel, and confirming his mission by numberless prodigies, by miraculous effusions of the Holy Ghost, who descended at his voice upon the faithful, and above all by the multitude of conversions which the Apostle himself called the apology of his apostolate, an apology written by the hand of God, a thousand times more convincing than any which could be written with corruptible ink (2 Cor. 3:3). Let us glorify, let us thank Our Lord for all these marvels; let us congratulate St. Paul for having so well corresponded to them, and let us ask the grace to imitate the Apostle.

FIRST POINT

✝ The Life of St. Paul was a Life of Entire Immolation to the Greater Glory of Jesus Christ

St. Paul was not one of those Christians who give only the half of themselves to Jesus Christ, and reserve the other half for their self-love, their comfort, and for things that give them pleasure; who give themselves in general to God in prayer and take back themselves in detail when it comes to practice. Our apostle began by emptying his heart of all attachment to this World and to human objects (Gal. 1:16), from all attachment to self-love and the opinion of men (1 Cor. 4:3), to everything which passes away (2 Cor. 5:18); then he gives up his heart entirely to Jesus Christ alone, to be wholly His by love, devotedness, and imitation. First, by love. Oh, how this great heart loved Jesus. Jesus was the whole of his life (Philipp. 1:21). The charity of Jesus urges me, he said (2 Cor. 5:14). I defy all creatures in heaven and upon earth to separate me from Him. Anathema be to him who does not love Our Lord Jesus Christ (1 Cor. 16:22). As for me, I give myself wholly up to His service; the whole of my person belongs to Him; I am His prisoner; the chains of His love hold me captive; I am delivered up to His grace that it may lead me where it will, chained by His spirit, from whom I will never separate myself (Acts 15:40; 20:27). He loves his good Master with all the affection of his soul; all the beatings of his heart are for Him; his hand delights to write the name of Jesus, and he repeats it as often as two hundred and forty three times in his fourteen epistles. Lastly, such is his love for Jesus that he desires two things only, one of them being to know always more perfectly the charity of his divine Savior, that he may love Him ever more and more (Eph. 3:19); the other to die, that he may go to heaven and live with Jesus Christ (Philipp. 1:23). Second, his devotedness is equal to his love; he devotes his body to Jesus Christ by mortification (2 Cor. 4:10), reducing it to servitude and crucifying it with Jesus Christ (Gal. 2:19). He devotes his whole soul and his life to Him entirely, going, at the risk of all kinds of dangers, of all kinds of labors, to bear His glory and His name throughout the whole earth, from Jerusalem to the confines of Illyria, and as far as Rome, whence he proposes to himself to go to Spain and to the extreme West. Would it be possible to be more devoted? Third, he belonged wholly to Jesus Christ by imitation. Love leads to the imitation of the person beloved. Therefore our apostle makes it his great study to imitate his good Master, and he succeeds so well that he is able to say to the faithful: "Be ye followers of me, as I also am of Christ." (1 Cor. 4:16; 11:1); "I live now, not I, but Christ liveth in me." (Gal. 2:20); and St. Chrysostom ventured to say: "The heart of Paul was the heart of Jesus Christ." Let us compare our love with that of St Paul.

SECOND POINT

✝ The Life of St. Paul was a Life Wholly of Immolation to the Service of his Neighbor, for the Love of Jesus Christ

We must bear it with respect, love, and joy. First, with respect. Nothing is more venerable than the cross. St. Paul placed his glory in it (Gal. 6:14).

St. John of the cross saw in it his Paradise upon earth. "What do you desire to have," Jesus Christ once asked him, "as a reward for all your great labors?" "Lord Jesus," he answered, "to suffer and be despised for Thy sake." And in point of fact, a soul which is crucified and weighed down under suffering is the image of Jesus Christ, the object of the complaisance of the heavenly Father, it is beautiful in the eyes of God and of His angels, worthy of the respect of heaven and of earth. It bears the seal of Paradise, the seal of the elect, and this is why, in the eyes of the saints, a good cross is worth more than all riches, a good affront worth more than all honors. Second, we must bear the cross lovingly. It is the consequence of what we have been meditating upon. Love follows upon esteem; we love things in proportion to the respect in which we hold them. Therefore we see that Jesus Christ passionately loved the cross; He was born upon it; He lived upon it; He died upon it, therefore the cross is most lovable; for, whatever men may say, the judgment of God is worth more than that of the world. Look again at St. Andrew, that illustrious lover of the cross; as soon as he saw it in the distance he cried out with transport: "O good cross, cross which I have so much loved, so much desired, sought after so greatly, I salute thee!" Third, we must bear the cross joyfully. To suffer patiently and without murmurs is the act of beginners; but in proportion as we study the cross we find in it our joy and our delight, we bless God for it, and we render to Him a thousand thanksgivings. We go farther still; we esteem ourselves to be unworthy of so great an honor, and we are plunged into profound astonishment that Heaven should have considered us to be worthy of so great glory. "The apostles went from the presence of the council rejoicing that they were accounted worthy to suffer reproach for the name of Jesus," it is written in the book of the Acts (5:41). Oh, how far are we from possessing the great sentiments of the saints: the respect, the love, the joy with which they welcomed the cross! *Resolutions and spiritual nosegay as above.*

July 2nd

FEAST OF THE VISITATION

SUMMARY OF TOMORROW'S MEDITATION

omorrow we will consider Mary, in the mystery of the Visitation, as a model: First, of strength of soul under trials; second, of perfect charity in regard to our relations towards our neighbor. We will then make the resolution: First, to exercise the most amiable and generous charity towards all those with whom we have relations. Second, to edify our neighbor by our words and our example, as the Blessed Virgin did in the house of St. Elizabeth. Our spiritual nosegay shall be the words of the Apostle: "Charity is patient, it is kind." (1 Cor. 13:4)

MEDITATION FOR THE MORNING

Let us transport ourselves in thought to the blessed house wherein the mystery of the Visitation took place; let us assist in spirit at this divine interview, at which Mary, by her words, sanctified John Baptist in the womb of his mother and glorified the greatness of the Incarnate Word; at which St. Elizabeth saluted Mary as the mother of God and proclaimed her honor and glory; at which, lastly, John Baptist leaped with joy at the voice of Mary and saluted Him of whom he was to be the precursor! Let us render our homage to St. Elizabeth and St. John Baptist; and from the midst of so many marvels let us endeavor to take back with us Christian courage and true charity.

FIRST POINT

✝ The Strength of Soul shown by the Blessed Virgin in the Mystery of the Visitation

A few days after the Blessed Virgin had conceived the Incarnate Word in her womb, instructed by the Spirit of God that a visit made by her to St. Elizabeth, her virtuous relative, would be a source of great graces to the whole of her family, she decides to undertake the journey. But, O Mary, what are you going to do? You are to undertake the impossible! Let us here admire the courage of the Blessed Virgin: First, she was obliged to quit her beloved solitude, which was her delight and her paradise upon earth; second, the journey is long from Nazareth to Hebron; she would have to traverse the whole of Judea: what fatigue for a young girl! Third, there were many mountains to be crossed: a fresh difficulty. Fourth, she was with child: what danger and also what suffering to make so long a journey in such a state! But difficulties only inflame her courage. As soon as she has been made acquainted with the will of God, she thinks only of obeying, and as soon as she has set out, she hastens on her road as quickly as she can; she flies rather than walks (Luke 1:39). It is the good pleasure of God she says to herself. Nothing costs one aught when one loves. What a beautiful lesson for the effeminate and cowardly souls who drag themselves carelessly along the paths of God, and give themselves negligently to the performance of duties. Such souls are not fit for the kingdom of heaven. God wills for His service only strong and generous souls, souls which can endure sacrifices. Do I belong to this number? Do I not spare myself too much? Do I know how to bear the annoyances, the disagreeables of life, contradiction, and suffering, without complaint or sadness?

SECOND POINT

✝ The Perfect Charity of the Blessed Virgin in the Mystery of the Visitation

First, her charity is engaging. As being the Mother of God, she was far above St. Elizabeth. It does not signify: she goes to her; she knows that charity always desires to be the first in honoring, in obeying, in giving; that it does not limit itself to rendering consideration in return for consideration, kindness in return for kindness, and that wherever it sees any good to be done it sacrifices the little sentiments of self-love and goes forward. Having reached the end of her journey, Mary is the first to salute St. Elizabeth, to congratulate her on the infant she bears in her womb, and, during the three months she remains with her holy cousin, she renders to her the most humble of services and shows herself full of consideration and amiable attentions towards every one. Second, her charity is wholly supernatural. It is not merely a worldly kind of politeness; it is not goodness of disposition, a purely human affection. If such had been the principles of her charity, it would have been a charity devoid of merit. Mary is charitable from a higher motive, from love of God and from a desire to please God. Before her departure God had said to her: "Arise, make haste, My beautiful one, and come." (Cant. 2:10) During her sojourn with St. Elizabeth He said to her interiorly: It would be pleasing to Me that you should do this or that, and Mary obeyed the voice of God. Oh, of how many visits do we lose the merit, because God is neither the beginning nor the end of them! Third, the charity of Mary is benevolent. It was proved on that day that God has made Mary a dispenser of graces. At the first word that she spoke when saluting St. Elizabeth, St. John Baptist was purified from original sin; he was enlightened with a heavenly light which revealed to him the presence of the Incarnate Word in Mary; he was inflamed with holy love which made him leap with gladness (Luke 1:41). Elizabeth, equally enlightened from on high, recognizes the Messias and proclaims His divinity (Luke 1:41-43). Lastly, Zacharias, who had been dumb for six months, recovers the use of his tongue. Let us learn from these marvels: First, that all graces come to us through Mary; that it is to Mary we must have recourse in all our needs; that it is in Mary we must place all our confidence. Let us learn: Second, that religion ought to preside in all our relations with our neighbor; that the truest and most intimate friendship is that of which God is the tie, the light, and the life, and in which we mutually excite one another to love God and to love virtue. *Resolutions and spiritual nosegay as above.*

See the meditations on the saints at the end of the fourth volume for meditations on St. Vincent de Paul (July 10th) and St. Mary Magdalene (July 22nd).

HAMON, A. J. M. BQ

Meditations for All the Days of the Year.

Reprinted by Valora Media 2011

www.ingramcontent.com/pod-product-compliance
Lightning Source LLC
LaVergne TN
LVHW020710110826
845149LV00012B/2199

* 9 7 8 0 9 8 4 5 0 7 5 2 8 *